Language Teacher Research in Asia

Edited by Thomas S. C. Farrell

Language Teacher Research Series

Thomas S. C. Farrell, Series Editor

TESOL Teachers of English to Speakers of Other Languages, Inc.

Typeset in Sabon and Adelon
by Capitol Communication Systems, Inc., Crofton, Maryland USA
Printed by United Graphics, Inc., Mattoon, Illinois USA
Indexed by Coughlin Indexing, Annapolis, Maryland USA

Teachers of English to Speakers of Other Languages, Inc.
700 South Washington Street, Suite 200
Alexandria, Virginia 22314 USA
Tel. 703-836-0774 • Fax 703-836-6447 • E-mail info@tesol.org • http://www.tesol.org/

Publishing Manager: Carol Edwards
Copy Editor: Terrey Hatcher Quindlen
Additional Reader: Marcella Weiner
Cover Design: Tomiko Chapman

ISBN 9781931185332
Library of Congress Control Number: 2006929363

Table of Contents

Acknowledgments

Thanks to the colleagues, friends, and teachers who supplied stories for this book. Appreciation is also extended to the TESOL Publications Committee, especially Marilyn Kupetz, Julian Edge, and Carol Edwards, and to the fabulous copy editing of Terrey Hatcher Quindlen. The unwavering support of our families made this book possible.

Series Editor's Preface

The Language Teacher Research Series highlights the role language teachers at all levels play as generators of knowledge concerning all aspects of language teaching around the world. This idea may seem alien to many language teachers. Often, they either think that they have nothing to say about their teaching or that what they have to say is of little significance. Teachers generally are accustomed to receiving knowledge from so-called *real* researchers.

In my opinion, language teachers have plenty to say that is valuable for colleagues around the world. One of the main reasons for the Language Teacher Research Series is to celebrate what is being achieved in English language classrooms each day, so we can encourage and develop communities of like-minded language teaching professionals who are willing to share these important experiences.

In this manner, the TESOL community can extend its understanding of English language teaching in local, regional, and international settings. The series attempts to cover as many of these contexts as possible, with volumes covering the Americas, Asia, Europe, the Middle East, and New Zealand/Australia. Each account of research presented in the Language Teacher Research Series is unique in the profession. These studies document how individual language teachers at all levels of practice systematically reflect on their *own* practice (rather than on other teachers' practices).

When practicing language teachers share these experiences with teachers in other contexts, they can compare and contrast what is happening in different classrooms around the world. The ultimate aim of this series is to encourage an inquiry stance toward language teaching. Teachers can play a crucial role in taking responsibility for their own professional development as generators and receivers of knowledge about what it means to teach English language learning.

How This Series Can Be Used

The Language Teacher Research Series is suitable for preservice and in-service teacher education programs. The examples of teacher research written by practitioners at all levels of teaching and all levels of experience offer a window into the different worlds of English language teachers. In this series we have attempted to impose some order by providing authors with a template of headings for presenting their research. This format is designed so that language teachers with varied expertise and educational qualifications can pick up a book from any region and make comparisons about issues, background literature, procedures taken, results, and reflections without having to work too hard to find them. The details in each chapter will help readers compare and evaluate the examples of teacher research and even replicate some research, if so desired.

This Volume

This volume of *Language Teacher Research in Asia* documents different forms of practitioner inquiry that involve systematic, intentional, and self-critical inquiry about language teaching in different Asian settings, including K–12, higher education, and courses in other formal educational settings. It will be interesting to compare and contrast these Asian research stories with studies from other regions in the series.

Thomas S. C. Farrell, Brock University, Canada

CHAPTER 1

Language Teacher Research in Asia

Thomas S. C. Farrell

In recent times language teachers throughout the world have been encouraged to reflect on their own professional development by engaging in such activities as self-monitoring their teaching, initiating an action research project, engaging in group discussions with other teachers, writing a teaching journal, analyzing case studies and critical incidents, participating in team teaching and peer coaching, and so on (see Richards & Farrell, 2005). This self-initiated professional development may be necessary because teachers have felt neglected when it comes to implementing new curricula or have felt a lack of ownership in the materials they are using, and as a result they may have also felt a lack of self-worth (Ruddock, 1991). In an address to English language teachers in Korea some 7 years ago, the well-known language educator Donald Freeman (1998) suggested that language teachers are best suited to carry out research in their own classrooms because they are "more insiders to their settings than researchers whose work lives are elsewhere" (p. 6). Freeman maintained that this form of teacher research is functional because the language teachers can "generate new understandings and knowledge" (p. 6) of their own workplaces.

In *Teacher's Edition,* an excellent language teacher journal in Vietnam, Doan Thi Kim Khanh and Nguyen Thi Hoai An (2005) surveyed 202 Vietnamese teachers of English to find out their attitudes toward classroom-based research. They discovered that teacher research has "not been accepted as a normal part of the teaching process" and "ordinary teachers appear not to think that they themselves can play a key role in doing research and generating knowledge" (p. 4). Of the 202 teachers surveyed, 60% responded that they had conducted some research. Of those who had conducted research, 53% reported that they had undertaken research only once and that in many of those cases it was a requirement of an advanced degree.

When asked to identify problems with conducting research, the respondents replied with three main reasons, which may be common regardless of location:

- Lack of time (31%)

- Lack of experience (31%)

- Lack of theoretical knowledge (26%)

The survey participants said that no course in their undergraduate teaching showed them how to carry out research on their own practice. So within the context of Vietnam, the lack of time (teachers may teach up to 12 hours a day), experience, and theoretical knowledge all seem to be valid problems associated with teachers conducting research on their own practice. If this same survey were conducted in other parts of Asia, similar results would probably be recorded. Time is probably the factor most often given by teachers for why they do not conduct research on their own practice. In the case of these Vietnamese teachers, lack of experience in conducting such research was given equal weight as a reason for not conducting teacher research.

So, even though language teachers in Asia have been encouraged to engage in their own teacher research, the actual process requires time, commitment, and a certain amount of skill. Naturally, many language teachers in Asia have at one time or another encountered some aspect of their professional practice in or outside the classroom that puzzled them, and that is a first step toward engaging in language teacher research. The next step would be to carry out a small-scale study of that puzzling aspect.

As Freeman (1998) pointed out, "Teacher research is about seeing what you do in your teaching and how it impacts on your students' learning" (p. 6). This is exactly the process followed by many language teachers who submitted manuscripts for inclusion in this *Language Teacher Research in Asia* volume. All of the submissions were of the highest quality and addressed very important aspects of language teacher research, and they could fill several volumes from Asia. Unfortunately, only a certain number of topics could be selected for the final collection.

Language Teacher Research in Asia thus presents research that was conducted by language teachers at all levels, from high school English teachers to English language teacher educators reflecting on their practice. The countries represented cover both north and south Asia. The chapters are presented in alphabetical order of the first author's name to indicate that no one topic and no one Asian region or country is more important than another. As you will see, the chapters follow a template so that readers can compare across chapters, looking at aspects such as the research issue, background literature, procedures, results, and reflection.

In the chapter "Teaching Character Depiction in Narrative Writing," Antonia Chandrasegaran and Siok-Chin Yeo outline the procedures they used to help high school students in Singapore improve their writing after conventional methods of teaching yielded less-than-encouraging results. The findings of their research suggest that teaching genre practices and the thinking underlying the practices can lead to better writing of the same genre.

Next, Sumalee Chinokul's chapter, "Expert and Nonexpert Teachers: Do They Use Different Processes While Learning to Teach?" discusses how one language teacher educator reflected on her role as teacher of the teacher when she was assigned to teach a course in methodology of English language teaching in Thailand. She conducted this research not as a classroom experiment but simply as part of normal classroom procedure. Her main research question was "How do expert teachers and nonexpert teachers differ in their processes of learning to teach English as a foreign language?" As a result of her research, Chinokul said that she gathered concrete evidence and samples to give course participants some benchmarks to help them further progress in learning to teach.

The chapter by Duong Thi Hoang Oanh, titled "Learner Autonomy in an Asian Context: Independent Learning and Independent Work at the University Level," explains how this English as a foreign language teacher addressed her observation that autonomy is seldom and ineffectively practiced in university English language classes in Vietnam. The author thought that she had encouraged students to work on their own. But, in practice, she found that she was still in control of her students' outside work and that the goal of this work was set by the teacher, not the students.

The chapter titled "The TESOL Methods Course: What Did They *Really* Learn?" outlines how a language teacher educator in Singapore, Thomas S. C. Farrell, explored how much his students learned as a result of taking his TESOL methods course. Although the students as a group had taken on new concepts as presented in the course, many individual postcourse concept maps indicated that the students had not yet linked these new concepts in any coherent manner.

In "Understanding Chinese Students' Teacher Dependence," Gao Xuesong (Andy) reports on an inquiry into a group of tertiary Chinese students' language learning experiences, with a focus on their teacher dependence during the learning process. The findings lend tentative support to his speculation that his students' dependence on their teachers might stem from strategic goals in a context in which education is widely viewed as a pathway for social promotion and teachers are seen as preselection agents.

The next chapter, "Challenging Tradition: Creating a Self-Access Language Learning Center in an East Asian Academic High School" by Chris Hale, outlines how the author created a self-access language learning center in a Japanese high school where teacher-centered, lecture-style lessons were the norm of classroom language instruction. The results suggest that regardless of the students' preference for teacher or student-centered learning, a self-study center can be beneficial in helping students achieve their goals.

Xuelin Liu and Christine C. M. Goh's chapter, "Improving Second Language Listening: Awareness and Involvement," outlines the steps the authors took to improve their learners' weak listening abilities. These teachers realized that in order to help their students improve these skills, the students needed to first become aware of their learning needs and comprehension problems. As a result of this research, the authors discovered that their students developed greater awareness of themselves as second language learners.

Next, Stephen H. Moore's chapter, "From Chalkboard to Lectern to Chalkboard: The Journey of an Applied Linguistics Lecturer," discusses how a language teacher educator in Vietnam attempted to delicately balance his roles as an applied linguistics lecturer and a former English teacher when confronting how to address his learners' language problems. Moore came up with various action plans that could help educators trying to interface between language and content learning and teaching in an applied linguistics course.

In "'I Want to Study TOEFL!' Finding the Balance Between Test Focus and Language Learning in Curriculum Revision," Patrick Rosenkjar reports on research undertaken to inform a comprehensive curriculum revision project that the author initiated shortly after being appointed director of a university program. As a result of revising the curriculum and surveying all of the stakeholders, Rosenkjar discovered that test anxiety and preference for explicit focus on forms still looms large in the minds of his Japanese students.

Timothy Stewart's chapter, "Bridging the Classroom Perception Gap: Comparing Learners' and Teachers' Understandings of What Is Learned," outlines the author's multifaceted approach to task evaluation undertaken to match teacher and learner impressions of task appropriateness in a Japanese university setting. As a result of his research, Stewart learned more than he had expected about himself as a teacher, his learners' expectations, and his course.

Wang Ge, in his chapter titled "Does Project-Based Learning Work in Asia?" discusses how he looked into the feasibility of using project-based learning (PBL) in China for English learning. Using the hot issue of the outbreak of the medical disease known as SARS in his classes, Wang developed a three-project approach to PBL, consisting of group discussion, a written report, and a writing task. His results indicate that the success of PBL is dependent on appropriate project planning, implementation, and assessment in language instruction.

The final chapter, "How Does Course Content Affect Students' Willingness to Communicate in the L2?" by Jennifer Weathers, describes how the author noticed various degrees of reticence among students in her oral English classes in China. Weathers outlines her attempts to get her students to speak more English in class by making various changes to her course content. As a result of her research, Weathers discovered that her students' responses seemed to confirm the important role that interest plays in her students' willingness to communicate in English.

This volume provides a small window into what TESOL practitioners are reflecting on in diverse settings in Asia. These TESOL professionals take enormous pride in their work, and now they also are willing to share their observations with other professionals. I hope that other teachers in the Asian context will not only read these wonderful articles but also replicate the topics they find most relevant to their context and compare the results. This approach is similar to one taken by a traveler who, before going on a journey, asks others who have visited his or her destination for their advice. In both situations, knowledge seekers can learn from others' successes and mistakes. To further that goal, this *Language Teacher Research in Asia* volume is designed to encourage more language teachers in Asia to embark on research and share their experiences with other teachers in the region and beyond.

Thomas S. C. Farrell is editor of the Language Teacher Research Series at TESOL and of this Language Teacher Research in Asia *volume. He is Associate Professor in Applied Language Studies at Brock University, Ontario, Canada. His professional interests include reflective teaching, teacher development, and methodology. His latest books are* Professional Development for Language Teachers *(coauthored with Jack C. Richards, 2005, Cambridge University Press) and* Success With English Language Learners: A Guide for Beginning Teachers *(2006, Corwin Press).*

CHAPTER 2

Teaching Character Depiction in Narrative Writing (*Singapore*)

Antonia Chandrasegaran and Siok-Chin Yeo

Issue

This study explores the question of how to help high school students improve their writing after conventional methods of teaching have yielded less-than-encouraging results. Conventional methods include remedial grammar exercises, vocabulary lessons, and classroom activities to stimulate a flow of ideas (e.g., free writing, brainstorming). In Singapore schools, where the English syllabus is genre-inspired, more and more teachers are teaching descriptions of the organisational structure of narrative and other texts. The common thread running through the conventional methods and the more recent genre-based methods of teaching writing is their focus on the finished product. Teachers tell students, for example, that a good narrative must have correct past tense verbs, vivid characterisation, and stages such as *setting* and *complication*. Then teachers expect their students to produce these features. Although such product information is useful for students who already have the composing skills to achieve the desired qualities, it is of limited help to students who do not. How can educators teach students the thinking and the ways of using language that produce the desired qualities? This chapter describes one attempt at finding an answer to this question.

The search for workable alternatives to product-focused methods of teaching writing motivated the two authors to explore, separately at first, the possibility of trying out methods that would focus student attention on thinking processes that align with particular genre practices. The second author, being a teacher with more than 10 years of experience with Singapore students, was aware of the disappointing limitations of additional remedial grammar lessons, vocabulary lists, and brainstorming for improving essay writing. Her classroom experience with narrative writing had shown that students could not use the grammar structures retaught, the new vocabulary learnt, and the ideas generated through brainstorming to create a text that readers could recognise as an interesting story. She wondered if the problem lay in her students' thinking processes. At the same time, having read about genre theory in a postgraduate course of study, she had a hunch that the solution might be to teach explicitly some of the discourse practices of short story writers. She discussed this hunch with the first author, a teacher educator, friend, and mentor, who suggested looking into a combination thinking and genre approach. In the rest of this chapter, the pronoun "we" is used to indicate actions and decisions taken by the two authors in consultation with each other.

One recurrent weakness that we noticed in students' narratives was a lack of purposefully selected detail that would construct vivid depictions of characters. Details either were absent or when present did not contribute to an overall effect. We hypothesized that students might learn to generate and select details judiciously if they knew how to think during the generation and selection process. If we could teach them the mental operations for establishing a point of reference for language and content choice, they might write better narratives. We further hypothesized that, to be effective, the thinking and mental posturing during the writing process would have to be presented to students as social practices of the narrative genre. Instead of approaching narrative writing as the production of correct sentences, the student would need to assume the role of a storyteller, whose social goal is to influence the reader's feelings toward the characters in the story. Otherwise, the story would tend to be little more than a skeletal recounting of events.

To test our hypothesis, we decided to focus on teaching methods of character depiction in the 7 weeks we had for conducting the research. We chose character depiction primarily because the characters in our students' stories tended to be pasteboard figures. Another reason for choosing character depiction is that a reader's response to a story is much influenced by the image that the reader constructs of the main characters, and that image is shaped by the writer's choice of language and meaning.

The main aim of the study was to find out if explicit instruction in specific genre practices and related thinking processes for constructing characters would improve students' narrative writing. The specific questions that drove the research were whether explicit teaching of genre practices and goal-directed thinking in depicting characters would

- Raise student awareness of the need to form a sociorhetorical intention when describing a character.

- Result in the use of a wider range of epithets (descriptive words) appropriately selected to match the student's rhetorical intention.

- Result in the creation of appropriate ideational tokens that evoke the qualities the student intends the character to display. (An ideational token is an expression that suggests, rather than directly describes, a character trait or the character's emotional state.)

Background Literature

From a cognitive perspective, writing is a decision-making process (Flower & Hayes, 1981) that requires "active thinking and problem solving" (Kern, 2000, p. 29). The problem to be solved in writing, according to Flower and Hayes, is the rhetorical problem consisting of the following elements:

- The writer's purpose—what effect the writer intends to create for the reader.

- The audience or target readers—their needs, previous knowledge, and so on.

- The context of situation in which the writing (and reading) take place (e.g., writing under examination conditions with an imposed word limit).

For the student asked to write a narrative, the rhetorical problem is how, within the time and word limit allowed, to generate and organise ideas into a story that the teacher would find interesting.

Flower and Hayes's (1981) research on writers' thinking processes led them to observe that "writing is a goal-directed process" (p. 377). Skilled writers engage in "goal-directed thinking" (p. 378) as a means to solving the rhetorical problem. Furthermore, the goals that guide the writing process of good writers are high-level rhetorical goals pertaining to writer purpose and reader effect, not local sentence-level goals. Applied to narrative writing, a high-level goal might be "I'll make the reader feel sympathetic toward the main character." Unskilled writers, on the other hand, tend to stay fixated on local goals such as spelling or sentence-level grammar accuracy (Hayes, 1996).

Although writing involves goal setting and goal-directed decision making, it is also a process of engaging in the sociocultural practices of a community of language users. Story writers, for instance, engage in the social practice of creating "a sense of suspense" in the reader, who then feels impelled to read on "to find out 'how it all ends'" (Rothery, 1996, p. 96). Producing suspense and creating sympathy or antipathy for a story's characters are among the practices that characterise the short story genre. The term *genre* is used here in the sense of goal-oriented social process (Martin, 1996). More than just a type of text with a certain form, a genre typifies and gives shape to the social activity associated with it (Bazerman, 2004). Students writing a story for their teacher are engaging in the social activity of storytelling, an activity present in all cultures. In the context of school-based writing, they also write to accomplish a social goal, that of securing the teacher's favourable judgment of the story and its author. It has been argued that reading comprehension is not complete if readers lack knowledge of genre conventions relating to discourse practices operating in a discourse community (Toledo, 2005). In the same vein, the writing process may not yield a successful product if the writer lacks knowledge of the genre conventions operating in the reader's discourse community.

The use of language to evoke emotive responses in readers is a genre practice that distinguishes narratives from other genres such as complaint letters or information reports. Language is often employed to create meanings pertaining to emotional and mental states, an area of meaning called *affect* (Martin, 1996). Most students know that affect can be communicated by means of adjectives (a *sad* man) or adverbs (shook his head *sadly*). There is also a less direct way, which is characteristic of narrative genres. According to Martin, affect is often connoted with ideational tokens. For example, *sleepless nights* would be an ideational token for *worried* or *anxious*. Teaching students to create ideational tokens when describing characters could inject some life into the pasteboard protagonists in their narratives.

By teaching students how to select and use language (such as ideational tokens) to create new meanings, teachers make explicit the language practices that are valued as characterising a particular genre. Often, teachers do not articulate their expectations in terms of grammatical structure but instead admonish students to "use the right words" or to achieve some other desired quality in the finished text (Schleppegrell, 2004). In the past decade, applied linguists such as Carter and McCarthy, working within the systemic functional linguistics tradition, have advocated the teaching of language in relation to its use in constructing social practices (Bloor & Bloor, 2004). For narrative writing, teaching language in relation to social practices means teaching students to use adjectives, noun phrases, and other structures to construct characters and events that evoke an affective response in the reader.

Based on the literature describing writing from cognitive and genre perspectives, we hypothesized that students' narrative writing would improve if they learnt the thinking that enables them to engage in the discourse practices of the narrative genre. There is research suggesting that teaching students cognitive strategies in story writing leads to improvement in the stories they write (Albertson, 1998). But if writing is a social activity (Christie & Misson, 1998), cognitive strategies and thinking skills should be taught in the context of genre practices. Strategy training, Kern (2000) notes, must be grounded in the context of specific texts and writing tasks. The question that presents itself at this point is how best to teach the thinking and genre practices of a specific genre, which in this study is the narrative essay. Among researchers who adopt the genre view of writing, there is a belief that the ways of thinking and using language associated with a genre can and should be explicitly taught (Christie & Misson, 1998). One method of teaching genre explicitly is "deconstruction," that is, guiding students through an examination of a well-written text of the target genre to discover "how the genre works to achieve its social purpose" (Rothery, 1996, p. 103).

Although there is debate on whether genres can be explicitly taught (Freedman, 1994), research points to benefits of explicit teaching. Rothery (1996) reported that primary school children learnt, through explicit genre instruction, to write factual genres such as report and exposition, "which have traditionally been considered beyond the abilities of primary school children" (p. 107). In another study, Williams (2000) found that the explicit teaching of functional grammar in relation to construction of a character in a story resulted in primary school children being able to articulate the significance of certain grammatical structures that mirror developments in a children's story. It is highly likely that deconstruction works because it involves awareness, attention, and noticing, which have been acknowledged as important processes contributing to success in language learning (Hinkel, 2002; Schmidt, 1995). Explicit instruction, through deconstruction, in genre practices and genre-related ways of using language may be particularly beneficial to Asian students for whom the ways of using language and creating meaning in a genre in English may seem less natural than those they are accustomed to in the same genre in their own language.

Procedures

Guided by insights derived from the literature previously mentioned, we decided to explicitly teach selected genre practices related to character depiction and the thinking processes for realising those practices. The thinking processes involved forming a rhetorical goal pertaining to reader effect and using this high-level goal for self-directing the choice of epithets and ideational tokens to construct a character.

The 33 students involved in the study were a class of 15-year-old Secondary 3 students in a suburban school in Singapore. Secondary 3 is the 3rd year of high school following 6 years of primary (junior) school. Like all mainstream public schools in Singapore, the school uses English as the medium of instruction. For many of the students in our study, English is not the home language or the preferred language of peer interaction. Even when it is, it tends to be the local colloquial variety, known as Singapore Colloquial English (Gupta, 1994), rather than the standard variety expected by language examiners. Nevertheless, most of the students could write understandable sentences despite frequent mistakes in grammar and usage. Their main problem in narrative writing was the inability to proceed beyond a sequential recounting of bare events; their stories tended to have a minimum of detail or none at all, or randomly chosen details. To address this problem, we used a series of writing lessons.

Before instruction began, the students wrote a story entitled "An Unhappy Wife." Writing took place in class in the students' usual 70-minute composition period. No feedback comments were given by the teacher on these preinstruction stories. A series of seven weekly lessons followed, each lasting 1 hour and 10 minutes, conducted by the second author. The lessons, planned with input from the first author, featured two main teaching and learning activities:

1. Deconstruction (Rothery, 1996) to observe how an expert writer selects language and meaning with the goal of creating a particular reader effect.

2. Group exercises to practise the goal-directed thinking and meaning-making processes observed during deconstruction.

The text used for deconstruction was a short story entitled "The Headache" by Ann Hunter (from the book *The Stench of Kerosene and Other Stories*, selected by Steve Bowls, Cambridge University Press, 1991). This story was chosen because its main characters are created through use of epithets (descriptive words or phrases) and ideational tokens (words that depict a character's qualities or emotions by describing behaviour or something in the environment).

The first lesson began with the teacher introducing and explaining three concepts: rhetorical goals and intentions, epithets, and ideational tokens. These concepts gave students a language for directing their thinking during character construction and for talking about this thinking in group work. The concepts were explained to students as follows:

- Rhetorical goals and intentions—Your aim, as writer, when describing a character. How do you want the reader to feel or think about the character? Example: To create a character the reader will feel sorry for.

- Epithets—Words for describing a character's appearance (*beautiful*), mood (*frightened*), personality (*tight-fisted*), or behaviour (*uncontrollable*).

- Ideational tokens—Words that create, in the reader, a certain impression of a character. The impression is created by describing something that represents the character's appearance, mood, personality, or behaviour. Example: *He stood up and gave her a sudden slap*— to depict a character as a bully and evoke disgust in the reader.

To ensure that every student was familiar with the story "The Headache," the rest of the first lesson was used for students' silent reading of the story. In the second lesson, deconstruction of the story began with teacher and students jointly studying how the author of the story selected details to paint a consistent picture of the main character, Joanna. The teacher asked questions to draw students' attention to the writer's rhetorical goal: What words did the author use to describe Joanna's appearance? Why did she use these words and not words such as *plain*? How does the author want the reader to feel about Joanna?

In Lesson 3, an exercise for group activity was set for students to practise the thinking involved in directing choice of meaning with a rhetorical goal. The exercise required them to pick, from a list, descriptive details that matched a given rhetorical goal and to justify that choice. The teacher went from group to group to check that the students' discussions on why a detail should be selected or rejected referred to the given writer goal. When students gave other reasons (e.g., It sounds better), the teacher guided the talk back to the rhetorical goal. Listening in to each group's discussion gave the teacher the opportunity to ascertain that all students understood what it meant to make goal-referenced decisions in writing.

In Lessons 4 through 6, the teacher guided students to notice how the writer of the deconstruction story realised her goal through the application of two genre practices: using epithets to construct a character and creating ideational tokens to evoke the character's qualities. Two lessons were devoted to each of these practices. Guided by the teacher's questions (e.g., The author uses the epithet *soft curls* to describe Joanna's hair. How does the author want us to feel about Joanna?), students identified exemplars of the genre practice and traced the relation of each instance of epithet or ideational token to the author's goal. After the teacher and students had jointly studied a part of the story, students worked on their own in groups to identify other epithets or ideational tokens that aligned with the author's goal in constructing the same character and other characters in the story. Students recorded their observations in a matrix that required them to describe how an epithet or ideational token created the intended reader effect. (See Appendix A for the epithet matrix.)

After each deconstruction lesson, students working in small groups practised the thinking processes and language skills they had learnt. In the second lesson on epithets, for example, students practised thinking up and selecting epithets for character depiction to meet a rhetorical goal of their choice. (See Appendix B for the exercise.)

When the lessons were over, the students did the same narrative writing task given at the preinstruction stage. They did not refer to their preinstruction story, which was written 7 weeks earlier and had not been returned to them. We decided to set the same task for postinstruction writing, so that there would be a common basis for comparing pre- and postinstruction stories. If a different task were given after instruction, it might have been difficult to distinguish whether the improvements were attributable to the lessons or to other reasons, such as the second task being easier to complete or providing a better stimulus.

In addition to the pre- and postinstruction stories, students wrote entries in a journal before instruction began, after each lesson, and after submitting their postinstruction stories. Class time was allocated for journal writing to ensure that all students made entries in their learning journals. The purpose of the journal entries was to track students' responses to the lessons, in particular their reactions to and understanding of thinking rhetorically and the genre practice of crafting characters with epithets and ideational tokens.

We analysed pre- and postinstruction narratives to discover if the instruction had any effect on the quality of character depiction. We looked for evidence of change in these abilities:

- Writing with a rhetorical goal and selecting details that match the goal.

- Selecting and using appropriate epithets and ideational tokens.

We first read the stories rapidly to obtain an impression of the student writer's intended rhetorical goal and then searched for discordant details (e.g., information about a character's appearance or actions) that did not fit the narrator's rhetorical goal. Discordant items included epithets and ideational tokens that did not fit the story. The rationale for identifying discordant items was that if writing is a goal-directed thinking process (Flower & Hayes, 1981), then students who directed their writing with a rhetorical intention would produce stories with no discordant details. The number of discordant details in each narrative was noted and compared across preinstruction and postinstruction stories. Based on the number of discordant details a story contained, we categorized it as reflecting a consistent rhetorical goal, a vacillating goal, or a vague or possibly nonexistent goal (see Table 1).

We read the essays again to count the number of epithets and ideational

Table 1. Categories of Rhetorical Goals

Rhetorical Goal	Indicators
Consistent (0 discordant items)	Depiction of character takes an obvious slant or position, and this position is maintained through appropriate choice of supporting details.
Vacillating (1–2 discordant items)	Depiction shifts from one polarity to another (e.g., from evoking disgust to admiration or neutrality and then back to disgust). Details chosen are conflicting.
Vague or nonexistent (3 or more discordant items)	Details of character do not converge on one effect.

tokens occurring in pre- and postinstruction essays. Inappropriate epithets and ideational tokens were counted separately from appropriate ones. Appropriateness was decided by considering the narrator's rhetorical goal, which we had identified earlier. Table 2 illustrates how discordant items, epithets, and ideational tokens (shown in italics) were identified.

Results

In Table 3, we have summarized how the findings relate to the research questions. Following the summary, more details from the findings are discussed in terms of what we learnt about teaching thinking and genre processes as a means of developing writing skills.

The drop in discordant details in the postinstruction stories (as shown in Table 3) suggests the influence of a rhetorical goal in the students' writing process after the lessons. Studies by Flower and Hayes (1981) have revealed that good writers make decisions by using high-level goals as a reference point. The students in our study must have learnt to form high-level goals when they were taught to articulate the effect they intended their story to have on readers.

Table 2. Identification of Discordant Items, Epithets, and Ideational Tokens

Excerpt From Student's Essay	Discordance, Epithets, and Ideational Tokens
"You never have time for the family," came the accusing tone of Mrs. Lee. Mr. Lee had been *slogging away* as the manager of a company. . . . "Don't you start interrogating me . . . or you'll regret it," *snarled* Mr. Lee. He *shoved her aside rudely*, sending her sprawling. . . .	Discordant item.[1] Appropriate ideational token. Aligns with goal to depict character as violent, uncaring.
One Sunday as Mrs. Lee was doing her usual shopping . . . she was *amused* to find her husband holding hands with another woman. . . . She went forward to her husband. "Why do you have to do this to me?" cried Mrs. Lee as she *tried to blink back the tears* that threatened to spill out.	Inappropriate epithet. Appropriate ideational token. Aligns with goal to depict Mrs. Lee as a long-suffering wife.

[1]Narrator's goal, gleaned from the story read as a whole, is to depict Mr. Lee as violent and uncaring of his family and Mrs. Lee as a long-suffering victim.

Source: Unedited excerpts from Student LHF's essay

Teaching Character Depiction in Narrative Writing (*Singapore*)

Table 3. Summary of Main Findings Answering Research Questions

Research Question	Findings
Did students become more aware of rhetorical goals?	Stories with discordant details dropped from 33.3% (preinstruction) to 12.1%.
	Stories with a consistent rhetorical intention increased from 72.7% to 87.9% after instruction. (n = 33)
Were there more epithets in the postinstruction essays?	Number of epithets rose from 106 (preinstruction) to 208.
Were more epithets appropriately chosen?	Appropriately chosen epithets rose from 88.7% to 93.3%. (n = 106 and 208 respectively)
Were there more ideational tokens in postinstruction essays?	Number of appropriate ideational tokens increased from 83 (preinstruction) to 164.

Writing with the intention to create a particular reader effect may have impelled them to vet ideas against their intention and to reject details that did not fit.

Although stories with a consistent goal increased from 72.7% of the preinstruction essays to 87.9% of the postinstruction essays (see Table 3), this rather low increase may not accurately represent the learning that occurred. The 72.7% may not be an accurate reflection of the number of students who wrote without a rhetorical intention before instruction because consistence of intention was measured by the absence of discordant details. The preinstruction essays tended to have few details to begin with, therefore the fact that a student was writing without a reader-effect goal could have been undetected in many cases. From students' journal entries, it appears that a significant number had learnt to conceive and use a rhetorical goal by the time they wrote their postinstruction essays. All 33 students commented in their journals on the rhetorical goal lessons. Some journal entries clearly suggested that the notion of rhetorical goal affected the students' writing processes. For an example, see Table 4.

Student AI's admission that she "just wrote whatever was in my mind" strongly suggests a writing process, before instruction, that was not guided by a rhetorical goal. Her portrayal of her postinstruction expertise as ability to "describe feelings . . . and characters further" seems to reflect a felt ability to generate "further" meanings in the direction set by some kind of mental goal she had. Her newly acquired skill has freed her from her previous dependence on "whatever was in my mind" as a method of generating text. Student AI and many of her classmates can be said to have made some progress in their learning journey as writers when they show, in their journals and postinstruction essays, evidence of using a high-level rhetorical goal as the reference point for composing.

Table 4. Journal Entries Depicting Changes in Writing Process

In Preinstruction Journal	In Postinstruction Journal
My mind was completely blank when given the topic. . . . I just wrote whatever was in my mind.	Now I'm able to describe feelings, people, and characters further than I have always done and written.

Source: Unedited excerpts from Student AI's journal

The increase in the number of epithets and appropriately created ideational tokens in the postinstruction essays (see Table 3) suggests that teaching genre practices and associated thinking processes equips students with the know-how to generate not just more content but more appropriate content. The increase from 83 to 164 appropriate ideational tokens—almost double—seems particularly impressive, considering the fact that there were only 7 weekly lessons taught to students who were academically average rather than high achieving. The students who used ideational tokens appropriately in character depiction must have guided their composing with a rhetorical goal, or their ideational tokens would not have aligned with the effect created by the other details of the same character in the story. A close examination of many postinstruction stories revealed an improvement in quality of character depiction that is not wholly captured by the Table 3 statistics on epithets and ideational tokens. See the example from Student LHF in Table 5.

Notice in the Table 5 excerpts that the husband in the preinstruction story, who is depicted as merely *angry*, is constructed as a more menacing figure in the postinstruction story. Ideational tokens relating to speech (*you'll regret, curses, threatened*) and actions (*snarled, shoved, sending her sprawling*) create a representation of the character's callousness. Besides demonstrating the effect of the

Table 5. Effect of Instruction on Use of Ideational Tokens

Preinstruction Story	Postinstruction Story
"You never have time for the family," shouted Mrs. Lee. . . . "I am working hard for a living not just playing around," exclaimed Mr. Lee, who was *angry* with his wife. Their children kept feeling scared whenever their parent quarrels with one another.	"You never have time for the family," came the accusing tone of Mrs. Lee. . . . "Don't you start interrogating me as if I'm a criminal or *you'll regret it*," *snarled* Mr. Lee in return. *He shoved her aside rudely, sending her sprawling across the floor* as she attempted to stop him leaving. *He uttered a string of curses and threatened to beat her up* . . . he left the house. Their children stood at the doorway looking. . . .

Source: Unedited excerpts (italics added) from Student LHF's "The Unhappy Wife"

lessons on ideational tokens, the postinstruction excerpt suggests the influence of a rhetorical goal during the composing process. The effort at creating an unlikeable character might not have been as well sustained if the student had not formed and kept to an intention to project the husband as violent. Similar improvements were noticeable in many other postinstruction essays written by class members.

It might be argued that the improvements illustrated in Table 5 arose from writing the same story a second time and not from learning about rhetorical goals, epithets, and ideational tokens. Although doing the same writing task a second time may produce some improvement in the second text, improvement across the class is likely to be random in nature, varying with individual capability and experience at narrative writing. If the instruction had not played a role in bringing about the more focused characterisation in the postinstruction stories, there might not have been such a drop in the number of stories with discordant details, from 33.3% to 12.1% (see Table 3). The significant drop suggests that many students had learnt to manage their composing process more deliberately as a result of learning to set reader-effect goals. They had learnt *how* to write, as one journal entry testifies:

> A lot of my classmates feel more confident now. I think all teachers should teach their students how to write. (Student SF)

The main finding of our study is that the participating students' narratives showed improvements in character depiction following lessons that taught them to form rhetorical goals and to use the goals to guide their choices of epithets and ideational tokens to construct the protagonists in their stories. A drop in the number of discordant items and a rise in appropriately used epithets and ideational tokens in the postinstruction essays together indicate the influence of a goal in the composing process. The findings suggest that teaching genre practices and the thinking underlying the practices can lead to better writing of the same genre.

Reflection

This study has given us the confidence to continue using the same eclectic cognitive-cum-genre approach to teaching writing, not only for narratives but for other genres too. The findings affirm our belief in the benefits of combining the explicit teaching of genre practices with demonstrations of the ways of thinking that produce these practices. Encouraged by the improvements in the postinstruction narratives, the first author has embarked on a research project to test the efficacy of teaching secondary school students the thinking procedures underlying the main genre practices in expository and argumentative writing.

Doing this research has convinced us that it is possible for language teachers to identify genre practices and some, at least, of the underlying cognitive operations responsible for the genre qualities they would like to see in students' texts. Teachers, by virtue of being readers of stories, news reports, and other genres that they ask students to write, are capable of observing and naming the thinking processes and genre practices that students need to learn so as to write effectively. It was through observation and introspection that we identified what to teach in our narrative writing lessons.

The process of planning and implementing activities to teach thinking and genre processes gave us immense satisfaction when we looked at the improvements in character depiction in the postinstruction essays. We realised how much students could benefit if we actually taught writing, instead of merely telling them to write and then correcting their mistakes. The students too seemed to feel a sense of empowerment after having ways of thinking and using language explicitly described to them, as the following journal entry shows:

> After learning epithets and ideational tokens I found a great improvement in my composition. I learnt to use them under different circumstances. . . . I don't feel so lost as before. (Student SL)

Teaching the thinking processes for creating the features of a genre takes the mystery out of writing.

We think there are two reasons that research studies like ours should be done in Asia. The first has to do with the fact that Asian students, who are mostly from non-English-speaking homes, may not have as much exposure as native English speakers to narrative and other genres written in English. Their unfamiliarity with the discourse practices of the short story genre, for instance, makes them the perfect subjects for studying the effects of teaching methods that spell out genre practices and the expectations of the community of target readers. Second, it is not difficult to find in Asian classrooms a considerable number of learners with a level of language proficiency that enables them to write understandable, though not error-free, English sentences and paragraphs. As language teachers, we could not help but wonder if these students' texts would take on more qualities of the target genre, despite surface grammar errors, if they were taught the thinking processes for producing the characteristic features of that genre. In other words, would their narratives resemble well-written short stories more closely if they had learnt the thinking processes that lead to vivid characterisation or an engaging complication? If the writing of Asian English language learners approximates a genre more closely after instruction in the discourse practices of that genre, we would be justified in advocating that all teachers (not just those in Asia) use the teaching methods that prioritise genre practices and genre-related thinking.

Antonia Chandrasegaran teaches at the National Institute of Education, Singapore.
Siok-Chin Yeo teaches at Yishun Secondary School in Singapore.

Appendix A: Deconstruction Worksheet for Study of Epithets

Name of character:_____

Writer's goal (intention)—complete one of the following:

To make the reader feel_____for/against the character.

To show up the character as a_____person.

Epithet Chosen by Writer	How It Achieves the Writer's Rhetorical Goal

Appendix B: Practising Choice of Epithets

INSTRUCTIONS:

Work as a group. Select one of the rhetorical goals in the left column. Suggest and select epithets to do the writing stated in the right column. You must aim to achieve the goal. Write a short paragraph (20–40 words) describing the character.

Rhetorical Goal	Describe the Character's
The reader will see this person as a very neat/untidy/kind/mean person. (Choose one quality.)	Appearance
Make the reader feel disgust/pity/a liking for this person. (Choose one feeling.)	Behaviour
Create in the reader contempt/admiration for this person. (Choose one effect.)	Thoughts

Expert and Nonexpert Teachers: Do They Use Different Processes While Learning to Teach? (*Thailand*)

Sumalee Chinokul

Issue

This research started when I reflected on my role as *teacher of the teacher* when I was assigned to teach the course Methodology of English Language Teaching. This course, held 3 hours per week for 15 weeks, is an elective in a graduate program leading toward a doctorate or master's degree in English as an international language at Chulalongkorn University in Bangkok, Thailand. Because the course is offered to master's and doctoral students, I found a huge gap between their levels of education, their learning and teaching knowledge, and their teaching experiences. Identifying teaching expertise can be problematic (Tsui, 2003) because of students' different experiences. However, I decided to try to categorize some as expert teachers and others as nonexpert teachers, so that I would then be able to provide them with more proper instruction. In other words, if I could estimate each student's *zone of proximal development* (Vygotsky, 1978b), then I would be able to provide scaffolding as they learned how to teach English as a foreign language (EFL). Therefore, I decided to conduct some research to increase my teaching effectiveness. My main research question was "How do these expert teachers and nonexpert teachers use different processes while learning to teach EFL in Thailand?"

Background Literature

Knowledge gained about teaching not only comes from teacher preservice courses but also is combined with the experiences of being a student. Wallace (1991) concluded that teaching ability is merged from both the received knowledge and experiential knowledge. Learning to teach requires that prospective teachers acquire knowledge about all facets of classroom life. This complex development is a result of teachers using knowledge and beliefs to make sense of themselves as teachers, their own teaching practices, their students, the content they are expected to teach, and the classrooms and schools within which they work. This process of meaning making continues through stages of the learning experience (Johnson, 1999). Learning to teach is a long-term, complex, socially constructed, developmental process that is acquired by participating in the social practices associated with teaching and learning. By combining such experiences, knowledge, and beliefs in the context of real classrooms, this learning forms the foundation for teachers' reasoning and the justifications for their classroom practices (Johnson).

From theoretical and practical perspectives, novice teachers go through difficult stages to become experts (Anderson, 1983; Randall & Thornton, 2001; Tsui, 2003). When they first begin to teach, they need to have conscious control over the content and the procedural process in their teaching. Their knowledge of classroom life tends to be limited to what they experienced as students and thus does not account for what they experience when they enter the classroom as the teacher. When their teaching becomes more autonomous and they construct their teaching knowledge based on intra-individual factors, interpersonal factors, and sociopolitical factors (Haste, 1987), they are better able to reconceptualize the content they are expected to teach from their students' perspectives and can develop a repertoire of reasoned instructional considerations to inform their classroom practices.

In my EFL teacher preparation course, the aim is to improve my students' beliefs, attitudes, and skills in teaching and learning EFL. I have realized that improvement in teaching entails changes—in this case, from less desirable to more desirable teaching practices. Such changes demand that the student teachers look critically at themselves and be prepared to change. Richards and Nunan (1990) noted that "experience alone is insufficient for professional growth, and that experience coupled with reflection is a much more powerful impetus for development" (p. 201). Therefore I decided to explore and investigate the beliefs the student teachers held, their received knowledge, their experiential knowledge, their practicum teaching, and their reflections on all of these aspects.

Zeichner and Liston (1996) convincingly encourage teachers to reflect on their teaching: "Teaching is work that entails both thinking and feeling, and those who can reflectively think and feel will find their work more rewarding and their efforts more successful" (p. xii). Through reflective teaching, practicing teachers and prospective ones examine and critically inquire about ends, means, and contexts of teaching. Reflective teaching thus helps teachers to examine practical theories; the experiences, knowledge, and values that they bring to teaching; and other issues that are pertinent to the teaching profession (Zeichner & Liston). Stanley (1998) suggested that reflective teaching is performed in five stages: engaging with reflection; thinking reflectively; using reflection; sustaining reflection; and practicing reflection. Viewing teachers as reflective practitioners assumes that teachers can pose and solve problems related to their educational practice. Because teachers are directly involved in the classroom, they bring perspectives about the complexities of teaching that cannot be matched by external researchers. Ghaye and Ghaye (1998) propose that reflection on practice is a process of continuous knowledge construction. With commitment, willingness, and enthusiasm to question the knowledge that is created and to challenge personal and collective values, teachers construct their professional knowledge. Reflection on practice is also regarded as a vital part of a teacher's meaning-making process when he or she attempts to improve the existing order and pattern of educational practice (Ghaye & Ghaye). Reflective teaching, through exploratory tasks and activities such as journal writing, peer observation, and action research, can foster critical self-examination, self-inquiry, and self-evaluation (Richards & Lockhart, 1994) as a means of professional development in English as a second language (ESL) classrooms.

Procedures

The research I conducted was not a classroom experiment but was simply part of normal classroom procedure and my reflection on my own practice. The aims of the Methodology of English Language Teaching course were to provide an opportunity for the course participants to critically understand major approaches and methods used in ESL/EFL teaching; to get accustomed to reflective thinking about our attitudes, opinions, and beliefs concerning ESL and EFL teaching; to develop competence in using various teaching techniques; to gain practical experience in conducting needs assessments; to be able to evaluate, adapt, and develop instructional materials and activities; and to learn how to effectively observe, teach, and assess EFL classrooms.

My approach was to put theory into practice and raise my students' awareness of their EFL teaching through an instructional model based on the 2R2C principle, which stands for reflective teaching, research-based instruction, constructivism, and collaboration. Students were made aware of and worked toward the pedagogical goals and content of the course in two ways: (a) by reflecting and using research in their own teaching and (b) by reflecting on and using research in their roles as students in my methodology course. Students were involved in selecting, adapting, and modifying the goals and content of the course among a range of options. Through this process, they were engaged in constructing their own knowledge about English language teaching methods while they collaboratively created the content for reflection and the lesson plans, materials, and tasks to teach to their own students. They learned and shared with classmates. Then they went beyond the classroom and made links between the course content and the world beyond through self-evaluation of their own teaching. The data for this study of students' processes of learning to teach were collected from course assignments (students' diaries or weekly methodology notebooks and lesson plans) as well as teaching observations and interviews. The examination of these issues arose from the following tasks that the students performed and that I responded to with feedback:

- Lesson plan evaluation forms
- Peer teaching evaluation sheets
- Self-evaluations
- Teaching observation checklists
- Semistructured interview questions
- Teachers' belief inventories
- Course evaluation forms

All the students did the same assignments and tasks. However, as the instructor of the course, I did select some students to be case studies so I could examine their processes of learning to teach while maintaining the usual routine classroom procedures as planned. Among the 26 graduate students who enrolled in the course, I chose four students designated as expert teachers and four students designated as nonexpert teachers to be the case studies. The term *expert teacher* in this study refers to a student teacher who was competent in teaching EFL, had experience teaching, understood the teaching context well, and was well qualified as an English teacher according to the criteria to measure expertise in teaching EFL (Chinokul, 2004). The term *nonexpert teacher*, on the other hand, refers to a student teacher who was not quite competent in teaching EFL, had not much experience teaching, did not understand the teaching context well, and was not well qualified as an English teacher as measured by the criteria. To maintain each student's natural process of learning to teach, I did not inform them about my project until the last day of the course. At that point, they all agreed to take part in my research.

I analyzed and interpreted the diaries, lesson plans, observation checklists, and interviews by looking for key words or phrases. Then I categorized the emerging data into three stages of the participants' processes of learning to teach EFL: past English language learning experience, learning in the methodology course, and real classroom experiences as a teacher. Teaching performance between the expert and nonexpert teachers was compared in terms of lesson plans (before teaching), teaching behaviors (while teaching), and reflection (after teaching).

Results

The results and discussions are organized according to the following concepts: (a) insights the participants gained from their past English language learning experiences, (b) insights they gained from the methodology of English language teaching course, and (c) insights they gained from their real teaching experiences.

INSIGHTS FROM PARTICIPANTS' PAST ENGLISH LANGUAGE LEARNING EXPERIENCES

Students in the expert and nonexpert categories seemed quite motivated to learn English. However, the expert teachers seemed to be more self-confident, and the nonexpert teachers seemed to be modest about their abilities as learners of English. The differences between the groups might be attributed to the expert teachers' tendency to be self-directed learners.

In interviews, the participants created metaphors to conceptualize themselves as language learners in the past. Expert teachers characterized themselves as being active and ready to change, and the nonexperts portrayed themselves as passive and waiting to receive instructions (see Table 1).

The insights from the expert and nonexpert teachers' experiences as language learners in the past, their exposure to the English language used outside classrooms, their confidence in using the language, and their active learning in the past may have created the differences in the teaching approaches they used in language classes once they became English teachers themselves. Nonexpert Teacher 2 stated in her diary entry: "When I first taught, I didn't know what the activities were like and how I could manage to use them in the class. This

Table 1. Participants' Characterizations of Their Past Language Learning

Expert Teachers (ET)	Nonexpert Teachers (NET)
ET 1: active learner	NET 1: subordinate
ET 2: explorer	NET 2: language user
ET 3: musician	NET 3: savings account
ET 4: sponge	NET 4: small bee

ignorance may be because I was taught by traditional teaching methods, and so I am afraid of taking any risks using activities in class."

INSIGHTS FROM PARTICIPANTS' LEARNING IN THE METHODOLOGY COURSE

The participants were asked to respond to a questionnaire (see Johnson, 1992) on the teachers' inventory approaches to English language instruction. They had to choose 5 statements out of 15 that most closely reflected their beliefs about how English should be learned and taught. I calculated the frequency of the chosen statements—reflecting their preferences for skill-based, rule-based, and function-based instruction—and then converted these numbers to percentages. The results revealed differences between expert and nonexpert teachers' perceptions of teaching approaches. The expert group put more focus on or tended to perceive as important rule-based and function-based teaching approaches. This seems to suggest that they focused on both accuracy and meaning. The nonexpert teachers focused more on skill-based and function-based teaching approaches, suggesting their tendency to focus on fluency and meaning. The difference was their preferences for promoting either fluency or accuracy, which is still a debatable and controversial issue among ESL and EFL scholars.

The participants expressed negative views about the theory-based class they had experienced before the methods course, and they expressed their need to clarify how to put theory into practice. In this study, there was evidence that expert and nonexpert teachers' perceptions about putting theory into practice changed to a certain degree when they learned from the instructor, from their peers, and from the thinking they put into their reflections.

The expert and nonexpert teachers learned about the processes of teaching from the ways the instructor handled the class. For example, they learned how to prepare lessons, manage and interact with students in class so as to encourage critical thinking, prepare the materials and organize activities in class, and evaluate and assess students' learning.

The nonexpert teachers learned the terms and concepts about teaching and learning and how to apply theory into practice from the viewpoints of expert peers. Some of the nonexpert teachers also were encouraged to put more effort into their processes of learning when they witnessed how hard their friends had worked to improve their teaching skills. The expert teachers also learned some new teaching techniques from demonstrations and videotape records of their friends' teaching, which were shown in class for discussions. Expert Teacher 2 said, "What popped up in my head while viewing the video was that technology is a very helpful tool, the personality of the teachers plus computer skills made the lesson much more interesting, and it could increase students' motivation as well."

Expert and nonexpert teachers admitted that they learned a great deal from writing their reflections in the methodology notebooks. Expert Teacher 4 mentioned that "I have to think a lot how to write something for weekly methodology notebook. Think about what I have learned today, and beyond that I have to think and relate what I learned today with information I had learned before. How is the new information different from the previous one? I have to be very critical whether I would agree or disagree with the points being raised. Why? How?"

I analyzed participants' reflections in their notebooks in terms of their ability to link theory and application by using an assessment for reflective journal activities adapted from the Web site Educational, Inspirational and Devotional Tools for Catholic Educators, Catechists, Parents, and Students (n.d.). I identified eight criteria for measuring the ability to link theory and application:

1. teaching awareness

2. response

3. communicative skills in English

4. reflection skills

5. reflection in relation to lecture content

6. reflection in terms of comprehension

7. ability to develop argument and opinion

8. reflection in terms of cooperation during activities or tasks raised in the lecture

Significant differences were found in five of the eight areas: 1, 2, 6, 7, and 8.

In addition, the data from students' reflections were also analyzed qualitatively, and the results showed the different strategies these expert and nonexpert teachers used in understanding learning and teaching concepts. These differences can be explained using the concepts of *deep* and *surface* approaches to learning, as illustrated in Figure 1. The expert teachers engaged in a deep approach to learning when they tried to understand and make sense of the teaching and learning concepts. In contrast, the nonexpert teachers simply related the concepts at a surface level by using the suggested procedures and did not really find the underlying reasons for the concepts.

With regard to learning in the course, the expert and nonexpert teachers thought it was important for them to put theory into practice, but they differed in their perceptions of effective teaching methods, their abilities to reflect on teaching, and their learning levels.

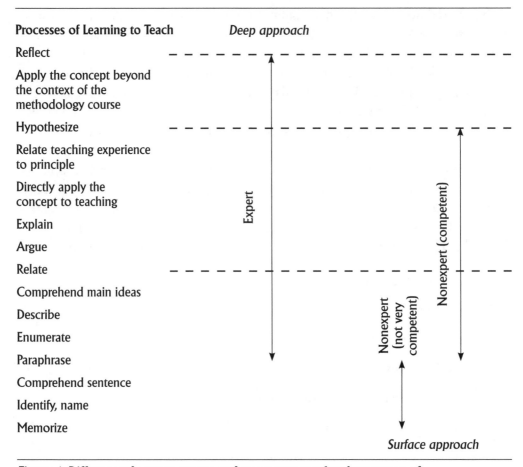

Processes of Learning to Teach

Deep approach

Reflect

Apply the concept beyond the context of the methodology course

Hypothesize

Relate teaching experience to principle

Directly apply the concept to teaching

Explain

Argue

Relate

Comprehend main ideas

Describe

Enumerate

Paraphrase

Comprehend sentence

Identify, name

Memorize

Expert

Nonexpert (not very competent)

Nonexpert (competent)

Surface approach

Figure 1. Differences between expert and nonexpert teachers' processes of learning to teach.

INSIGHTS FROM PARTICIPANTS' REAL CLASSROOM TEACHING EXPERIENCES

Qualitative analysis of the lesson plans written by the expert and nonexpert teachers demonstrated observable differences in their objectives, content, teaching steps, tasks and activities, and monitoring and evaluation of the learning outcomes, as shown in Table 2.

The qualitative analysis of lesson plans to some extent explained the differences between the groups' lesson plans. Because mental lesson planning was practiced by some of the expert teachers, I could have more accurately evaluated their plans if they had explicitly shown the details. Expert Teacher 2 commented that "effective detailed lesson planning probably may be a good idea but it should be flexible so as to allow for the teacher's creativity during the class. . . . Many teachers will only focus on the content, and so they forgot what their students need."

Table 2. Analysis of the Lesson Plans

Issues	Expert Teachers	Nonexpert Teachers
Objective	• was specific, clear, and measurable • identified what, how much, when, and how to teach	• was broad, pluralistic • had no relation among activities
Content	• focused on meaning and understanding • integrated content and skills • oriented toward problem-solving skills • focused on independent content, did not rely on textbooks	• focused on minor skills • separated content and skills, skill-oriented • was heavily dependent on the textbooks to develop materials and content for the class
Teaching steps	• provided ample opportunities for students to integrate new knowledge with established knowledge • focused on the process rather than product • focused on learner-centered activities • provided choices for learners • encouraged the students to go on learning • used collaborative learning • conducted implicit lesson planning • devised and provided the maximum of practice	• focused on the outcome of the product or something more concrete • focused on teacher-dominant activities • used teacher as the only learning resource • conducted explicit, detailed lesson planning • focused on the transmitted content rather than what the students could learn
Tasks/ activities	• showed variety, were entertaining • drew from various resources	• were predictable, patterned • were not quite challenging
Monitoring/ evaluation of the learning outcomes	• controlled or monitored the quality of students' output as well as length of time they needed to accomplish the expected learning outcomes	• tended to allow the activities to go naturally • rarely used monitoring techniques to control the activities to reach the expected learning outcomes

From the findings, the implication for instruction about the before-teaching phase was that I needed to help the students see the importance of planning, teaching, and evaluating, and see how all these elements could be linked to create a well-organized overall lesson.

I compared the quality of the experts' and nonexperts' classroom teaching behaviors to examine the differences. Target classroom teaching behaviors were evaluated and given scores from 1 to 5 points, depending on the quality. This analysis of the actual classroom teaching revealed that the experts outperformed their counterparts with regard to overall classroom management skills, clear explanation, techniques to help increase students' motivation, appropriate seating arrangements, the teacher's circulation in class, group management skills, and the encouragement of active learning.

In addition, I analyzed a videotape record of the students' teaching, using a checklist of teaching behaviors observed. To record features of teaching behaviors, I used a minute event matrix. In other words, I viewed the videotape and paused it to check the appearance of target behaviors every minute. Target behaviors for this analysis were the teacher's strategies in questioning and giving feedback, the teacher's actions with regard to establishing students' motivation, classroom management, and transitions between activities. Some teaching behaviors observed in expert teachers were more likely to create effective teaching and learning—for example, effective use of questions, connection between the students' background knowledge and new knowledge, and links between activities used. Some teaching behaviors practiced by the nonexpert teachers, such as allowing a long period of silence or confusion in class, seemed unlikely to produce effective teaching and learning outcomes.

These findings were consistent with the results of a detailed qualitative analysis of the expert and nonexpert teachers' teaching behaviors in class, as illustrated in Table 3.

The findings from observing the experts' and nonexperts' teaching behaviors were important, because they showed the teaching qualities both groups needed

Table 3. Analysis of Teaching Behaviors in Class

Expert Teachers	Nonexpert Teachers
· accurately linked what was planned with the expected learning outcome and demonstrated the ability to write lesson plans	· demonstrated limited ability to write lesson plans unless guidance was provided
· used position and proxemics adequately · circulated in class adequately	· asked students to sit in rows or prearranged groups · remained at podium as teacher's main position · did not circulate in class very much
· provided useful feedback	· did not provide any useful feedback (e.g., gave yes or no answers)
· pointed out the main structures or issues · focused on the deep approach	· provided only the main lists or facts · did not provide any links to the main teaching points

Table 3. Analysis of Teaching Behaviors in Class *(continued)*

Expert Teachers	Nonexpert Teachers
· based the teaching content mainly on integration of thought and knowledge	· focused on overview of the issue · did not demonstrate any deep understanding of the subject matter
· considered the context and the students when teaching problems needed to be solved · was well informed about the students' expectations and limitations	· focused on the content rather than the learners when teaching problems needed to be solved · focused on covering what was stated in the lesson plan
· was flexible and able to predict when a problem occurred	· was not quite flexible
· carried out teaching steps smoothly and naturally	· sometimes allowed teaching steps to become unnatural
· provided students with appropriate strategies to understand the language · encouraged the students to think and raise critical questions or issues	· demonstrated intention to transfer the content written in the lesson plan · provided surface feedback · focused on memory of the language patterns that appeared in the texts
· dealt with inappropriate or disruptive students' behaviors	· avoided dealing with inappropriate or disruptive students' behaviors
· evaluated the main concept	· evaluated the minor points and facts
· used teaching and evaluation procedures to help create a good classroom environment concerning involvement	· provided necessary answers for the students, thus removing opportunity to think or present problems
· encouraged cheerful classroom atmosphere	· promoted uninteresting classroom atmosphere · maintained predictable teacher and student roles

in order to become better teachers. For me, as the teacher of the course, the observations demonstrated areas that the student teachers needed more practice in.

After the period of instruction, the expert and nonexpert teachers attended postinstruction conferences with me, during which they were asked to complete self-evaluation forms and submit reports. The data from their self-evaluation forms and their reports were then analyzed for students' ability to link theory and practice (using the assessment I developed). This assessment was categorized into 3 levels:

- Level 1—the ability to give details related to teaching theory (scores ranging from 1 to 3 points).

- Level 2—the ability to give and prove hypotheses using theory (scores ranging from 4 to 8 points).

- Level 3—the ability to link the rationale of the teaching principles with practical aspects (scores ranging from 9 to 10 points).

The self-evaluation results showed that the expert and nonexpert teachers' abilities to link theory and practice were significantly different. The expert teachers' abilities were at Level 2, and the nonexpert teachers' abilities were at Level 1. However, the results from their later written reports did not reveal significant differences.

Therefore, I placed expert and nonexpert teachers at Level 2. Nonetheless, when the data from their weekly methodology notebooks were analyzed, they revealed some interesting differences in behaviors. The expert teachers were more likely to engage themselves with an experiment to find or confirm their curiosity in teaching. However, that was not the case for the nonexpert teachers, who were more likely to defend their teaching in an effort to gain acceptance from their teaching instructor.

These findings from the after-teaching phase had interesting implications for me as the instructor of the course. How can I help my students improve their ability to the desired Level 3? In teaching, I may need to make all student teachers aware that the important part of the training is for them to improve their teaching. Thus, there is no need for them to be defensive.

Reflection

As a teacher you have reflected the image of teachers = teacher + hero. I like the way you commented and gave feedback to our teaching. It was so encouraging. You did not try to flatter us but you would back up with reasons. Here I am not trying to flatter you either, but I am trying to find the reason why I like your approach. (Expert Teacher 3)

Using the findings to answer my main research question, which was "How do the expert teachers and nonexpert teachers use different processes while learning to teach EFL?" helped me focus my teaching on the expert and nonexpert groups. To reach my goal of learner training, it was necessary to collect information about teaching behavior and practices objectively and systematically and to use this information as a basis for making decisions about whether I should change the teaching aspects I focused on in my methodology course. I observed the students teaching, asked them to write journal entries for 15 weeks during the course, and interviewed them. With this information, I was in a better position to estimate each student's zone of proximal development and be able to project his or her potential level (Vygotsky, 1978b).

The insights into the differences between the two groups in classroom management skills as well as their strategies for controlling teaching outcomes and feedback led me to an alternative way of monitoring their teaching and providing more concrete target teaching behaviors that the learners required. I became more aware of alternative ways to teach the nonexpert teacher group to promote cooperation in the learning process and encourage them to apply a deeper approach to learning, become aware of the limited range of teaching strategies that they had been using, realize that they needed to develop better classroom management strategies, learn the value of evaluating themselves, and learn more about their strengths and weaknesses as teachers. I recognized that I needed to help them understand that, as language teachers, they should make more room in their instruction for the teaching of learning strategies. Doing so would empower students to learn independently from the teacher and make the most of classroom experiences.

With the findings, I got concrete evidence and samples to give course participants some benchmarks to help them improve their progress in learning to teach. For example, I noted the differences their friends had made in each others' learning processes, the impact of creating a learning environment in which students learn and share with each other, the characteristics of a role model for effective teaching, and ways to shift from teacher-centered to student-centered learning to encourage students to construct their own knowledge.

I found that by using the instructional model 2R2C I could challenge both groups to learn and to feel that the knowledge they gained from the course would be useful for their professional growth. Nonexpert teachers could learn effective strategies practiced by other nonexpert teachers and expert teachers. Expert teachers could serve as valued mentors to their less-experienced classmates. Through the same process of critical reflection used by novice teachers, the expert teachers became more thoughtful about their own teaching. The activities in class such as weekly writing in methodology notebooks (journals), videotaping lessons, and observing peers triggered student teachers' self-appraisals, facilitated their reviews, and helped them set goals for further development. From the evidence, the expert and nonexpert teachers learned that "knowledge about language teaching and learning is in a tentative and incomplete state, and teachers need regular opportunities to update their professional knowledge" (Richards & Farrell, 2005, p. 2). Still, they need to deepen their content knowledge and learn new methods of teaching; devote themselves to examining new standards being proposed; and seek innovative ways to improve their students' achievement, promote quality teaching, motivate their students, and create significant learning experiences for their students.

I found that a collection of cases such as those of my students, focusing on a particular kind of problem or issue, can be a valuable teacher training resource for novice teachers. Learning to analyze cases based on descriptions of how teachers deal with issues encountered in the classroom can provide a basis for arriving at valuable insights and principles. This type of analysis enables teachers to verbalize and share the problem-solving strategies used in teaching (Richards & Farrell, 2005).

In general, the experience of conducting this research was very positive. Being challenged to respond to learners' needs in a practical and immediate way (as I interacted with and responded to their reflections in their weekly methodology notebooks) was very rewarding for me and the learners. I learned a great deal about my own teaching and about my students. I was fascinated by the power of the information I gained and by my students' critical minds and feelings of success or failure. My findings seem to confirm Richards and Farrell's (2005) comment: "Classrooms are not only places where students learn—they are also places where teachers can learn" (p. 2).

As a researcher and teacher at the same time, I felt more engaged in what I was doing. I found my class meaningful, purposeful, entertaining, and full of mysterious learning and teaching elements that required my problem-solving skills as a teaching researcher. I demonstrated to my colleagues and graduate students how participating in classroom research and taking joint responsibility for plans, processes, and outcomes can enhance the effectiveness of teaching and the relevance of learning. The ideas of exploring research into teaching and how teaching can show us new ways to do research might prosper in the classroom. I personally witnessed the value of being a scholar in the field, yet I feel there is a lot more to learn about myself as a teacher, my work in teaching and research-ing, and my students' interests and learning processes. This may be an important aspect of reflective teaching—the process can help develop knowledge and theories of teaching that are essential for growing professionally as an effective teacher and researcher.

Sumalee Chinokul teaches at Chulalongkorn University, Thailand.

Acknowledgment

I would like to thank Robert Troyer and David Brooks for their constructive comments to help edit the original version of this chapter.

CHAPTER 4

Learner Autonomy in an Asian Context: Independent Learning and Independent Work at the University Level (*Vietnam*)

Duong Thi Hoang Oanh

Issue

This study arose from my experience as an English as a foreign language (EFL) teacher in Vietnam, where there are considerable challenges in encouraging students to learn and work independently. The Vietnamese seem to believe that learning can happen only in a classroom under the supervision of teachers. Learning is usually organised within the classroom and during class time and is checked strictly by the university. The most common type of Vietnamese classroom is one in which the student sits in a fixed row in class, tries to understand what the teacher and textbook say, and then repeats this information as correctly as possible in an examination. Teachers provide information for the students to learn by heart for examinations. The teacher or the book gives out knowledge to the students, like pouring water from a so-called full pitcher (the teacher full of knowledge) into a so-called empty glass (the student's mind). In such a context, the prevailing model of teaching and learning is "teachers teach and students learn." In class, students are expected to listen rather than participate actively. Therefore, the knowledge learned is limited, and the students are not motivated to learn beyond the exam.

This model of teaching and learning creates a passive attitude in students and a general overreliance on teachers for knowledge transfer and guided forms of practice, leading to a serious lack of learner autonomy. Recently, learner autonomy has become one of the aims of the Vietnamese education system in an effort to promote education reforms. As Nguyen Dinh Ca (2000) and Nguyen Quang Cao (2005) observe, one of the changes necessary for students is the capacity to think and learn independently and turn the learning process into a self-teaching process. However, my experience and observations convince me that autonomy is seldom and ineffectively practised at my university in Vietnam. In such a context, I implemented this research in my two speaking classes, which focused on the oral presentation activities of 4th-year university students. These classes ran three periods per week and were part of a bachelor of arts in English programme. My goal was to gain insight into how learner autonomy relates to these classroom practices. Therefore, my main research question was to see whether independent work or independent learning was practised in my speaking–oral presentation classes and how it took place. I was largely researching my own practice, but I also wanted to find out what other teachers in the same teaching context were thinking about the same issue.

Background Literature

The concept of learner autonomy—also referred to as independent learning, self-directed learning, and self-study—is well documented in related literature, although it has sparked considerable controversy (Thanasoulas, 2000). According to Wang and Peverly (1986), autonomous learners have the capacity for being active and independent in the learning process. They are also able to identify and formulate goals, change goals to suit their own learning needs and interests, use learning strategies, and monitor their own learning.

Other authors share similar arguments. For example, Thanasoulas (2000), Mariani (1997), Dickinson (1992), Kohonen (1991), Little (1991), and Holec (1985) all state that autonomy is the capacity for detachment, critical reflection, decision making, and independent action with an individual, gradual, never-ending process of self-discovery. However, autonomy does not mean individualism and a neglect of the social context, because personal decisions are necessarily made with respect to social and moral norms, traditions, and expectations. There are two kinds of autonomy: individual autonomy, which stresses individual learning styles and preferences, and social autonomy, which recognises that learning takes place through interaction and collaboration. Thus, autonomy includes the notion of interdependence and cultural awareness, and therefore different cultures place different emphases on learner autonomy (Kohonen, 1991; Sinclair, 1997).

Many authors discuss the role of the teacher, stating that an independent learning process cannot be effectively realised without teacher intervention and guidance (Holec, 1985; Hurd, 1998). According to Little (1995b), the pursuit of learner autonomy requires "a shift in the role of the teacher," aiming "to bring learners to the point where they accept equal responsibility for this coproduction, not only at the affective level" but undertaking "organisational initiatives" as well (p. 175). One of the challenges in current EFL learning is the shift from an instructivist way of teaching and learning, in which teachers play the active role, to a constructivist approach, in which students construct their own knowledge (Stracke, 2004; Wolff, 1994).

Moreover, independent learning is "a desirable goal for physiological, pedagogical, and practical reasons," according to Cotterall (1995, p. 219). It also is integral to maximising the diminishing resources for language programs (Hurd, 1998). Furthermore, Little (1995b) argued that "genuinely successful learners have always been autonomous" (p. 175). Being autonomous is vital for students' effective functioning in society, because it prepares them with necessary skills that are transferable to their future studies and careers (Hurd, 1998; Knowles, 1975).

Hurd (1998) noted that teachers have different interpretations of independent learning and its role in the learning process. Whereas many teachers agree with the concepts previously mentioned, others see independent learning as a self-access package linked to class work, with clear instructions for usage, or as students working in groups independent of teachers. Littlewood (1999) suggested two levels of self-regulation in autonomy. The first one is proactive autonomy, which regulates the direction of activity as well as the activity itself. With this approach, learners are able to take charge of their own learning, determine their objectives, select methods and techniques, evaluate what has been acquired, and establish a personal agenda for learning (see also Holec, 1985; Little, 1995a). The other level is reactive autonomy, which regulates the activity once the direction has been set. With this approach, students do not create their own directions. However, once the instructor has initiated a direction, learners can organise their resources autonomously in order to reach their goals (Littlewood, 1999).

In my study, I defined independent learning as making students responsible for deciding what is to be learned, when, how, in what order, and by what means, and for setting their own goals and measuring the degree to which they have been effective in attaining them. In this process, the teacher acts as facilitator to help learners achieve independence and decreases involvement as student expertise increases. I define independent work as directed work. Students are required to work on some specific task, assignment, project work, or homework, and teachers are responsible for providing a significant input in terms of setting up the task, monitoring it, and assessing its value.

Procedures

The data were collected through document review, class observations, and interviews.

DOCUMENT REVIEW

I started my study by collecting, reading, and taking notes about documents related to learner autonomy, including those on curriculum development, recent changes, and evaluation. I also considered administrative documents, such as proposals, progress reports, agendas, announcements, minutes of meetings, and other internal documents. Throughout my research, I consulted other important printed and online materials, such as journals and mass media articles, to keep me updated about developments in my country and elsewhere that were relevant to my study.

CLASS OBSERVATIONS

I observed my two classes, which consisted of 99 students who were studying at the upper-intermediate level of English. Ten 90-minute sessions were videotaped. I used an unstructured class observation method to observe the classes (not to follow any fixed plan or structure), with a detailed record of observational notes that included reflective and analytical observations (Gorman & Clayton, 1997). I kept daily teaching logs and aimed to describe the classes' activities objectively and in detail. The videos were of great use as I reviewed specifically what the students and I had been doing in class, focusing on elements related to independent learning. They helped me make insightful reflections about my own classroom practices. To aid the observation process, I asked students to keep journals for my speaking classes so I could use them as a resource. I asked students to write down (ideally) everything that happened in these classes, especially the highlights and what they liked most and disliked most about the class activities. I collected these journals every 2 weeks, read them, took notes, and then returned them to the students with my feedback the following week. The students seemed to understand that journal writing was part of their learning process and a good way to communicate with the teacher, given the large class size, so they enthusiastically kept regular journals. Sometimes I also asked other teachers or students to comment on what had been happening, and I compared their responses with my notes and the students' notes.

INTERVIEWS

I used in-depth semistructured interviews to collect insightful data rather than facts and figures (Oppenheim, 1992). I interviewed six students from two classes. I interviewed each subject three to four times, at the beginning, middle, and end of the course, with each interview lasting from 15 to 30 minutes. I also interviewed two teachers, Miss Que and Miss Sa, three times, at the beginning, middle, and end of the course, with each interview taking about 30 minutes. Vietnamese was used in data collection, then translated and paraphrased into English. All interviews were tape-recorded, accompanied by personal notes to aid in transcription. I had no fixed questions, but I was equipped with a list of general topics or areas around which the interview was to be conducted as unobtrusively as possible. During interviews, I also used a reflective approach (White, 1999), trying to give regular feedback to the participant to make sure that comprehension was complete on both sides.

I used these three main tools to collect the data, and then I classified and categorised it. I used multiple sources of data to identify patterns and avoid bias toward one set of data.

Results

My analysis of the process of teaching and learning revealed several interesting patterns related to the practice of learner autonomy and the questions about whether independent work or independent learning was practised in my speaking–oral presentation classes.

INDEPENDENT WORK OR INDEPENDENT LEARNING?

The data revealed that although I was aware of the differences, in practice I usually made no distinction between the concepts of independent work and independent learning. The video of my class observations and the interviews with the two teachers showed that we used many terms to refer to students working independently of the teacher: *autonomy, self-study, self-reliance, learn independently,* or *work independently.* The terms *independent learning* and *independent work* were used interchangeably.

The students' participation in my class activities showed that they reacted very positively to the tasks I assigned to them and that they performed in class based on my directions for homework or assignments. Observing my own teaching, I recognised that I rarely asked the students to think about what they should do in their time outside class to back up their class activities.

Other teachers said they had similar experiences. For example, the teachers I interviewed said they aimed for independent learning, but their description indicated that what actually happened was independent work. In one case, Miss Sa said she aimed for "students' autonomy" and "self-reliance," so she gave the students the tasks and the students worked on the tasks on their own time. In another, Miss Que told her students, "Self-study is important, so you have to work on your talk, look for materials on your own. Don't wait for me to take

you to the library; you go yourself to develop your independent learning habits."
My colleagues and I reflected that we used the terms *independent learning* and
student autonomy, but we never talked about students setting their own goals
or helped students design their own learning plans. It was clear that we usually
interpreted independent learning as students working outside the classroom
on teacher-assigned tasks. Through oral presentation tasks in these speaking
classes, we set the goals, facilitated student control, and gave out-of-class task
assignments.

TEACHER AS FACILITATOR

For student oral presentations, I tried to be a facilitator, instructing and influ-
encing students to develop their independent working capacity. It was obvious
that presenting a talk encouraged students to work and manage their own time,
make use of all resources, and enhance self-reliance and autonomy. They had
to work independently, although I would offer help if students had difficulties.
However, I recognised that I usually gave students tasks to perform on their own
but dictated the purposes of the work. The common practices I applied included

- Teacher-provided clues, letting students explore each task.

- Teacher-provided optimal opportunities for practice in and out of class,
  with prepared and unprepared talks and with peer and teacher evaluations.

- Opportunities for students to speak in front of the class.

- Invitations for students to create topics and contexts suitable for raising an
  issue, presenting it, and discussing it.

Therefore, students worked on their own but usually under my strict direction.

GOAL SETTING BY TEACHER

During class time, my students and I discussed and set learning goals. I usually
started my class with, "Oh well, what should we learn today? What do you
expect to achieve from this class?" However, most of the time it was me who
directed the process, by hinting about the immediate goals the class should
achieve. In some classes, I set up the goals beforehand so that the students could
recognise, understand, and be able to act on them. My conclusion is that if I had
not presented these goals, students would not have identified them themselves.
For example, in one class, I asserted that the goal of our task was to learn
techniques to attract an audience's attention during a talk. In their interviews,
the students agreed that before I had clarified that goal, the students had thought
that presenting was separate from interaction with an audience and that interaction with the audience was of little or no value. They became more aware of
their aims and tried to work out ways to attract an audience's attention.

The two other teachers I interviewed set goals differently in their classes. In her class, Miss Que worked from a checklist of goals she prepared before class. In her class, Miss Sa introduced goals to the students, but students could ask for clarification or negotiate the meaning of a goal. In both classes, the teachers asked students for input. During my time teaching, I never observed a student nominating a goal that had not already been mentioned by the teachers.

STUDENT CONTROL IN SPEAKING ACTIVITIES

My class observation data showed that oral presentation as a speaking activity helped enhance students' control of their class performance. Specifically, students were in charge of organising and implementing their activities, taking control of the preparation, and conducting the presentation.

Preparation

In the preparation phase, I usually defined what was to be done and the boundaries in doing it, limiting the degree of freedom of students' activities outside class. The students received some instruction on preparing for their presentations in class and then worked out of class to collect materials and rehearse. I only introduced access to resources and gave advice. Students searched for relevant materials, and their group members produced outlines, assigned group tasks, and found visual aids.

The students I interviewed said that preparing for their presentations forced them to collect relevant materials themselves. Finding enough information was the biggest problem. The journals revealed the challenges students confronted in collecting data. One student wrote

> To present successfully, we had to work very hard: to collect materials from many sources of information such as the library, Internet, some committees, and observing real situations. I find it helpful and interesting. We feel confident to have first-hand information based on our research. The task gives me a chance and an excuse to communicate with important officials of the city and I did it well: it's really very good for my self-confidence, social skills, and future work skills.

Another student had a less pleasant experience, commenting

> We had a "hard" time. For real information and statistics, we contacted the Board of Trustees. However, they do not hold such information, so they advised us to go to the City People's Committee, then Children Care Committee. It took us four times to meet with the right person! However, we managed to get what we wanted on our own.

I appreciated the students' efforts. I believed that when students went to the state offices to ask for information, the data obtained would be more vivid, updated, and even accurate than those collected from locally printed materials. Surprisingly, the students managed the tasks well on their own.

Many students commented that they rehearsed a lot on their own time and before or after class. Many attributed their success to frequent rehearsals, as noted in these journal entries:

- "We practised many, many times until we ran out of voice. The success of our groups depended on our careful preparation and rehearsal."

- "We practised and practised at home many times, watching and correcting one another, and felt confident."

- "We gain success! Although I knew the content of the story because we did it over and over again, I still felt very surprised impartially. Everybody laughed. We talked fluently."

Presentations

The students said that presentations were rare opportunities for them to demonstrate their speaking ability, maturity, and independent work. Unlike other speaking activities, which were closely guided and monitored by teachers, oral presentation activities enabled students to take responsibility and produce appropriate performances. In making presentations, students played all the roles: owner, author, director, actor and actress, evaluator, and audience. They emphasised that presentation was a particularly effective activity because it was the only opportunity for them to be completely in charge of class time and activities. During a presentation, a student was in charge of the class, including asking and answering questions and facilitating comments from peers.

DIFFICULTIES IMPLEMENTING INDEPENDENT WORK

Sometimes it was difficult for me to implement independent work because the students showed a low level of initiative and overreliance on teachers. Generally the students were reluctant to work without teacher pressure. It was observed that with very simple assigned tasks, such as home reading assignments, students might say naturally and innocently in class "I haven't read it yet." If students were allowed to do a task themselves, nothing would be done properly. If the students were given some options to choose from, some usually looked bewildered and did not know what to do.

For example, one teacher, Miss Que, complained that although she offered students freedom, most of them did not want to accept that freedom. Students wanted the teacher to decide what they should do and to give detailed instructions. To them, the teacher was the master of the subject. Students were weak at applying new things, did not have a reading culture, and only went to class to listen to the teacher's explanations. I realized that the level of dependence on the teacher varied according to the level of the students. But only a few advanced students could work independently, and weaker ones needed careful instructions from the teacher.

My observations convinced me that there is also a serious lack of systematic support and application of autonomy at an institutional level in Vietnam for students working on their own. After class, students have to rely on their own arrangements in terms of time, space (e.g., where to study—no space has been set out specifically for group studies at the university), and resources. Teachers are present at the university only during classes and administrative meetings. The schedules for teachers are almost completely limited to academic activities, with no specific time allocation for consultation with students. University officials checked whether the teacher was following the timetable, but they did not consider the possibility of students doing independent work outside class hours. When students needed help or consultation, they had to contact teachers by phone or even go to teachers' homes to ask for advice. In addition, the library and departmental reading room were small, with limited resources that did not meet the demands of the students.

STUDENTS' PERCEPTIONS OF INDEPENDENT WORK

In their interviews, the students said that they liked the freedom and appreciated the level of independence and responsibility they were given. My speaking class activities showed that the atmosphere was very lively, with numerous student contributions. Students said that oral presentations were "interesting" or "fantastic," that students "never feel tired," and that "time flies." The students enjoyed suggesting different answers or opinions, laughed and teased one another, and enjoyed being active and argumentative in class. Van said enthusiastically, "Some groups propose many interesting ideas completely different from the teacher. It makes my lesson today even more useful and relevant. I like to see our different ideas accepted by the teacher!" Many students shared similar impressions, such as the following:

- "Classmates have many questions."

- "There are different ideas, but most groups have logical explanations. It's fun."

- "I liked the lecture today very much, especially the way the lecturer arranged her lecture, and we do argue with her!"

- "We do have different opinions, which makes the class richer."

Han and Xuan reflected that when giving a talk, they could learn more because they had more control of the class situation. They were motivated because they could choose their own topics and had more freedom. Quy also commented that working independently was the strongest motivation for students to actively participate. However, as Thu observed, students were confused sometimes because they were not used to working and making decisions on their own. Students had internal conflicts about expectations, and some felt bewildered when left to carry out tasks on their own.

Reflection

Observation of my classroom practices revealed that although teacher-dependence was thought to be the norm in Vietnam, independent work was a focus of these speaking classes. Students were typically encouraged and expected to finish teacher-directed assignments by themselves. Therefore, I concluded that the focus was on independent work, not independent learning. I realised that although my colleague teachers and I thought we encouraged students to work on their own, in practice, we were actually driving the process and setting the framework. The goals were not designed by students through negotiation with teachers but were set by teachers. The students recognised and understood these goals and then acted on them. General goals were set out for all students, with no distinction between students' different interests, purposes, or proficiency levels. The students might well have been learning in the process, but the focus was on doing tasks, not on the learning. In independent learning, students should be shown *how* to do something, but they have to decide *what* to do. In my case, students were expected to work independently following the framework set by the teacher, under the teacher's direction. In this respect, the teacher was in control of the whole regulated process, with the students working independently.

As a result, although some class activities helped students establish and develop independent work habits, there was little focus on independent learning. This type of independent work is not the ultimate aim for learner autonomy. Teachers need to include and implement independent learning in the teaching and learning process, starting with independent work. This is only the first step in developing students' ability to direct their own learning during the remainder of their time at the university and during their future careers.

Based on the lessons learned, I will try to incorporate independent work into more classes, with the aim of creating independent learning. I will discuss goal setting and learning strategies with students at the beginning of the course, and the scope will allow for development and change. For example, in the classes I teach, I always start my course with the question, "What do you expect from the course?" Then I summarise their suggestions on the blackboard. After that, I tell the students what I expect of them, and we get to a common understanding by the end of the period. This type of conversation is repeated and adjusted during the course.

For some classes of relatively small size, I try to arrange student and teacher dialogue, in which every student is interviewed by the class teacher (about 5 minutes each) at the beginning and toward the end of the course. The two interviews have different purposes. The first one is to establish and clarify objectives, and the second one is to assess and discuss the student's goals and progress and to offer advice for any adjustments needed. For larger classes, I organise group interviews, with students choosing the group to be in for the interview. That way, the time allocated for interviews can be shortened but produce a similar outcome.

Teachers aiming to promote independent learning must remember that the focus of teaching includes instruction in methods of learning as well as what to learn. Other important skills could be strengthened and developed through class activities, such as time management, the use of available facilities, strategic competence, and research-based skills. Even with large class sizes, I organise lessons in an interactive and communicative way. Pair and group work are encouraged, so students work independently of the teacher. Different ways of independent work and independent learning are implemented through the assignment of tasks to be undertaken within and outside the classroom.

The most essential element of the independent learning process is for students to set their own targets and then make their own decisions to reach them. They should not just do the task independently but actually plan and implement their own learning programme as individual learners. In that way, they can do completely different things in their own time to reach their own goals.

To encourage students to work on their own at home, I ask them to keep record booklets. This task adds an element of monitoring to the learning process. At the start of the course, each student is guided to design a two-part personal record booklet. The first part is for recording personal objectives, and the second part is for recording activities and progress during the course. The booklet encourages students to critically judge their language performance and helps them monitor their evolving language competence. The booklet also provides a starting point for discussion of participants' experiences in the course and can serve to prompt out-of-class practice. I often design some class activities related to student record booklets and constantly check their status.

Through my study, I recognised that in some cases my colleague teachers and I demonstrated contradictions between what we said and what we did, and even between what we said on different occasions. For example, although we claimed to facilitate students' self-reliance in their studies, we did not feel confident that the students would do the assigned tasks without being checked. Therefore, we ended up giving students time to fulfil the set tasks in class. My lesson from this finding is that I should trust students and let them know I trust them to do what is best for their studies. On the other hand, some discipline in the first stage would also be worthwhile. If the students fail to do the tasks assigned prior to class time, let them suffer the consequences (by being unable to follow the class activities or being given low marks), while the teacher works only with the well-prepared students. Unprepared students will soon learn that the teacher does not tolerate laziness and lack of cooperation. This strategy has proven to work in my classes, provided I am patient and consistent and do not actually ignore the unprepared students. (I just pretend to!) Then, being well prepared and ready for class becomes a habit and part of the class routine, and I no longer have to check the students' work as the course progresses.

Duong Thi Hoang Oanh teaches at Hue University, Vietnam.

CHAPTER 5

The TESOL Methods Course: What Did They *Really* Learn? (*Singapore*)

Thomas S. C. Farrell

Issue

Research has indicated that preservice teachers come to any teacher education program with prior beliefs about teaching and learning (Shulman, 1987). These beliefs have been accumulated from a variety of sources, including their past experiences as students in the school system (called apprenticeship of observation), and may filter what they are exposed to in the teacher education program (Lortie, 1975). Hence, differences are likely to exist between what teacher educators think is important for their students to learn and what the students actually learn as a result of taking a course. As a Western language teacher educator in Singapore at the time of this study, I was the coordinator of a methods course for English as a second language (ESL) teachers that focused on the theory and methods of teaching reading to secondary school students. After delivering the course for some time, I wondered what the preservice teachers had learned as a result of taking the course. Of course, the preservice teachers all had to complete an assignment that usually consisted of developing a lesson plan for a reading class along with the rationale behind the plan. However, I had no other way of gauging the real impact of the course on teachers' beliefs. Had they, for example, filtered the educational concepts they were presented with through their prior belief systems? If yes, were they conscious of this filtering? Which beliefs had they accepted, which ones had they rejected, and why?

These are very important questions. As Joram and Gabriele (1998) argue, it is essential that teacher educators take prior beliefs into account "because any new material taught will have to compete with, replace, or otherwise modify the folk theories that already guide both teachers and pupils" (p. 176). So, I set out to find a different method of evaluating the course's success in terms of its impact on preservice teachers' beliefs. After some research, I decided to use concept maps to gauge the impact of this TESOL methods course.

The preservice teachers were enrolled in a 1-year program, called the Post Graduate Diploma in Education (PGDE), to certify them as secondary school teachers in Singapore. Preservice teachers take a 10-month program in which they experience teaching practice and theory classes. Preservice teachers in the English language teaching stream take theory courses in the teaching of reading, writing, grammar, and listening and speaking. The reading course consists of nine classes (18 hours of class time over 9 weeks) of instruction on reading theory, teaching strategies, and current concepts. The course emphasized the following concepts in current reading theory: schema theory, the role of prior knowledge, psycholinguistic theory and reading, metacognition and self-monitoring techniques, text structure, techniques to promote the use of effective reading strategies, vocabulary teaching, and actual lesson plan writing and critiquing. Additionally, the course included various methods of evaluating reading comprehension in the Singapore examination system.

Background Literature

The evaluation tools I used, concept maps, are diagrams that show relationships among concepts within a specific domain of knowledge (Novak, 1990). Meijer, Verloop, and Beijaard (1999) define concept mapping as a "technique for capturing and graphically representing concepts and their hierarchical interrelationships" (p. 62). The technique of concept mapping—sometimes called "tree technique" (Mergendoller & Sacks, 1994, p. 589)—originally comes from the field of cognitive psychology and was transferred into educational research to understand how teachers use their knowledge to carry out the complex task of teaching. Van Bruggen, Kirschner, and Jochems (2002) suggested that concept mapping can be a very effective way to relate new concepts to a person's current knowledge and to encourage his or her involvement in the learning process. Within educational research, concept mapping has also been used to trace conceptual changes in students who take a course or program of study and has even been used successfully to trace changes in preservice teachers' conceptions about teaching English reading (Meijer, Verloop, & Beijaard, 1999; Mergendoller & Sacks, 1994).

Although several studies (e.g., Horton, McConny, Gallo, Woods, & Hamelin, 1993) have suggested that concept mapping in education can result in meaningful learning, not all researchers have agreed that concept maps are a valuable research tool for tracing conceptual changes in learner teachers. Kagan (1990), for example, has argued that concept mapping to investigate teacher thinking is too complex and time consuming. She further argued that the use of concept maps puts too much emphasis on short-term changes in teachers' cognition and that these concept maps are usually compared to a target map, such as the instructor's map. Kagan wondered if comparing students' and instructors' course concept maps rendered them invalid.

Although concept mapping may be a complex and time-consuming way to look at cognitive changes in teacher thinking, this study used concept maps as evidence of knowledge growth rather than as a reflection of cognitive structure (Morine-Dershimer, 1993). In other words, I used a nonstructured approach to stimulate students when there was no prepared list of concepts on the teaching and learning of English reading. With this nonstructured approach, the preservice teachers were asked to generate concepts related to the reading process and the teaching of reading comprehension in Singaporean secondary schools. For the purposes of this study, the word *concept* is defined as a mentally conceived image of what the preservice teachers understand to be important in teaching reading, including their beliefs.

Procedures

On the first day of class, the 20 preservice teachers were asked to construct a concept map of the reading process and the teaching of English reading in Singaporean secondary schools. Fischer, Bruhn, Grasel, and Mandl (2002) suggested that students construct their own concept maps, rather than have a precourse map prepared by the course instructor, to ensure greater ownership of the learning process. The first maps students created were for diagnostic purposes; they would give me an indication of the preservice teachers' beliefs about the reading process and how to teach reading to secondary school students. Even though my students did not have the subject matter knowledge, they did have experience as students in the school system and as successful readers (otherwise they would not have been in the PGDE program). They were all shown an example of a concept map and given a detailed explanation of this map. They all received the same written (and orally explained) directions with the example concept map.

On completion of the maps, they were asked to share their answers during a peer group discussion and reflection session. At the start of the following class, and in order to clarify what they wrote in their concept maps, I conducted a class interview (Wilson, 1997). I led a discussion and encouraged the preservice teachers to further explore their perceptions, attitudes, feelings, and ideas about the reading process. Most of the class participants contributed to the discussion.

Each preservice teacher's map was analyzed as follows: Each concept was numbered and a frequency count was noted along with any connections made to other concepts (Taylor & Coll, 1999). Taylor and Coll conducted a similar qualitative analysis of concept maps as a tool for monitoring student learning in science. In my study, each preservice teacher drew a concept map that answered the following question: What does teaching reading to secondary school pupils involve, and how would you do it? I totaled the number of concepts from the 20 individual student maps and constructed a precourse group concept map. The group map provided an indication of what the class as a whole believed about teaching reading.

On the last day of class I distributed a blank concept map with the same question as the map given on the first day of class and asked that each student construct a postcourse concept map. I had told them on the first day of class that they would be receiving their precourse maps back at the end of the course but not that they would be asked to construct a postcourse map. After they created postcourse maps, I returned their original precourse maps. Then I asked them to compare the two versions. When they had finished their comparisons, I asked them to write down the differences they had noted between the two maps and to state the reasons for these differences. I analyzed the individual postcourse maps using the same procedures as with the individual precourse maps, and then I constructed a group version of the postcourse concept maps. However, because the individual postcourse concept maps were much more detailed and sometimes had many different concepts, I found this process time consuming. I also discovered that I would have to use different categories for the postcourse concepts because the level of detail differed from the precourse maps. One final procedure, which I had not planned, was that I interviewed a number of the participants because some of the concepts they put on their maps were not explained clearly.

Results

PRECOURSE CONCEPT MAP

The group composite concept map I constructed from the students' individual precourse maps is shown in Figure 1. Figure 1 illustrates that the group ($N = 20$) had no shared understanding of what it means to teach reading. The issues in order of frequency were comprehension (15); motivation (9); vocabulary (7); reading aloud (4); grammar (3); and an other category, which included many diverse items such as role plays, drama, silent reading, and speed reading.

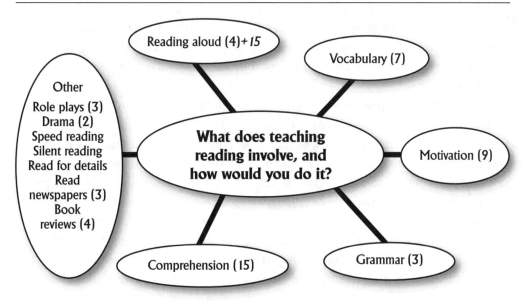

Key: Number in parentheses shows how many preservice teachers included that topic in their concept maps. Number in italics (+15) represents students who later thought the concept should be included but did not include it in their concept maps.

Figure 1. Precourse group concept map showing frequency of topics.

Comprehension was chosen by 15 of the preservice teachers. Many of them just wrote the word *comprehension* with no explanation. In a class discussion that followed, I asked why they wrote comprehension and what its meaning was. Many said that teaching reading for them meant that the students read a passage, answered some questions—usually 10—and the teacher then "ran through" the answers. They said that this type of reading class was typical of what they had experienced as students in the system and that they would probably teach reading in a similar way.

The next concept, motivation, was picked by nine preservice teachers. They said the concept meant that "teachers must inspire the students to read," but they did not say how. When asked to explain what motivation was, many preservice teachers said that the teacher should cultivate and encourage an interest in reading. They said that the teacher should explain the benefits of reading to the students. However, none of the preservice teachers was able to come up with an exact method of motivating students to read except explaining the benefits of reading.

Vocabulary was the next most valued idea for teaching reading to secondary school students, with seven preservice teachers placing it in their maps. Again, most of them just wrote the word *vocabulary* with no explanation. When asked what way they would teach vocabulary, many said the teacher should get the students to underline whatever words they did not understand. Then the teacher could explain the words, or the students could look them up in their dictionaries. Again, they mentioned that this was what most of them had experienced when they were students. Some mentioned that they could get the students to memorize words because that is the way they were instructed in vocabulary acquisition.

Another issue the preservice teachers included was reading aloud. In fact, many said that even though they did not include it in their initial concept maps, they now thought that it should be included. During the discussion, 15 more students raised their hands in agreement, for a total of 19. However, they did not add this concept to their maps. When asked why they valued this strategy in a reading class, the preservice teachers stated that they themselves had been trained with reading aloud in their own school days and that it would be good for their students' pronunciation development. Three preservice teachers included grammar in their maps. They stated that grammar should be highlighted during a reading lesson, but they did not indicate how this should be accomplished.

This precourse concept map gave me some indication of these preservice teachers' underlying beliefs about the teaching of reading. It showed me that many of them did not have explicit knowledge of reading strategies even though they themselves were fluent readers. It was also an indication that many of these teachers had to draw on their experiences as students in the school system to complete their precourse concept maps and show how they would teach reading in the Singaporean secondary school system.

POSTCOURSE CONCEPT MAP

A postcourse group concept map was constructed from the preservice teachers' individual maps, as shown in Figure 2.

Overall, the postcourse group concept map was more extensive and slightly more complex than the precourse group concept map. The teachers together included 10 headings in their final concept maps. Shah's comments best represent the general differences between the pre- and postcourse maps. She said that her experiences as a student in the school system had influenced her initial precourse concept map. Shah continued, "Before this course, my ideas were based on my own personal experience as a student in secondary school. That time there were no lessons to teach us reading. Now I have learnt that there are reading strategies and ways and activities to carry out teaching." Many of the other preservice teachers made similar reflections that traced the origins of the concepts in their precourse maps to the way they experienced reading classes when they were students: all testing and no teaching of how to read. As Evelyn said, "Knowing now that reading strategies exist and we can teach students these is all new to me."

Except for the topic vocabulary, which was expanded from the combined

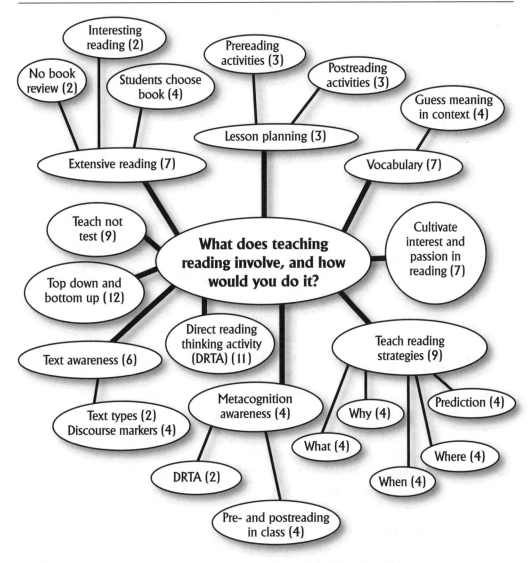

Key: Number in parentheses shows how many preservice teachers included that topic in their concept maps.

Figure 2. Postcourse group concept map showing frequency of topics.

precourse map, most of the other topics were different from the ideas presented in the precourse concept maps. The new topics in the postcourse map included extensive reading, teach reading strategies, text awareness, lesson planning, metacognition awareness, direct reading thinking activity (DRTA), top down and bottom up, teach not test, and cultivate interest and passion in reading. Many of these new topics were representative of issues highlighted in 2-hour segments during the course. Additionally, six of these ideas were directly related to the teaching of reading: (1) text awareness, (2) teach reading strategies,

(3) lesson planning, (4) extensive reading, (5) vocabulary, and (6) metacognition awareness.

Top down and bottom up, and DRTA were the most popular concepts, appearing in 12 and 11 postcourse concept maps, respectively. However, the teachers did not elaborate on these topics. Teach reading strategies appeared in nine postcourse maps, with a secondary level represented by what (four maps), where (four maps), when (four maps), why (four maps), and prediction (four maps).

Seven preservice teachers included extensive reading and vocabulary as important concepts for teaching reading, and both topics had two-level representations. The second-level topics for extensive reading were students choose book (four maps), no book review (two maps), and interesting reading (two maps). The second-level technique for vocabulary was guess meaning in context, which was only a slight change from the precourse map. Cultivate interest and passion in reading also appeared in seven maps, but with only one-level representation.

Text awareness was included in six postcourse maps, with a second level showing examples such as recognize discourse markers (four maps) and text types (two maps). Three of the preservice teachers noted the importance of lesson planning, with secondary levels labeled prereading activities (three maps) and postreading activities (three maps).

Two topics on the postcourse concept maps were related to the delivery of lessons; these were teach not test and cultivate interest and passion in reading. Nine of the preservice teachers included teach not test as a separate concept in their postcourse concept maps. All 20 of the preservice teachers commented about this occurrence when asked to write about the changes they noted from the precourse maps. They said that they suddenly realized that what mostly happens in reading classes is testing reading, by having the student read a paragraph and answer the 10 questions that follow, rather than actual teaching of reading.

Comparing this postcourse group concept map with the precourse map, I noticed a complete absence of reading aloud, grammar, and comprehension. I wondered if this might indicate a change in beliefs about teaching reading as a result of taking the module. Yen Wha, for example, noted that reading aloud can be a problem for the reader and the other students. She said, "Reading a passage aloud is not very effective, as the students who are not reading will switch off and even the student reading may not understand what he or she is reading."

One major disappointing aspect of the group postcourse concept map was the lack of complexity, which can be seen in the branching (spokes) and minimal levels of ideas presented. In fact, only eight of the teachers' maps had two-level representations, which included the idea or concept (such as vocabulary) at the first level and the method (such as guessing meaning in context) at the second level. None of the teachers' maps had any third-level examples or techniques that represented these methods. Another disappointing feature of the postcourse concept maps was that the different ideas presented were not connected in any unified way (see Ken's concept map in Figure 3 as an exception). Here it seems that the preservice teachers failed to make connections between theory and pedagogic purposes in any meaningful manner.

When I attempted to analyze individual concept maps to see how each teacher internalized the course, I found it difficult to group them into coherent categories. Each teacher seemed to have gained something different from the course. However, I was able to set two broad categorizations in terms of levels of representations: Level 2 maps, which indicated a more sophisticated understanding of the concepts, and Level 1 maps, which indicated only a surface understanding of reading concepts. This continuum from Level 2 to Level 1 is represented in the following individual concept maps, Ken's Level 2 map (see Figure 3) and Raymond's Level 1 map (see Figure 4). I interviewed Ken and Ray about the contents of their maps.

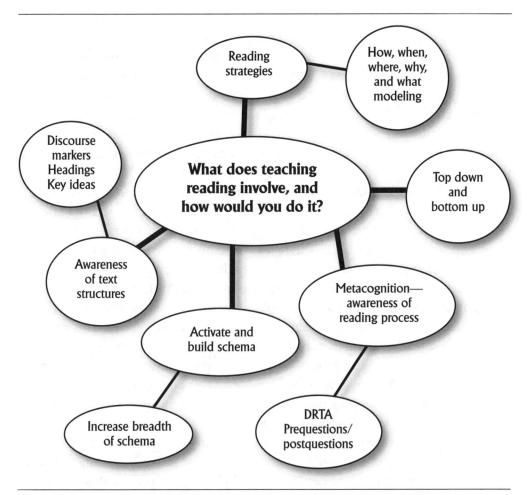

Figure 3. Example of a Level 2 map, from Ken's postcourse concept map.

Ken's postcourse map shows a more structured understanding of what he learned from the course. He has taken various concepts that were presented to him during the course and reproduced them in a two-level representation. Level 1 concepts are awareness of text structures, reading strategies, top down and bottom up, metacognition—awareness of reading process, and activate and build schema. Four of these five concepts had examples of techniques or activities attached to them. Reading strategies, for example, had an attached representation indicating that the teacher should model these strategies by showing students "how, when, where, why, and what the strategies are," Ken explained in an interview. He said that as a result of taking the course he had a "greater knowledge of technical terms" and that this allowed for "a more accurate expression of ideas." Ken further elaborated on the importance of discussing the process of reading and reading strategies with students: "Discussions on the reading process leads to a higher level of metacognitive awareness as to the personal process of reading." Ken said he did not really elaborate on the postcourse map because he did not need to; he said he "knew what each spoke meant" to him. During the interview, Ken did elaborate on the contents of the map, but he said that he was doing this for me as a researcher rather than for himself.

As I discovered, he had a more complete picture of how he would teach reading within an interactive approach, which included both top-down and bottom-up activities. He was also aware of how he would teach various reading strategies and how these fit into the "big picture of reading and learning how to read." The interview seemed to have yielded more information about Ken's concept map entries and led me to believe that he had a deeper understanding of the course than he had represented on his concept map.

As a result of explaining his own concept map, Ken seemed to have gained a greater conceptual clarity about the course he had just taken. During the discussion, he became more aware not only of his own conceptions but also of some knowledge gaps and some inconsistencies. Thus, an important finding of this interview was that in the future I should consider having all the preservice teachers explain their concept maps. This practice might enable them to critically reflect on the concepts they included. Posing questions to have students justify parts of their concept maps can help them discover inconsistencies. This process of uncovering teachers' beliefs may be a crucial step in concept mapping.

Based on these findings, I now wonder if the context influenced what the preservice teachers were prepared to put on paper. Their culture does not encourage students to put their thoughts in writing, because then those words are in a public domain and open to scrutiny. It may well be that the preservice teachers do not want this scrutiny. In fact, the school system itself does not encourage people on either side of the desk, students or teachers, to voice their opinions in public. Therefore, this culture obviously would have a bearing on these findings.

One worrying factor regarding the postcourse concept maps was the fact that many of the individual maps were unstructured, one-level maps. In fact 12 (60%) of the maps were Level 1 maps, and only 8 were Level 2 maps. These numbers indicate that many of the preservice teachers might have had only a haphazard recollection of what the course was about. Ray's Level 1 map (as shown in Figure 4) was representative of this side of the continuum.

Raymond's representation of concepts is minimal and his placement of ideas such as activate schema, predicting, teach not test, and discourse markers shows some understanding of teaching reading. However, because there is no elaboration, his map remains at Level 1. When I interviewed Ray, his answers seemed to indicate that he has more depth to his understanding of the concepts he presented in his map. For example, regarding the issue of teach not test that appeared on his map, he said: "The main idea is to teach reading, not test reading. Usually a comprehension text only tests students' reading ability. How can we teachers transform this into a teaching activity?" He then proceeded to use all the other concepts in his map together to explain what teachers should do when teaching reading:

> First, students need to be taught to be able to predict by looking at the title of the passage and the topic sentences. This helps them skim for gist, and construct meaning. Then they need to be taught appropriate word identification strategies. Students must finally be able to self-monitor own reading and demonstrate independent learning.

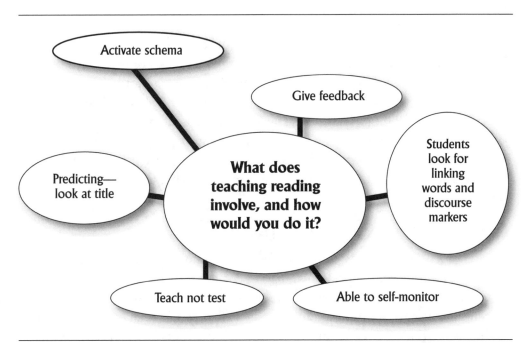

Figure 4. Example of a Level 1 map, from Raymond's postcourse concept map.

The interview did yield more information about Ray's understanding of the course; for example, he expressed a more coherent view of how he should teach reading in general terms. Yet he still could not explain coherently how he could teach reading in terms of specific methods, techniques, or activities. Many other concept maps were of this haphazard nature, indicating that most students probably had not yet linked the concepts presented to them during the course in any coherent manner.

Reflection

One important reason for undertaking this study was to find out if the course had any impact on the learner teachers. Obviously, the module had some impact, but how much and of what quality? The postcourse group concept map indicated that many of the students were indeed able to use appropriate terms associated with the teaching of reading to secondary students in Singapore. Another indication that the course had an impact was the presence of two-level maps from eight of the learner teachers. The two levels showed that they were trying to connect concepts with methods, techniques, and activities that would enable them to implement these strategies in class, thus integrating knowledge gained during the course.

However, individual concept maps showed that the students internalized the course in different ways. The example of the Level 1 concept map shows that some students did not have a very coherent representation of what it means to teach reading. Many of these students could have acquired a superficial knowledge of the terms linked to the teaching of reading, such as top down and bottom up, but not have fully conceptualized them in terms of teaching reading. Furthermore, I now wonder if the Singaporean cultural norm *Kiasu* played any role in these postcourse maps. *Kiasu* means "fear or dislike of losing out to others" (Brown, 1999, p. 123). This fear could have had an effect on the participants when they attempted to include any idea from the course rather than leave the postcourse concept map blank. As a result, I am not sure if I can say that all of the learner teachers have grasped the essentials of what the course was trying to convey.

WHAT I LEARNED ABOUT THE COURSE

I have decided to follow a new maxim for this and future TESOL methods courses: less rather than more. I plan to present fewer new concepts to the group during the semester, but I will go into more detail when explaining each new concept: the origins, meanings, and suggested ways to use such concepts. I will allocate more time to finding out how these new concepts agree or clash with my students' prior knowledge or beliefs, and will address any differences in detail.

For example, for the reading methods course, instead of just lecturing about how to use reading strategies with such methods as the DRTA, I will get them to actually use the DRTA in the classroom and experience it for themselves.

I will follow the "less rather than more" maxim for all the other TESOL methods courses, so the learner teachers will have more of a qualitative, experiential knowledge of the various concepts presented during the course. Thus, information generated from the initial concept maps and the interviews will shape the future content of the curriculum.

WHAT I LEARNED ABOUT THE METHOD

In the last decade, there has been a call for language teacher education programs to acknowledge student teachers' prior knowledge and personal understandings as having an influential role in developing them as teachers (Almarza, 1996). Thus, teacher education courses "should aim to provide space and means by which student teachers can bring up and examine their pretraining knowledge in order to see how it relates to teacher education knowledge, so that learning is more meaningful" (Almarza, pp. 73–74). Concept mapping offers language teacher educators in Asian settings one method of bringing these prior experiences to a level of awareness.

The results of this case study have indicated that concept mapping, both at the beginning and end of the course, has raised the level of the learner teachers' awareness about their own beliefs and prior experiences related to learning and teaching reading in an Asian setting. The precourse map is important because teachers' beliefs often remain at the tacit level and are "often unconsciously held assumptions about students, classrooms, and the academic material to be taught" (Kagan, 1992, p. 65). In fact, the preservice teachers admitted that they had never been asked their opinion in any of the other education courses prior to this one. They suggested that it is not a common Asian practice to ask students what they believe about a subject before they study it.

However, it is essential for learner teachers to become aware of their prior beliefs, because these beliefs serve as a "lens through which they view" (Richards, 1998, p. 71) the subject matter during the course. Unfortunately, research in Western settings has indicated that if learner teachers are not made aware of their preexisting beliefs, then they may only refine these preprogram beliefs instead of restructuring them as a result of taking a course. In this way, the learner teachers confirm what they hold to be true and deny anything that conflicts with what they believe (Hollingsworth, 1989).

The postcourse concept maps are important too for the learner teachers to see what changes have occurred to their beliefs and the impact of the course on their prior experiences with the subject matter. Teacher educators play an important role here as well by having the learner teachers articulate what the changes mean to them as a result of taking the course. It is important for the learner teachers to be aware of the differences of fine-tuning existing beliefs (which means little change from the beginning) and restructuring many of their beliefs (most desirable).

However, as the findings of this case study suggest (especially the interview with Ken), precourse and postcourse concept mapping should be supported with learner teachers' explanations of their own maps. Because time constraints may not allow interviews with each learner teacher, instructors can ask course participants to collaborate in pairs or groups to construct concept maps. Teacher educators can then record the resulting discourse about the concept-mapping task.

Learner teachers should be given some guidelines to follow when interacting with peers. They must articulate their thoughts about the concepts they are putting in the precourse maps as well as their prior experiences with these concepts and why they want to include them. They should also try to articulate the reason for the changes between the precourse and postcourse concepts maps. If learner teachers are allowed to articulate the concepts in discussions at the beginning and end of the course, they will have more opportunities for critical reflection during the methods course.

The process of having preservice teachers make and discuss concept maps has allowed me to gauge their conceptual changes as a result of taking the reading methods course. The information gathered from the concept maps and follow-up interviews might also be useful to inform other teacher educators in Asia (and other regions) about how preservice English language teachers internalize the curriculum in TESOL methods courses. Furthermore, concept mapping (precourse and postcourse) is useful because it encourages the teacher and students to reflect before and after the course. In the context of my courses in Singapore, I asked preservice teachers to construct concept maps so they could then become more aware of their understanding of the course material and thus take more charge of their own meaning-making about teaching English reading in Singapore.

Thomas S. C. Farrell teaches at Brock University, Ontario, Canada.

CHAPTER 6

Understanding Chinese Students' Teacher Dependence (*China*)

Gao Xuesong (Andy)

Issue

This chapter reports on an inquiry into a group of tertiary Chinese students' language learning experiences with a focus on their teacher-dependence in the learning process. All participants in the inquiry are from a low-profile tertiary vocational college where I teach on the Chinese mainland. After reviewing research literature on Chinese students from high-profile institutions (e.g. Cheng, 2002; Cortazzi & Jin, 1996), I believe that these students are relatively weak in language skills and competence to improve language skills. At the college where I teach, there are always tensions between students and teachers related to their roles in the teaching and learning process. For example, during teacher-evaluation sessions, our students complain about teachers providing insufficient support for the learning process beyond the classroom.

My colleagues have been deeply troubled by these students' high expectations and have complained that our college probably has the most dependent college students across the Chinese mainland. The solution many teachers have proposed is to develop students' learning skills and make them more autonomous. This sounds like a reasonable solution. Nevertheless, I was not convinced that skills training alone could make my students autonomous and independent in learning. Therefore, I wanted to have a better understanding of my students' dependence on teachers, especially the students' conceptions of the teacher's role in the learning process.

Background Literature

Opinions concerning Chinese students' teacher-dependence are diverse in the literature. Some researchers (Cortazzi & Jin, 1996; Hu, 2002; Wen & Clement, 2003) have identified the Chinese cultural tradition as an essential explanation for Chinese students' outward behaviors and attitudes toward teachers. They argued that Chinese students are socialized into a culture demanding obedience and respect for authorities such as teachers and that the Chinese cultural tradition grants the teacher a status equal to emperor or father (Cleverley, 1991; Cortazzi & Jin, 1996; Hu, 2002; Schoenhals, 1993; Wen & Clement, 2003). In contrast, other researchers (e.g., Cheng, 2000; Stephens, 1997) contended that the same Chinese cultural tradition also values students who ask questions and actively seek learning opportunities; hence they can be active, resourceful, and independent from teachers. These researchers (e.g., Cheng, 2000; Dooley, 2001; Littlewood, 1999; Stephens, 1997) maintained that educators should explore the impact of social contexts on language learning and not assume influences from a fairly monolithic conceptualization of Chinese traditional culture.

Because empirical studies directly focusing on Chinese students' teacher-dependence are still few, it is worthwhile to take a close look at two such studies, one by Cortazzi and Jin (1996) and one by Cheng (2002). Cortazzi and Jin explored Chinese students' conceptions of their teachers by asking 135 students an open-ended question: What do you expect from a good teacher? Based on the students' responses, they identified the attributes in Table 1. The students' image of a good teacher, the researchers observed, aligns with traditional Chinese culture.

Based on Cortazzi and Jin's (1996) widely cited exploratory inquiry, Cheng (2002) developed a questionnaire to investigate whether Chinese students' own culture of learning, instead of frameworks from Chinese cultural traditions, influences their conceptions of a good teacher and the teacher's roles. In Cheng's study, culture of learning was defined as learners' expectations, attitudes, values, and beliefs about what constitutes effective learning. Cheng's research participants differed from Cortazzi and Jin's, because they were college students specializing in English language. Comparing the findings from the two studies, Cheng argued that different learning contexts enabled the students in his study to have a different culture of learning from those in Cortazzi and Jin's study. Cheng found that his participants put much less emphasis on teachers' deep knowledge and their knowledge-imparting responsibilities. However, they highly valued the teacher's ethical devotion and care for students as well as the teacher's role in developing them into effective language learners.

Although both studies open a window for me to understand Chinese students' expectations of teachers, their findings are of limited help as I interpret my own students' teacher-dependence. First of all, Cortazzi and Jin (1996) did their

Table 1. Chinese Students' Expectations of a Good Teacher (*N* = 135)

A Good Teacher	Percentage of Respondents
Has deep knowledge	67.0%
Is patient	25.0%
Is humorous	23.7%
Is a good moral example	21.5%
Shows friendliness	21.5%
Teaches students about life	17.5%
Arouses students' interest	17.0%
Is warm-hearted and understanding	16.2%
Uses effective teaching methods	16.2%
Is caring and helpful	14.8%
Explains clearly	6.7%

Source: Adapted with permission from Cortazzi and Jin (1996, p. 187)

data collection in 1993, thus their data may not reflect recent cultural changes stimulated by increasing marketization and emerging consumer awareness in the society as a whole or by changes in China's education sector, which has led to profound shifts in Chinese youths' cultural values and attitudes toward authority (Garrott, 1995; Kang, 2003). Second, Cortazzi and Jin's (1996) and Cheng's (2002) studies are methodologically limited by their failure to ask participants to explain the reasons for their responses. Thus, it is impossible to verify other possible interpretations of participants' answers in both studies. Cheng's use of predetermined questionnaires may also have reinforced certain perceptions of a good teacher and the teacher's roles while undermining others. Third, both studies used participants from elite universities on the Chinese mainland, which means they were successful winners of the stressful academic race in secondary school. The question remains: What about my students at the college, who were comparatively losers of this competitive academic game?

Procedures

I started my inquiry with an initial research question: What did my students depend on teachers for or expect teachers to do for them? In the data-interpretation process, I decided to add two more questions, because their answers might shed further light on the research issue. First, I was struck by the mismatches between my students' expectations of teachers and their teachers' actual fulfillment of these expectations, some of which I found deeply worrisome. As a result, I developed a second research question: How did their teachers fulfill their expected roles? In addition, during interviews, my students happened to make a critical evaluation of their dependence on teachers. These emerging comments indirectly provided answers to the third research question, which I was even more concerned to address: Do students think that they should be independent from teachers in learning? Why or why not?

Because questionnaires or open-ended questions were limited in helping me understand the research issue better, I decided to use a biographical/narrative approach as well. Many researchers (Benson, 2005; Johnson & Golombek, 2002) have found the biographical/narrative approach, which involves collecting and analyzing learners' recollections of their experiences, helpful in capturing learners' voices and enhancing understanding of learners' realities. Although such a research approach involved time-consuming in-depth interviews and limited the number of research participants, it enabled me to gain a deep knowledge of the research issue while avoiding imposing certain preconceptions on my students and particular frameworks on the data interpretation.

In a 1-month period, I interviewed 14 student volunteers from my own classes, either in pairs or alone. All of them were female and in a 3-year diploma program in English and business. There were two rounds of interviews: The first interview, lasting about 45 minutes, was semistructured (see the appendix for sample questions). The interview covered specific questions related to their memories of teachers and significant people who influenced their English learning in the past. I used the follow-up interviews, which lasted 20–25 minutes, to clarify specific issues that captured my interest after reading the first interview transcripts. To increase the trustworthiness of students' accounts, I assured them that I would keep their narratives confidential and separate their participation in the inquiry from their final course assessments. I conducted both rounds of interviews in Chinese so that they could speak without any linguistic hindrance, and I recorded the interviews on tape for verbatim transcription.

I took a grounded-theory approach in interpreting the data (Strauss & Corbin, 1998). During the process, I searched for all the students' references to *teachers* in the data. For instance,

He was a serious teacher in class. But after class, he could be your nice friend. In fact, many students like such teachers. (Jing Jing, September 19, 2004)

I highlighted the words *serious, nice,* and *like,* because they suggest that an ideal teacher in this particular student's opinion should be nice and strict. I identified the initial coding categories by carefully reading through one interview transcript, and I refined the coding categories by applying the initial categories in interpreting the other interview transcripts. The process of data analysis was also interactive, and further categories of analysis emerged from the data. First, references to nice or good teachers in the past helped define the attributes of a good teacher, reflecting what these students wanted teachers to do for them in the learning process. I then critically analyzed positive and negative images of teachers to identify particular patterns in teachers' actual fulfillment of students' expectations. Finally, students' reflexive comments on teacher-dependence, especially at their college, were interpreted to see whether they wanted to be independent from teachers in the learning process and why or why not.

Results

The in-depth biographical interview method allowed my students to explain what they needed teachers for, how these teachers actually participated in their past learning experiences, and why they wanted to be independent at the college.

Emerging from the data is a distinctively paradoxical image of an ideal teacher (see Table 2), which echoes a Chinese traditional saying 亦师亦友 [*YI SHI YI YOU*, being both a teacher and friend]. The image of the ideal teacher along with the data suggest that my students expected a teacher to fulfill four roles in the language learning process: friendly supporter, authoritarian teacher, exam-oriented learning expert, and role model. Except for the last one, these roles seem related to the competitive nature of the educational process and my students' desires for better academic performance in terms of exam scores (Cleverley, 1991; Dooley, 2001; Ross, 1993; Schoenhals, 1993; Turner & Acker, 2002). In particular, teachers were expected to empower their students emotionally and give them the resolve to cope with stressful exam preparations.

In the first place, students wanted teachers to provide emotional support to sustain their learning in the learning process. This phenomenon may not be surprising considering the fact that learners as well as their teachers regarded English as one of the most important academic subjects in the race for qualifications (Pennycook, 1994; Zhao & Campbell, 1995). Because of a lack of strong intrinsic motivation, teachers' emotional support became an important source of motivation for these learners. Like Xiao Rong and Ling Li, they frequently mentioned their gratitude to teachers who had inspired and motivated them in learning English at school and college:

> English teachers gave me special attention. They would say "Wonderful. Go Go!!!!" It was always like that. (Xiao Rong, September 17, 2003)

Table 2. My Students' Perceptions of Ideal Teachers (*N* = 14)

Teachers Should	Number
Be nice, motivating, caring, and supportive friends.	14
Be strict and willing to compel us to work hard.	10
Be able to advise us on learning, particularly on preparing for exams.	9
Be role models (oral competence, interesting teaching methods).	9

And the following describes a college English teacher:

> She doesn't put up the kind of authoritarian appearance that other teachers do. She is really close to us, like a friend, not like a teacher. . . . We really like to listen to her teaching. (Ling Li, September 27, 2003)

A well-established student–teacher rapport helped create a motivating learning atmosphere in classrooms and gave an extra but much-appreciated push to help students learn English beyond their classrooms. Teachers' constant and close attention often made learning more meaningful to these students:

> My teacher always praised me for it. I thought it was nice so I became interested in learning English. (Xiao Yan, September 24, 2003)

> The more praise I got from my teachers, the more interested I became in learning English. Without their attention and praise, I would not do well in learning English. (Shen Ling, September 22, 2003)

Second, students needed teachers to force them into making intense learning efforts to deal with exams and fierce competition as they reached for educational goals. The data indicated that students had ambiguous attitudes toward exam-oriented learning. They disliked studying for exams because it was boring, demoralizing, and stressful. On the other hand, they knew that they had to achieve good grades in exams to continue their education, attain their desired educational qualifications, and even find good jobs (Zhao & Campbell, 1995). A teacher who was just a supportive friend might not have the capacity to help them overcome their ambiguous feelings toward exams. Therefore, they needed tough teachers who could coerce them into working and push them through the nerve-breaking exam preparation process. They made the following types of statements to express such expectations of teachers:

> If teacher forces us to do something, then we will do it. . . . Those good teachers would be very strict with you and control your learning tightly. (Ying Ping, September 19, 2003)

> I need somebody to supervise my learning. If there is somebody who supervises my learning, I will learn. (Hui Ling, September 19, 2003)

Third, students depended on teachers to advise them how to learn English and especially how to prepare for high-stakes English exams. Yet all the students except one denied the suggestion that they should be spoon-fed by teachers. Because the interviews took place when students were preparing for the College English Test (CET) exams, they explicitly spelled out their dependence on teachers who understood how to approach exams:

We have an exam-oriented curriculum to survive. . . . We also need some knowledge for the test. . . . If I cannot pass CET-4, what is the point of spending three years here? The college will not issue me a diploma without a CET-4 certificate. (Ling Li, September 27, 2003)

In order to help us pass exams, teachers should help students increase knowledge about exams. (Luo Jing, September 26, 2003)

Fourth, students looked for teachers to be role models in learning English. In my students' past learning settings, English teachers were the few available English-speaking adults. Therefore, they viewed teachers who displayed a high level of competence in English with great admiration. Such teachers were often noted for their innovative and interesting teaching techniques, which made classroom experiences enjoyable for my students:

She was a really brilliant teacher. She is doing a postgraduate degree now. . . . She speaks good English, very fluently. (Ling Li, September 27, 2003)

She speaks good English. . . . I wonder when I will become like her. (Jian Li, October 7, 2003)

COMPARING EXPECTATIONS TO REALITY

Not all teachers could live up to the image of the ideal teacher conceived by my students. For instance, many teachers who taught them were poorly trained, partly because most of my students came from secondary schools in rural areas and small towns, where schools had fewer resources and teachers were underqualified (Cleverley, 1991; Hu, 2004; Ross, 1993; Schoenhals, 1993). Moreover, the data revealed that there were disturbing mismatches between these teachers' actual roles and my students' expectations. Although teachers displayed a friendly face of YOU [友, friend] to a selected number of students, they exhibited a harsh face of SHI [师, teacher] and had been strict controllers with the larger group of students.

Teachers as Friends

Most of my students reported that teachers normally initiated a personal relationship with a limited number of students—about a dozen students out of a 50-student class, according to Wen Min (September 17, 2003). These students often described themselves as good learners. They were attentive listeners, active in answering teachers' questions, and willing to participate in classroom activities. For instance, Shen Ling won her teacher's support by outperforming others in class. She had attended private English lessons before she started learning English at her secondary school:

I was able to answer questions asked by the English teacher at school because I had learnt them all before. She was deeply impressed. From then on, she paid a lot of attention to me and always praised my performance. Therefore, I felt that I could do well in English. (Shen Ling, September 22, 2003)

In other cases, particular teachers believed that certain types of students had more potential for academic performance than other students. Yan Jun had a female English teacher as her homeroom class teacher (*banzhuren*), who thought that boys could achieve better results than girls if they were pushed to do so:

She often went to talk to the boys. . . . They were usually quite naughty. So she bribed them into working hard by all measures, such as inviting them for meals at her home. (Yan Jun, September 20, 2003)

There were many benefits for these lucky students who received the teachers' special favors. For example, with the teachers' special attention, they were often granted higher status among their peers, such as being appointed as class representatives for English teachers, as happened to Li Ping:

On my first day of learning English, when the teacher was explaining vocabulary to us, I listened carefully and answered her questions loudly. After class, the teacher told me to collect assignment books for her. . . . The homeroom class teacher told me that I was just appointed by her as the class representative. From that moment on, I felt that I should work hard on and do well in learning English. (Li Ping, September 21, 2003)

Another example cited was access to extra learning resources—such as exercise books or learning methods—that contributed to enhancing these learners' academic performance:

At that time, there were many student contests. He gave me some good exercise questions to prepare for these contests. (Shan Hong, September 26, 2003)

There was a teacher who showed greater care for me. . . . In comparison with other students, he thought that I was quite good at English. . . . He wanted me to work harder at that time. He not only gave me extra exercise, more exercises than others, such as a book he thought helpful for my learning. And also he taught me some learning methods . . . and so on. (Dan Feng, September 27, 2003)

However, teachers' selective favor had worrying consequences. Those students who were unable to receive teachers' support felt frustrated to have teachers who showed their concern for other students more than them. They complained about receiving insufficient attention, saying their teachers "always liked to call [on] some students who talked a lot in class. I seldom got my turn to speak"

(Shan Hong, September 26, 2003). One student even associated this lack of attention with her falling grades, saying her teacher was particularly nice to boys:

These boys quickly improved their grades in exams. However, girls like me who used to have good grades started falling behind. . . . I think that I need to compete to attract teachers' attention. It is not difficult. If your grade is good and active in class, teachers would pay attention to you. (Yan Jun, September 20, 2003)

Chinese teachers have been noted for their readiness to use strategies to enhance competition among students (Schoenhals, 1993). Teachers' selective favors might have been one measure for them to encourage student competition for better learning. However, as revealed in Yan Jun's quote, these preferences also seemed to create tensions among students. Fierce academic competition had already made academic life depressingly stressful for these students. Because peer relationships were tense, they had to resort to seeking teachers' support in dealing with most of their academic problems. Consequently, they became much more dependent on teachers than necessary had there been mutually caring peer relationships.

Teachers as Authoritarian Figures

In addition to being a nice friend to selected students, English teachers in the interview data were also described as authorities who had immense power over the students when they were at secondary school. They often dictated learning activities and the content of learning and had little desire to accommodate learners' own choices in language learning. They adhered to a routine of rigid exercises, dictation, memorization, and simulation:

At that time, teachers forced us to memorize all texts. We had to do vocabulary dictation each day. (Hui Ling, September 19, 2003)

This teacher . . . often asked us to do more exercises, previews, reviews, and so on. Then there were simulation papers for exams. . . . We did many simulation exam papers. (Xiao Yan, September 24, 2003)

In my junior high school, the teacher did not teach anything about grammar. He said that we would not be able to understand it after all. He just got us to recite texts in our textbooks. Every single text. The teacher wanted you to memorize and recite them. (Wen Min, September 17, 2003)

The teachers appeared to accept that they were expected to do whatever they could to enhance learners' language learning, which in most cases meant working to boost exam scores. My students indicated that such authoritarian teachers

---

were almost indispensable to them as they coped with the learning demands. As long as exam pressure was there, they would expect such teachers to help them maximize their exam results. In many cases, they appreciated such teachers, although it was often painful to follow their directives:

> The teacher worked very hard so that we might go to university. She had to do so. She was afraid that we were not motivated enough so she organized class meetings everyday. . . . Because she had a tight control of our learning, I started realizing that I had to work hard, too. (Dan Feng, September 27, 2003)

> Our teachers (at our secondary school) were like. . . . If you completed your today's work, you could go home. If you didn't, stay on, although there were no compulsory evening tutorials. . . . We memorized texts only for reporting to teachers. But we were grateful to teachers in exams. Why? For example, there was *cloze* in English exams, which were normally based on English texts. . . . If we could memorize all the texts, it was not difficult for us at all. . . . We were exhausted sometimes but we felt grateful to teachers. (Jing Jing, September 19, 2003)

However, the same students would question such teachers' authoritarian stance when they failed to achieve better exam performance for their students. In general, my students implied that they were less than happy with their teachers at secondary school because their low exams scores allowed them to enter only a fifth-class institution. As an example, Shen Ling led a peculiarly open but subtle rebellion when she found that her teacher was failing to help her achieve learning objectives. This example suggests that some students not only maintained their independent thinking but also acted on it:

> At that time. . . . That teacher! Ha! He was funny! He asked us to read the vocabulary list every morning. On Monday, we should read the sections *A* to *F*. So we should start from *G* on Tuesday. But he forgot!!! So we started reading *A* again. . . . It seemed that we could never manage to read all the sections. . . . And it was the final review time! We were really angry. . . . So we organized ourselves . . . and read the whole list from *A* to *Z* in one go! (Shen Ling, September 22, 2003)

ACKNOWLEDGING THE NEED FOR INDEPENDENCE

Despite my students' desire for friendly support and disciplinary intervention from their teachers, they knew that they were responsible for their own learning outcomes. Although they still wanted teachers to use all means (through praise or cajoling, award or punishment) to keep them working hard and prevent them from going astray, students gradually felt that they needed to take more control of their own learning. They found that such independence was finally possible at college, because learning and teaching were organized differently compared with secondary school. At the college, teachers had less control over the time and space of their English learning, and alternative learning resources were more readily available:

> There are some differences between the high school and college. At college, we should rely on ourselves, all on ourselves. There are not many lessons. We have more free time. At high school, there was no time after study. (Yan Jun, September 20, 2003)

> Teachers do not have a tight control of us here. There are great differences in the levels of teachers' control at high school and college. (Wen Min, September 17, 2003)

> Here . . . there is a library, where there are many books to borrow and read. There is a lot of information there. . . . Here I rely on my own will and my own self-will. . . . In the past, I think that I relied on teachers. (Xiao Yan, September 24, 2003)

My students said that at secondary school they felt that teachers were justifiably authoritarian because the students were "young" (Dan Feng, September 27, 2004). However, once students were at college and perceived themselves as adults, they recognized that they needed to excel in English of their own accord:

> After coming to the college, we have become grown-ups. . . . It is no longer possible for us to learn under teachers' close control. At that time, we needed it because we were learning the basics. Now we have learnt the basics and need to expand our knowledge on the basics. (Jing Jing, September 19, 2003)

Finally, some students emphasized that they should be independent in learning in the future. They believed that they would be at a disadvantage if they relied on others after graduation:

> The society after my graduation is a big classroom, where I will have many things to learn. If I follow my teachers' instructions to walk every step, or I only do what my teachers tell me to do, I will be in an awkward situation in the future. (Shen Ling, September 22, 2003)

Reflection

So far, I have examined what kind of roles my students wanted their teachers to play, how teachers fulfilled their roles in my students' past learning experiences, and what caused them to desire independence. I found that my students were dependent on teachers for emotional empowerment and exam-related tips that could help them survive and succeed in the competitive educational process.

I also discovered worrying mismatches between my students' expectations of teachers and their teachers' actual involvement in the learning process. These discrepancies seemed to have made some learners even more teacher-dependent and others to start critically examining teachers' roles. Furthermore, I learnt that most of my students wanted to be independent even if they were not.

Integrating the multiple findings from this inquiry, I realized that my students' teacher-dependence was possibly strategic in nature, because my students appeared to have utilized teachers' support and intervention to solve their short-term academic problems and do well in the academic race. In some sense, their teacher-dependence could be a paradoxical feature of a local version of autonomy shaped by cultural traditions and educational contexts (Littlewood, 2001).

As I kept reflecting on these findings, I began to critically assess the institutionalized roles of teachers and some of my colleagues' actual roles in the learning process in relation to my students' teacher-dependence. First, teachers have institutionalized roles as academic gatekeepers in a context in which education and English learning are widely considered ways to achieve social and economic advancement (Cheng, 1996; Dooley, 2001; Pennycook, 1994; Zhao & Campbell, 1995). Academic competition is ferocious and the stakes are high for Chinese students. They live and study in a system that tends to concentrate resources and opportunities for a few elite students or institutions on the top of the social and educational hierarchies (Dooley, 2001; Ross, 1993; Schoenhals, 1993). For my students, their educational experiences were stressful and demoralizing because their past institutions and the college had offered few opportunities for further education and social promotion (Hu, 2004; Postiglione, 2005; Shen & Li, 2004). In other words, my students felt that they had to depend on teachers in learning.

Second, some of my colleagues' actual roles in the learning process also seemed to have made students dependent. Most of the English teachers whom students reported on were also my students' homeroom class teachers (*banzhuren*), who not only had pedagogic expertise to help students move up educational and social ladders but also had micropolitical power to control students' academic and daily lives (Dooley, 2001; Lo, 2001; Ross, 1993; Zhu & Liu, 2004). Students regarded the selective attention teachers gave to potentially successful students as a crucial force motivating them to strive for academic achievement. This attention also provided these fortunate learners with a competitive edge over other learners in terms of extra learning resources, opportunities, and advice. These teachers' authoritarian power certainly compelled my students to do their utmost in the excruciating and often demoralizing exam preparation process. Although my students had fond memories of nice but strict teachers, the students were prone to criticizing teachers who failed to meet their expectations (Cleverley, 1991; Schoenhals, 1993). This criticism seemed to make my colleagues feel threatened.

Like Cheng's (2002) study, my inquiry is another attempt to present a contextual perspective on Chinese students' dependence on teachers, in contrast to Cortazzi and Jin's (1996) normative view. My findings are limited to my classroom and are not intended to challenge any previous research findings on Chinese learners, because this inquiry involved only 14 students. Still, I believe that most language teachers will find similar inquiries valuable and relevant to their teaching, although these studies can be time consuming. As teachers, it is important for us to know what Chinese students are like. But it is even more important for us to understand what our individual students are like. Such inquiries provide an avenue for teachers to develop deep knowledge about individual students.

Such studies can also help teachers negotiate with students about their respective roles in the teaching and learning process, if such inquiries include dialogue. As I learnt from my own students, they depend on us for emotional empowerment and technical know-how, especially in relation to assessment. Although it is relatively easy for us to share technical know-how, students' dependence may not disappear even if we try to help them build learning skills and strategic competence. Fostering emotional empowerment requires time, energy, patience, and empathy. What teachers really need to do is commit a substantial amount of energy and time to listening to students' past and current learning stories and seeking mutual understanding about teachers' and students' roles. The inquiry itself can be a starting point for this effort.

Meanwhile, teachers also need to raise their critical awareness of the political, ethical, moral, and pedagogic aspects of teaching practices. The confrontational accusations among students and teachers are by no means particular to my college alone. In many educational settings, whether teachers like it or not, they function as preselection agents. Furthermore, the stratification of learners by academic results often leads to social stratification as well. Therefore, teachers should not be surprised if students attack them and hold them responsible for perceived failures.

Gao Xuesong (Andy) is currently pursuing his doctoral degree in applied linguistics at the University of Hong Kong.

Appendix: Interview Schedule

1. Can you share with me your past English learning experiences?

2. When did you start learning English? And how did you like English at that time?

---

3. How did you learn English at your junior (senior) middle school?

4. How about your life at your junior (senior) middle school?

5. What was an English lesson at your junior (senior) middle school like?

6. Could you share with me your memories of your English teachers?

7. Any other memories of significant people or events related to your English learning at your junior (senior) school?

8. How are you learning English at college?

9. Any changes in your life and study at college in comparison with the past?

10. What was an English lesson at college like?

11. Any interesting events or people at college you wish to talk about?

CHAPTER 7

Challenging Tradition: Creating a Self-Access Language Learning Center in an East Asian Academic High School (*Japan*)

Chris Hale

Issue

The focus on learner autonomy has increased along with efforts to increase student motivation in English foreign language learning. The growth in the number of self-access centers appearing on Asian university campuses provides evidence of this attention. Such centers allow students to choose their own learning materials based on unique learning interests and needs. They also offer researchers who are interested in autonomy a convenient opportunity to analyze learner behavior. Although self-access centers have been a part of the language learning landscape for years at universities and language institutes and the amount of research that exists on their impact is extensive (see Cotterall & Reinders, 2001; Sturtridge, 1997), apart from some notable exceptions (e.g., Miller, 1999), research on the effectiveness of self-access centers in senior high schools, and in particular East Asian high schools, is comparatively limited.

The gap in research may be the result of teacher researchers in primary and secondary schools feeling intimidated by the challenges associated with creating, funding, and monitoring a self-access language learning center. In addition to these concerns, there is pervasive evidence that the secondary education system in much of East Asia, and Japan in particular, is heavily teacher centered and tied to the age-old tenets of the grammar-translation method (Hato, 2005; Rohlen, 1983). Gorsuch (1998) calls this system, in which the teacher holds unquestioned authority, *yakudoku*. In such an environment, a learning center designed to encourage students to take more control over their learning may be viewed by administrators and some teachers as an affront to the status quo, and such a view could therefore limit a center's chances of success.

The research on autonomy and East Asian students can be characterized as inconsistent at best. Many researchers (Benson, Chik, & Lim, 2003; Ho & Crookall, 1995; Jones, 1995; Turner & Hiraga, 1996) note that autonomy is often perceived as a Western construct that has questionable appropriateness in East Asian cultures where students are accustomed to regarding the teacher as holding unquestioned authority. Other research has emerged suggesting, essentially, that students do indeed desire autonomy. However, with pressure to produce students who perform well on entrance examinations, institutions are often unwilling to provide students with autonomous learning opportunities (Littlewood, 2000; Pierson, 1996).

In an effort to reconcile these views, I created a self-access language learning center in a Japanese academic high school in which teacher-centered, lecture-style lessons are the norm of classroom language instruction. Taking a group of 14 students, I assessed their attitudes toward the method of instruction at the school and observed their activity in the center over an 8-month period. My primary interest was to see if students accustomed to learning English through *yakudoku* would find value in autonomous language learning in a self-access center, and whether their time spent in the center would address their own stated language learning needs. It is my sincere hope that teachers interested in learner autonomy, and perhaps contemplating establishing self-access centers in their own schools, will find the results of this project informative and useful. Keeping in mind those educators who may attempt to replicate any part of this study, I have tried to be as detailed as possible about exactly what I did and how the students responded.

Background Literature

As stated previously, there is a great deal of inconsistency in the research dealing with autonomy in East Asian contexts. Some (primarily Western) researchers have formed the impression that East Asian students are passive and unresponsive to autonomous learning situations. In a study conducted at a Sydney university by Braddock, Roberts, Zheng, and Guzman (1995), 60% of the staff viewed the international Asian students on campus as passive and indifferent in class while rating international students from North America and Europe much more favorably. Cortazzi and Jin (1996) found similar sentiments at a Chinese university among Western teachers who complained that their students were shy and passive. Flowerdew and Miller (1995) and Ferris and Tagg (1996) have linked this behavior to East Asian cultural values, which hold teachers as unquestioned authoritarians and arbiters of learning materials and students as passive receivers of information.

Cheng (2000) and Liu and Littlewood (1997) have argued against the notion that East Asians are culturally programmed to be passive learners. These researchers have cited student surveys that indicate a strong desire for active participation in classes and particularly in group activities that allow students to be more assertive in expressing their opinions. Cheng reasons that it is more appropriate to say that *some* students prefer teacher-centered learning and that, if given the appropriate environment, "most learners can be active and participative" (p. 439). Littlewood (1999) found similar opinions among Chinese students who were generally quite critical of their teachers and the teacher-centered curriculum. Widdows and Voller (1991) surveyed students at four Japanese universities and found a "dichotomy between what students want to learn and experience in university English classes and what they are actually taught there" (p. 134). According to these researchers, East Asian students can benefit from a setting in which the teacher is not seen as the sole information "knower" (McKay, 2000, p. 55) and students are given a voice in directing their own learning.

Aoki and Smith (1999) argued against the notion of comparing East and West at all, asserting that cultural stereotyping serves only to disempower students and limit their potential for change. Autonomy—much like human rights—is a desire of all people, they reasoned, regardless of national origin. Aoki and Smith concluded that Japanese students, like students anywhere in the world, will respond positively to autonomy when ambitious educators break from tradition and endeavor to renegotiate the "rules of engagement" (p. 20) by providing students with learning opportunities that reduce their dependency on teachers.

Any research project that attempts to deal with autonomous learning in the Japanese high school context must take into consideration the formal learning environment found in the schools. There has been much written describing the secondary education system in Japan as heavily teacher centered and intertwined with the grammar-translation method (GTM), which ranks translation prowess above oral fluency in the educational hierarchy (Benson, Chik, & Lim, 2003; Hato, 2005; Rohlen, 1983). Gorsuch (1998) refers to Japan's English education pedagogy as translation-reading.

In an attempt to clarify exactly how formal secondary education is conducted in Japan, Gorsuch (1998) observed two fairly typical classroom environments and noted that the method of instruction was heavily influenced by the wash-back effect of university examinations. Her research showed that the "preparation for university entrance exams [is] the highest education priority" (p. 11) in Japanese high schools. Her findings coincide with what Rohlen (1983) found 15 years earlier: "The criterion of efficiency in preparation, of meeting competition by gearing education to the [university] examinations, reaches deep into nearly every corner of high school education" (p. 108). In such an environment, it is considered counterproductive to allow students to choose for themselves what and how to study, for doing so would neutralize the teacher's "control over language learning activities" (Gorsuch, 1998, p. 27) and risk underpreparing students for the examinations.

Medgyes (1992) found that one of the main causes for teacher-centered, translation-heavy instruction in Japan is "a state of constant stress and insecurity [among teachers] caused by inadequate knowledge in the language they are paid to teach" (p. 348). Therefore, teachers are more comfortable in classes conducted in their first language, Japanese, that involve translating English passages into Japanese. Such a classroom dynamic caused Gorsuch (1998) to conclude that "instruction sequences appeared to [be] more as lessons in Japanese than English. . . . [and] the teachers focused on helping students to think about and create meaningful Japanese, rather than meaningful English" (p. 20). The implication is that in English language classrooms in Japan, more value is placed on being astute in Japanese than in English.

Procedures

SETTING

I created the center in an academic public high school in eastern Japan, where I had been working for approximately 4 years. I secured a rarely used audiovisual room, which at the time was being used primarily for storage. I equipped it with materials related to listening, reading, writing, and grammar. The room was already outfitted with cable television, two TVs, a VCR, a DVD player, sofas, and a coffee table. In addition, I brought in two relatively unused audio CD players from the English department. The high school possessed a wealth of authentic materials in the form of graded readers, English magazine and newspaper subscriptions, textbooks, listening programs, and movies. The resources easily numbered several hundred, but they were scattered throughout the English department with no apparent cataloging system. I placed all of these materials in the center, where I organized them according to skill area and difficulty (beginner, intermediate, and advanced). To better distinguish which materials learners were utilizing, I decided to make two clear categories for all materials in the center: authentic and grammar-based. For this study, grammar-based materials were defined as English learning materials written in Japanese. They included the following:

- University practice entrance exams (generally a complex reading passage followed by comprehension questions in Japanese).

- English grammar and sentence structure texts (written in Japanese).

- Reading and translation exercise texts.

- Vocabulary texts (which present an English word followed by a Japanese definition and sample usage).

Authentic materials were defined as containing only English, including the following:

- Daily English newspapers.

- Weekly news magazines.

- Novels or other books (including graded readers).

- Novels or other books on CDs and audiotapes.

- Movies on videocassettes and DVDs.

- English cable TV programs (from Fox, CNN, and BBC).

- English-only textbooks (written for use in English as a second language classrooms where grammar is not the focus).

At this point, I should note that I had no budget whatsoever for procuring center materials and equipment. All of the center's materials either belonged to the English department or were donated by other departments in the school. This point is significant, because educators often cite budgetary concerns as a reason for not establishing centers at their institutions.

PARTICIPANTS

Students had 7 hours of classroom English instruction per week, and 6 of those were taught by Japanese teachers of English who used GTM as the primary form of instruction. I observed this tendency during 2 weeks of the students' English lessons (14 hours in total), which resembled Gorsuch's (1998) definition of *yakudoku*. In other words, the teachers stood at the front of the class and lectured about English in Japanese. Students were called upon to answer translation-related questions based on a numerical seating chart (students were numbered 1 to 40). I interviewed the 11 English teachers at the school after this 2-week observation period and asked if what I had observed was indicative of the type of English lessons students normally engaged in throughout the year. The teachers answered that it was. The students also had one class a week with me, a native speaker of English. My classes were taught entirely in English, and the objective was to participate in small-group and communicative activities. As a result of these observations, I made the determination that the majority of

English class time for the students in this study (six of seven classes, or 85.7%) was spent engaged in *yakudoku* (see Table 1).

For this study I focused on 14 senior-year students (out of a class of 40) who enrolled in my elective English course (the remaining 26 students opted for an elective math course). The class met for 1 hour per week, and students were also required to spend 1 hour a week in the self-access center. The required time in the center amounted to 32 hours per student over 8 months, which is the typical number of months Japanese seniors attend formal classes. This requirement was meant to represent a reactive autonomous learning experience. That is, students did not choose when to study autonomously, only what and how to study. The requirement also served to integrate the center into the curriculum, enhancing teacher and student involvement (Benson, 2001).

My goal was to document proactive autonomous learning in the center, which involved students choosing for themselves when and how often to visit the center. Therefore, I observed the center's use at lunchtime and after school, when visits were completely voluntary and time spent there did not count toward a student's weekly 1-hour requirement.

DATA COLLECTED

Following the multidimensional methodology structure for data collection developed by Gardner and Miller (1999), an approach designed specifically for evaluating self-access language learning centers, I collected qualitative and quantitative data. Before introducing the students to the center, I distributed a questionnaire with items designed to elicit attitudes about the approach of the school's English curriculum. One item in particular asked students to rate on a Likert scale of 1 to 5 their attitudes regarding classes in which teachers lecture and students are expected only to listen and take notes. I also asked students if they desired more opportunities to use English communicatively. Student responses on the precourse questionnaires helped me to determine their attitudes toward teacher-centered learning and subsequently monitor their use of materials in the center. In particular, I categorized learners according to their responses to the questionnaire items in Figure 1.

In addition to questions relating to the curriculum, I included questions to

Table 1. Class Time by Lesson Type

	Yakudoku	Group/Communicative
Hours per Week	6	1
Hours per Year	192	32
Percent of Total Class Time	85.7%	14.3%

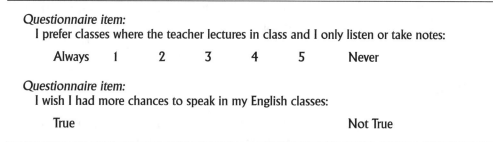

Figure 1. Items from precourse questionnaire on learning preferences.

enhance awareness about learning goals by asking students to state the subject areas they wanted to address in the center: reading, writing, listening, or grammar. I conducted interviews to better ensure that students' answers to the questionnaire items accurately represented their opinions. Interviews were recorded to MiniDisc and transcribed. I then gave students a formal introduction to the center, pointing out the various materials available in each skill area. I also instructed students how to operate the audiovisual equipment.

For each hour spent in the center (class time and voluntary time), students completed a study reflection sheet on which they detailed the exact resources used as well as what they learned or discovered during the studying process. This reflection sheet served the dual purposes of increasing learner awareness and providing a detailed record of center resources being used. Each week I reviewed the reflection sheets and wrote comments to students about what they did and learned. In no way did I intend these dialogues to direct students away from their chosen areas of study. Rather, my comments were meant to serve as a continuing dialogue with students and to answer any questions that might have come up during their study time in the center. Reflection sheets were copied for research purposes, and originals were returned to students within 1 week. At three scheduled interviews throughout the 8-month study, I asked students to comment on the materials they were using in the center and to indicate if the materials were sufficient or effective in aiding their study of their chosen skill areas. At each interview I asked students to reflect on their time spent in the center in order to establish if they were finding the center valuable to their overall learning routines.

At the end of the research period, I gave students a second questionnaire. This time, I asked if they had found the center's materials useful and, if so, which ones and in what way. For students opting to use the center on their own time, I posed questions to determine why students chose to use the center when doing so had no relation to the 1-hour weekly requirement. Follow-up interviews were conducted to give students the opportunity to clarify and expand on their answers to the questionnaire. I recorded these interviews in MiniDisc format and transcribed them in their entirety. Student comments presented in this study were edited for fluency only; content has not been altered.

Results

The results of this study indicated that even among the small group of subjects, diverse learning preferences were represented. Generally, three distinct types of learners emerged: those who preferred the lecture-based, grammar-translation approach typical of the English classes of the school; those who disliked the *yakudoku* approach; and those who disliked *yakudoku* yet found little practical value in studying nongrammar-related materials. Yet again, a small number of learners indicated no clear learning preference. Responses to the precourse questionnaire item asking students to rate their preference for teacher-centered learning proved an accurate barometer of how they would use the center over the 8 months (see Table 2).

In the results section, I will focus on the two groups of students at each end of the spectrum indicating the clearest opinion regarding *yakudoku* (those answering either 1 or 5 on the precourse questionnaire). The results show that students' study patterns while in the center reflected their attitudes toward grammar-based classroom learning. Students who preferred GTM primarily used the grammar-based resources, and students who found the least value in GTM used a wider variety of resources, primarily authentic materials. Because all learners generally responded positively on surveys and in interviews to spending time in the center, and based on the number of hours spent in the center voluntarily after school, I concluded that the center was largely successful in supplementing the learning routines of students who had different preferences and needs.

Table 2. Questionnaire Responses Showing Opinions About *Yakudoku*

Questionnaire item:
I prefer classes where the teacher lectures in class and I only listen or take notes:

Always   1   2   3   4   5   Never

	Prefer *Yakudoku*		Preference Unclear	Dislike *Yakudoku*	
	1	**2**	**3**	**4**	**5**
Responses	3	1	2	3	5
Percentage	21%	7%	14%	21%	36%
	28%		14%	57%	

Note: Figures do not equal 100% because of rounding.

LEARNERS WHO PREFERRED GTM

Of the 14 students, only three (21%) indicated on precourse surveys (and confirmed in follow-up interviews) that they "strongly" preferred learning English through lectures and note taking. On the question asking if they wished they had more chances to speak English in classes (Figure 1), all three indicated that they did not. These students preferred the predictable nature of teacher-centered classes because they felt uncomfortable when asked to speak in front of others. One student remarked that "the teacher might only call on us once during a class, so we can feel relaxed." Another student commented that she did not like the classes with a native English speaker because he often gave students group work that required them to speak in English: "It just feels strange to speak to other Japanese in English. In my normal classes [with a Japanese teacher] we never have to do that."

For the three students to whom English competency equated to mastery of grammatical minutiae, they overwhelmingly chose to utilize the center's grammar-based materials. In the initial months of their required time in the center, I observed that they experimented with other materials, such as movies and authentic novels and magazines. As the semester progressed and entrance examinations loomed, however, they gravitated toward the grammar materials they assumed would better prepare them for the tests, particularly the university exam test-prep texts. The three students' use of grammar materials noticeably increased following summer break, a season when high school students prepare in earnest for entrance examinations. A student explained that even though she liked the variety of materials available in the center, she felt it was a waste of time to venture away from the resources that best prepared her for university entrance exams. "I like the materials here, like TV and magazines, but right now it is important to focus on exams," she said. The other two students made similar statements regarding the importance of studying for entrance exams using grammar-based materials.

With 32 total hours per student over the 8-month study, the three students who preferred GTM spent a combined 72 hours (75%) of required center time studying grammar-related resources. They interacted with authentic materials a combined 24 hours (25%) (see Figure 2).

For those three students, the number of hours spent with authentic materials was considerably smaller than the number of hours spent with grammar materials. However, the number is nonetheless significant considering that these students indicated a strong preference for *yakudoku*. When asked why they chose to study the authentic materials, the students replied that when there was little pressure to memorize anything for a test, they allowed themselves on occasion to, in their words, "have fun" and just watch the TV or "relax" by "skimming" an English magazine.

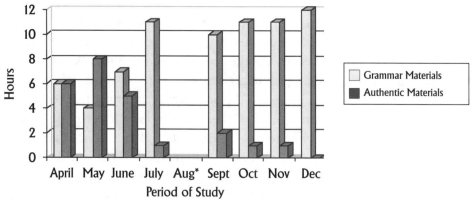

*summer vacation, no data

Figure 2. Materials used during required center time by three students with a strong GTM preference.

LEARNERS WHO DISLIKED GTM

Of the 14 participants, five (36%) indicated a strong dislike of *yakudoku* (see Table 2). On the question asking if they wished they had more chances to speak English in classes, all five indicated that they did. The five students indicated "boredom" as the main reason they disliked their grammar-based English classes as well as a lack of emphasis on "real" English. The five students wanted to focus on other areas of English, rather than the translation of difficult texts characterizing their traditional English classes. One student said that "in class we never practice listening. The teacher just explains everything in Japanese. That's OK, I guess, but I want to improve my listening." Another student stressed that although she understood the importance of studying grammar in class for entrance exams, she worried that if she were to travel abroad she would be unable to use English communicatively. She said she wanted to join an English conversation school (*eikaiwa*) to overcome the deficit. All five students indicated that they were looking forward to studying other aspects of the language while in the center. Two were planning to attend American universities after graduation and said they were interested in watching American TV programs, which would allow them to focus on pronunciation and colloquial expressions.

The five learners began the semester using the authentic materials, particularly the movies and novels, and the trend remained consistent throughout the 8-month study. Students tended to alternate between the various resources in the center, often choosing two or more areas (e.g., listening to English music and reading graded readers) in a single 1-hour session. Students engaged the grammar materials as well, although far more sparingly than the authentic materials. Use of the grammar materials by the five students increased only slightly following the summer break. During required center time (32 hours per student over the 8-month study), these five learners spent a combined 112 hours (70% of their time) with authentic materials and 48 hours (30% of their time) with grammar materials (see Figure 3).

The amount of time spent with the grammar-related resources was considerably less than time with authentic materials but was significant considering the five students indicated a strong dislike of grammar-translation learning. Students indicated that although they wished they could have spent all of their time with authentic materials, the demands of their grammar-based English classes and impending entrance examinations influenced their use of the grammar materials in the center. One student expressed a sense of conflict between what she wanted to do in the center and what she believed she should be doing: "I really need to be thinking about *juken* [studying for entrance exams] now. It is too bad because studying grammar is not useful for improving natural English, which is what I want to work on." Other students rejected the idea of studying grammar materials in the center completely: "I know some people are worried about entrance exams, but all they are doing is learning how to take tests, they aren't actually learning *anything*." Another commented that studying in the center was the only chance for her to really interact with English at a level appropriate for her: "I really like the [graded readers] because I can understand them. Reading easy books is fun."

VOLUNTARY USE OF THE CENTER

For all students, voluntary use of the center at lunch time and after school increased dramatically throughout the 8-month study. The students indicating the strongest dislike of GTM used the center more often than other students in the study, as shown in Figure 4.

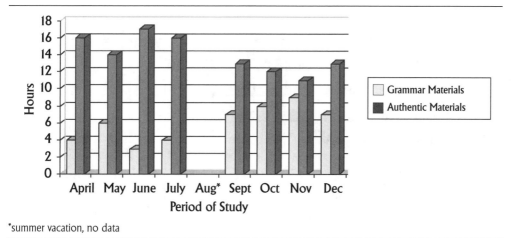

*summer vacation, no data

Figure 3. Center use in required hours for five learners indicating the strongest dislike for GTM.

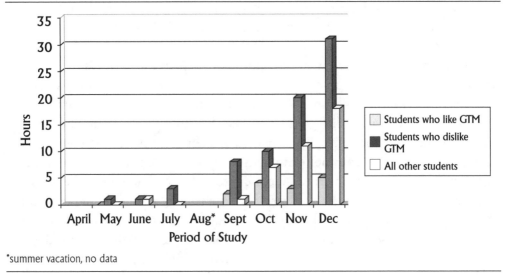

*summer vacation, no data

Figure 4. After-school center use in hours for all students.

VOLUNTARY USE BY STUDENTS WHO PREFERRED GTM

The three students who preferred GTM spent a combined 19 hours in the center at lunch or after school over the 8 months. The prime reason for coming to the center on their own time was that it was a "comfortable place." This reason ranked slightly higher than the "need to study for a test" or "liking the materials," which each had two responses (see Figure 5). One student explained that with a comfortable sofa and chairs the center did not "feel like a classroom." Another credited the air conditioning as a key reason for coming to the center on her own time, saying, "This is one of the most comfortable places in the school during summer."

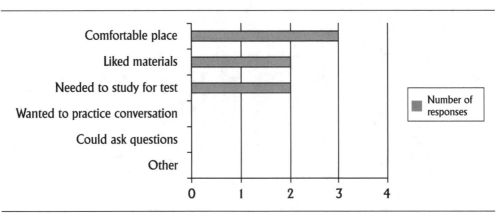

Figure 5. Reasons for coming to the center after school and at lunch time for three students indicating a strong preference for GTM.

VOLUNTARY USE BY LEARNERS WHO DISLIKED GTM

The five students indicating the strongest dislike of GTM spent a considerable amount of time in the center on their own, a trend that increased steadily over the 8 months. The five students spent a combined 79 hours in the center at lunch time or after school over the 8 months (60 more total hours than the grammar-centric group). The increase was in part the result of pressure to prepare for the impending Test of English as a Foreign Language (TOEFL) and entrance examinations, but more surprisingly it also arose from a growing sense of ownership of the center. All 14 students in the study were aware that they were participating in a closed study and that the center was created for their use exclusively. One of the five students illustrated this sense of ownership by proclaiming the center as "ours." She said it would be a waste if she did not use it. Four of the five students began to come to the center nearly every day after school, and one invited schoolmates unrelated to the study to join her in the center to watch English movies or TV programs. Their reasons for the high rate of use were diverse, with the most important being, again, that the center was a "comfortable place" (see Figure 6).

STUDENT IMPRESSIONS OF SELF-ACCESS LEARNING

All but one of the 14 participants in the study responded favorably to spending time in the center. In response to the question about which materials were most useful, the three learners who preferred the teacher-centered curriculum indicated that the grammar-based materials available in the center were most useful, followed next by magazines. The five learners indicating a strong dislike for teacher-centered learning responded with more variety to the question, indicating that the authentic materials, particularly the daily newspaper, weekly magazines, and cable television were most useful (see Figure 7).

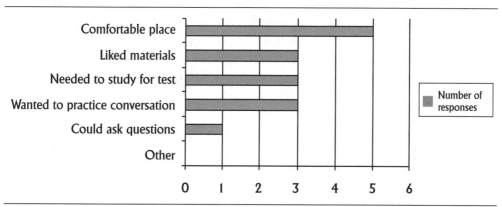

Figure 6. Reasons for coming to the center after school and at lunch time for five students indicating a strong dislike of GTM.

Most useful materials for three students who preferred GTM (multiple answers possible):

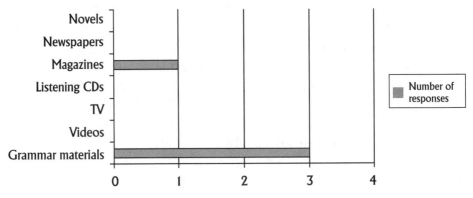

Most useful materials for five students who disliked GTM (multiple answers possible):

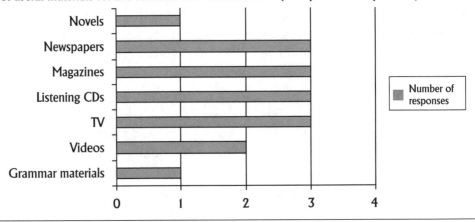

Figure 7. Center materials that students found most useful.

In the final questionnaires and interviews, students overwhelmingly agreed that the center played an important role in aiding them in their preferred mode of English study. Students also all indicated that my comments on their hourly study logs were helpful by giving them direct feedback and support on what they were discovering during the self-study process. One student said, "I liked the way you explained idioms I heard in a movie using easy English." Another wrote, "Your comments helped me to find just the right listening materials for me."

Reflection

The results of this study indicate that regardless of students' preferences for teacher or student-centered learning, a self-study center can be beneficial for students, provided that the center is comfortable and has a variety of resources.

A self-study center can help students achieve their goals, whether those goals are tied to the extrinsic demands of entrance examinations or the intrinsic rewards of effective communication. In this study, students comfortable with teacher-centered learning felt more familiar using grammar-based materials. The students uncomfortable with *yakudoku* expressed more concrete learning objectives, saying, "I want to improve pronunciation," and "I need to increase listening comprehension."

It was not the aim of this study to criticize or laud one type of learning preference. Rather, I wanted to see in what ways students with different learning styles and philosophies could find value in self-access learning. I believe the study was successful in illustrating that high school students would use a self-access center if they had access to one. I found that all students gradually began to spend more time in the center beyond the requirement, which led to a sense of ownership, especially among students who disliked *yakudoku*. And although the students who preferred the passive learning environment of the classroom spent considerably less time in the center after school than the other students, it was no less significant that they found enough value in autonomous learning to use the center as much as they did.

It has been suggested that East Asian students are reticent and passive and may therefore reject Western-style autonomy. I am concerned, however, that this characterization may serve to marginalize students who do not fit into this rather narrow stereotype. Such generalizations have the potential to discourage educators and institutions from attempting to establish self-access learning centers, particularly in high schools where teacher-centered curricula are often the norm. Despite the relatively small number of participants in my study, disparate learning styles were clearly represented, making it impossible to formulate sweeping generalizations about East Asian students being naturally prone to passive learning. In fact, the majority of participants exhibited clear *proactive* autonomous learning behaviors, such as using the center after school or bringing their own materials to supplement those available in the center.

Although enthusiasm for the center varied among the participants in this study, I was surprised by some students' candid comments in interviews about the school's English curriculum, particularly among students who disliked *yakudoku*. One student complained that "for six years we have been studying English that way—it has been a total waste of time." Another student was even blunter in her criticism: "Somebody needs to tell them [the teachers] that what they are doing is wrong. Students should tell them, maybe, but we can't. The system needs to change." Whether these complaints have merit is not the issue here. What is striking is that such opinions as these hardly exemplify a passive acceptance of teacher-centered learning. Such frank responses indicate that self-access learning centers are needed in Japanese high schools, where diverse learning styles and preferences are clearly represented but appropriate avenues for development are not always provided. Of the 14 students in this limited study, a majority indicated a strong (5 students) or moderate (4 students) dissatisfaction with GTM. Although a detailed examination of this finding was not within the scope of this project, the students' responses certainly contradicted the impression that East Asian students are comfortable with the notion of "teacher as knowledge giver."

The decision to create and maintain a self-access center in a Japanese high school has not been without its challenges. Principal among these has been to convince colleagues and school administrators that providing a place where students are in control of their own learning is beneficial to the students and the institution. According to Littlejohn (1985), for a self-access center to be effective, it is imperative that teachers in the institution where it exists actually believe in it and promote it. Unless the English instructors believe that such a center would enhance learning, they are unlikely to endorse it to their students. Keeping this in mind, I interviewed colleagues prior to undertaking this endeavor. All of them were generally supportive of my "little experiment," but at the same time they expressed reluctance to integrate the center into their own class curricula. They were concerned that students would be lost if left to their own devices and would give up rather quickly. My research contradicts this fear and, in fact, shows that interest in the center among students increased steadily over the 8-month study.

Seeing the center flourish, my once-skeptical colleagues have now begun to advocate its use among their own students, and the English department has even earmarked a modest annual budget to expand the center's resources and keep them current. With these funds I have been able to purchase two TVs and several hundred graded readers for the center. As with any new concept, support often comes only after something is shown to be of value.

Chris Hale teaches at Takezono High School in Tsukuba, Japan.

CHAPTER 8

Improving Second Language Listening: Awareness and Involvement (*Singapore*)

Xuelin Liu and Christine C. M. Goh

Issue

As teachers, we were concerned about our learners' weak listening abilities. Traditional ways of teaching listening in course books tended to focus on comprehending the contents of listening passages. We were convinced that to help our students improve their listening abilities, we needed to first become aware of their learning needs and comprehension problems. We began systematically finding out what these were, and based on that understanding we began transforming our ways of teaching. Rather than merely carrying out the listening activities in course materials, we were involved in creating learning tasks that focused on the listening process.

The students were enrolled in an intensive English language programme in our institution aimed at tertiary students from China. The group consisted of 19 Chinese English as a second language (ESL) students from the first author's regular listening class. Of the 19 students, 6 were male and 13 were female, and the average age was 18. Before coming to Singapore, they had 6 years of language learning experience and at the time of enrollment had intermediate-level English proficiency.

In the past 10 years, about 200 to 300 students enrolled in this programme each year. We found one thing to be consistently true: The majority of these students had poor listening comprehension abilities. Our observation is supported by the results of centralized assessments at the beginning of each intake and our own experience teaching these students. Many of them had problems with perceiving chunks of speech, understanding gist, and recognizing key words. Most of them also suffered from listening anxiety. As these students were preparing for undergraduate studies in English-medium universities, poor listening comprehension would inevitably jeopardize their success.

One of the reasons for their poor listening ability was the lack of adequate input and opportunities for practice before they arrived in Singapore. In China a great deal of emphasis is still placed on the written language, and resources for listening are too expensive and hard to come by for many learners. The established practice of focusing solely on examination subjects, insufficient exposure to aural input, and the lack of expertise in teaching listening on the part of many teachers have contributed to this situation.

Besides these contextual factors, the learners also had to contend with a challenge faced by all language learners—the transient nature of the spoken language. Listening comprehension has its distinctive features: real-time processing, and phonological and lexico-grammatical features (Flowerdew, 1994). A reader can take time to read a text back and forth. However, a listener has no control over a listening text because it must be processed as it is uttered. Listeners also have to deal with rapid colloquial speech (Brown, 1990) and a range of registers, including stress, intonation patterns, hesitations, and false starts. To further complicate the matter, listeners have to use particular sets of knowledge to cope with lexico-grammatical features that are peculiar to spoken text (Flowerdew, 1994).

Some research has been conducted among Chinese ESL learners in Singapore (e.g., Goh, 1997, 1998), leading to recommendations for teaching. One such recommendation was to raise learners' metacognitive awareness about the listening process. The study reported here was an attempt to do just this. We hoped that this intervention, if successful, could offer us and ultimately other teachers in the programme a new way of teaching listening.

Background Literature

According to Flavell (1979), metacognitive knowledge refers to an understanding of the ways different factors act and interact to affect the course and outcome of cognitive enterprises. It can be classified into three major categories: person, task, and strategy. Building on Flavell's work, Wenden (1991) applied metacognitive knowledge to second language learning. She defined person knowledge as the learners' general awareness of the effects of factors such as age, learning style, and aptitude on language acquisition; task knowledge as what learners know about the nature, demands, and purpose of learning tasks;

and strategic knowledge as knowledge about what facilitates and inhibits language learning. Metacognitive knowledge influences approaches to learning and affects the course and outcome of learning (Holec, 1987; Horwitz, 1988; Wenden, 1987). In the article "Metacognitive Knowledge and Language Learning," Wenden (1998) emphasized the influence of metacognitive knowledge on the self-regulation of learning. She stated that person knowledge can affect learners' choices related to learning objectives and how they evaluate their learning outcomes.

Chinese learners' metacognitive knowledge about listening was first systematically explored through Goh's (1997) extensive analysis of the listening diaries of 40 students in Singapore. The students were reported to have a high degree of metacognitive awareness. They not only were aware of their learning processes but also had specific beliefs about the various factors that enhanced or impeded their listening comprehension. In addition, they could verbalize their own theories of approaching listening in the target language and observe their own cognitive processes in their own listening. Goh suggested including process-based discussion as part of the course curriculum to involve students in thinking about the process of listening.

In a study among learners of French, Vandergrift (2003) used several listening tasks to guide his students through the process of second language (L2) listening. He then examined the effects of these tasks by asking the students to reflect on their usefulness in assisting their comprehension and raising their metacognitive consciousness of the listening process. The study showed that learners were successfully guided in using prediction as a key listening strategy and demonstrated the motivational effects generated from this type of process-oriented listening. The study is a good example of how teachers can effectively help promote metacognitive processes through specially designed listening tasks.

Our research is based partly on this study by Vandergrift. Inspired by the success reported in his study, we hoped to obtain similar encouraging results with our Chinese learners.

Procedures

Before the research was carried out, we collected some baseline data to help us ascertain the students' listening comprehension needs. The initial cycle of our study had two phases and spanned a period of more than 3 months.

The first phase investigated listening strategies that were available to the students through the use of a questionnaire as well as delayed reports about survey interviews that they conducted as part of another course requirement. The baseline data helped us understand the general patterns of the students' strategy use. Based on the information from the first phase, we devised a series of intervention lessons for the second phase. We obtained data through two research instruments: a process-based listening guide (Vandergrift, 2003) and a self-directing listening guide (Goh, 2002).

We adopted this procedure for a number of reasons, two of which were in accordance with Mendelsohn's (1995) strategy-based approach. First, the procedure not only gave our students a good understanding of how they handled comprehension but also informed us of their approaches to comprehension. Before teaching students additional listening strategies, Mendelsohn suggested that teachers raise students' awareness of their own listening strategies, which he called "metastrategic awareness." Students should know what listening strategies they have before acquiring additional tools of comprehension. Second, the procedure provided scaffolding for the students. Mendelsohn also advocated providing assisted listening. He suggested including a series of guided exercises that instruct learners in the use of strategies. Our assisted and self-directing methods of teaching listening work toward the goal of learner autonomy. Finally, our procedure focused on the role of the teacher not only as a provider of comprehensible input but, more important, as a teacher of listening strategies. We hoped that the effects of the intervention activities would encourage teachers to break away from the traditional practice of teaching listening and to devise more such process-oriented listening tasks. The following sections present a detailed description of the procedure for each phase of the study.

PHASE 1: FINDING OUT HOW STUDENTS LISTENED

In Phase 1, two short open-ended questionnaires were used to find out what students did during listening and their reflections on their experiences. The first was used after students completed classroom listening tasks. We asked these questions:

- What are the important things you did to understand the text you just heard?

- What did you do to check your listening comprehension?

- What problems did you have?

We chose three passages from the students' course materials that were at appropriate proficiency levels and would likely relate to their experiences. The three texts covered the themes of invention, food, and advertising. Each week the students spent about 35 minutes listening to a text twice and answering the related questionnaire. They completed the three listening texts in 3 weeks.

In addition, we administered a similar questionnaire after the students conducted an oral survey for their oral communication project. The aim of this questionnaire was to find out what the students did to understand conversations outside the classroom. Students conducted their interviews in public places such as shopping malls, train stations, and schools. After they had completed their oral surveys, they were given the questionnaire in their listening class. We asked the following open-ended questions:

- Are you satisfied with your performance during the interviews?

- Reflecting on your performance during the survey interviews in English, what were the important things you did to understand the people you interviewed and to check your listening comprehension?

- What problems did you have?

It took the students half an hour to complete these questionnaires.

After we categorized the strategies used in the two settings, we held a sharing session to show the students that they had rich knowledge about listening comprehension that they could apply to aid their comprehension in different situations. This session also provided an opportunity for students to learn what their classmates did to tackle listening tasks. After students shared their listening strategies, we taught them additional listening strategies based on the inventory in Goh (2002). Each week we introduced three or four new strategies, and the students practiced using appropriate listening tasks.

PHASE 2: TEACHING STUDENTS TO LISTEN STRATEGICALLY

In Phase 2 of the study, we conducted two process-oriented lessons to sensitize students to the process of L2 listening and to teach them how to listen strategically. The first type was guided-listening lessons using a framework based on Vandergrift's (2003) listening practice activity table as a framework for carrying out the listening tasks. This framework includes prediction, first listen, second listen, third listen, and personal reflection.

To help facilitate the listening tasks, we simplified Vandergrift's (2003) seven-step procedure and used five steps for guiding students through the L2 listening process. In our last and personal reflection stage, we focused on students' perceptions of the activities and strategies they used to understand the texts instead of asking them to write the strategies they would like to use the next time. We were more interested in their feedback on the effectiveness of the activities. Table 1 shows each step for conducting the guided lessons. The two texts the students listened to were taken from their course materials. One was about common problems in adolescence; the other was about intelligence and whether it is linked to nature or nurture. The first author guided the students through the two lessons in 2 weeks. Before the lessons, students were given a briefing on how to proceed with each step. Each guided session lasted about 50 minutes.

In addition to these guided-listening lessons, we planned self-directing

Table 1. Steps for Guided-Listening Tasks

Step	Activity
Step 1	Prelistening activity—Before listening to the text, students worked in pairs and predicted possible words and phrases they were most likely to hear. They then wrote the information in the Prediction column.
Step 2	First listen—As students listened to the text, they underlined what they had anticipated in the Prediction column and entered new information in the First Listen column. They also compared predictions and what they understood. Difficult points were identified for the second listen.
Step 3	Second listen—Students worked in pairs to solve problem areas and entered information they comprehended in the Second Listen column. The teacher-facilitated discussion that followed subsequently served to check comprehension and share strategies.
Step 4	Third listen—Students listened to the text for the third time in order to check if they had missed any important information.
Step 5	Personal reflection—At this point students reflected on the effectiveness of the lesson. They entered in the last column their feelings and views about the guided-listening process and some strategies they had used to understand the text.

Source: Based on Vandergrift's (2003) process

listening activities. We modified Goh's (2002) guide for self-directing listening (see Appendix A). The guiding questions that helped the students manage and regulate their own listening comprehension were printed in a self-study sheet for them to refer to individually at any time during listening. Based on level appropriateness and topic familiarity, we selected two texts from BBC World Service's Learning English magazine radio programme (BBC, n.d.) and made arrangements for two classrooms to be used, one for each listening text. Students chose the topic they were interested in and participated in the listening activity in the designated classroom. They were free to listen to their texts as many times as they preferred and were in total control of the session.

As they listened on their own, students answered prompt questions before and after the texts to make prelistening preparation and plan their strategies for future listening. They also evaluated their own performance in terms of strategy use as well as comprehension. They compared actual strategies they used with those they planned to use and tried to find out if those strategies were effective. Students received transcripts of the recordings so they could evaluate their comprehension by identifying areas they had and had not understood. While students were listening, the first author moved between the rooms and observed the students. Both groups completed their tasks within 50 minutes. Table 2 outlines the steps for the self-directing listening sessions.

Table 2. Procedure for Conducting Self-Directing Listening Tasks

Step	Activity
Step 1	Selecting listening texts—Recordings that suited the students' proficiency levels and related to their experiences were preselected.
Step 2	Choosing the topics—Students were informed of the topics of the listening texts. They chose the topics they were interested in and formed groups according to the texts they chose.
Step 3	Making prelistening action plans—In their respective rooms, students set goals for listening; predicted contents, words, and difficulties; and considered appropriate strategies for their listening passages.
Step 4	Listening to the passage—Students listened to their passages. They checked comprehension, shared notes, verified main ideas and details with one another, and discussed difficult points.
Step 5	Conducting postlistening evaluations—Students compared their strategies, evaluated their comprehension, identified problems, and planned strategies for future use.

At the end of the intervention sessions, we elicited students' oral reports. We intended for the reports to indicate any improvements in students' strategy use and metacognitive awareness. We hypothesized that after learning additional strategies and participating in process-based assisted listening, the students would demonstrate a higher degree of metacognitive awareness in student-centered activities and use more listening strategies. The preliminary results were also used for evaluating teaching and planning a follow-up cycle of metacognitive instruction.

Results

In this section we present three sets of results. We begin with listening strategies identified from Phase 1 of the study. Next are the students' responses to the guided-listening lessons. Finally, we present results from the self-directing listening activities.

LISTENING STRATEGIES

To organize the students' listening strategies revealed in the first phase of the study, we used Goh's (2002) inventory of listening strategies and tactics. We found that different tasks resulted in the use of different strategies. The type of listening strategies and the frequency of use changed between the interviews and the classroom (see Appendix B for listening strategies in two situations).

When conducting survey interviews, students used more cooperation strategies (social-affective) than they did in the classroom. These included asking for information and explanations and asking the speaker to slow down so the student could interact with the person during the conversation. Students used more metacognitive strategies in coping with classroom listening tasks than in the interview conversations, although in both contexts they applied four subcategories of metacognitive strategies: prelistening preparation, directed attention, selective attention, and comprehension monitoring. As for cognitive strategies, the students did not report using any in the conversations, although they used four types in the classroom listening: prediction, visualization, contextualization, and elaboration. We think students did not report using cognitive strategies in conversations because they were focused on getting the conversations going.

The students encountered many problems in the two contexts. Some of their problems in the conversations were associated with the socioaffective domain: feeling anxious and shy and having a lack of confidence. Other problems in comprehending classroom listening texts seemed to be at the lexical and semantic level. Students had difficulty with vocabulary and sentence structure. Factors such as speed, memory load, and attention span were also reported to have affected their comprehension.

GUIDED-LISTENING LESSONS

The students demonstrated positive responses similar to the ones Vandergrift (2003) reported from his students in Canada. On the whole, our students were in favour of using guided-listening tasks. There were few negative comments (see Table 3). Some reported that prelistening activities contributed to better comprehension and that the listening tasks activated students' background knowledge. Others said that they became familiar with listening strategies through this systematic approach and that group discussion seemed to be an effective way of achieving good comprehension. Many students expressed the desire to have more such listening lessons in the future.

An encouraging finding was that the students responded more positively to the second guided-listening activity than to the first one. In fact, the number of positive comments on the second task doubled those on the first one. This increase could indicate that when students became more familiar with the approach, they were even more disposed to process-oriented listening lessons. A few students, however, did not respond favorably to the activity, saying it was a waste of time and that prediction was helpful only in test situations. These students seemed more concerned with the content of a text than learning how to listen.

Table 3. Sample Student Comments on Guided-Listening Tasks

Reflection After First Guided-Listening Lesson	
Positive Comments	**Negative Comments**
a. It was a more efficient way of listening.	a. I got only a general idea.
b. Prelistening activities helped me to understand better.	b. I cannot get much content.
c. I hope to have this method of listening often.	c. My prediction was not mentioned.
d. Discussions helped us to check main ideas and details.	
e. I could get a good comprehension of the text and a clearer structure of the text.	
f. It enabled me to have a focus: first on main ideas, second on details.	

Reflection After Second Guided-Listening Lesson	
Positive Comments	**Negative Comments**
a. The method makes listening easier, and we become more confident.	a. Prediction was useful only for tests.
b. It makes us more familiar with listening strategies.	b. It was a waste of time.
c. We can improve listening comprehension step by step.	
d. Background knowledge is so important. This method activates that.	
e. Prediction is very important because we can have a good preparation.	
f. The teacher helped us to pick up main points and helped us understand bit by bit.	
g. We can understand more through discussions.	
h. I can concentrate on listening.	
i. I can learn how my partners listen to English.	
j. I hope I can have more such listening activities.	
k. Second listen made me improve a lot.	
l. I can learn how to take notes/improve note-taking skills.	

SELF-DIRECTING LISTENING ACTIVITIES

In this part we analysed the strategies that students reported using to find out how they managed their listening when given an opportunity. We also analysed whether students' introduction to additional strategies and participation in the two guided listening tasks had any effect on their strategy use and metacognitive awareness. When we compared how the students handled classroom listening tasks in Phase 1 with how they managed self-directing listening tasks in Phase 2, we found an increased number of strategies reported (see Appendix C). Their expanded repertoire of strategies appears to support our preliminary hypothesis that process-based discussions and lessons would heighten students' metacognitive awareness and could lead to an increased use of strategies. Our key findings include the following:

- There was an increase in the students' use of cognitive strategies. They varied tactics for contextualization strategies and reported more strategies for making inferences.

- The students used more cooperation and confidence-building strategies in the social-affective category. They cooperated with each other in their own listening by discussing difficult areas with classmates, asking for help, and sharing information.

- They developed greater person knowledge by consciously using more confidence-building strategies such as overcoming nervousness, thinking positively, and encouraging themselves.

- The use of three subcategories of metacognitive strategies—selective attention, directed attention, and comprehension monitoring—was expanded considerably. In addition, they used more metacognitive strategies.

Reflection

This two-phase study demonstrates that metacognitive instruction can enhance learners' metacognitive consciousness about listening comprehension and diversify the use of listening strategies. Generally, learners' awareness about listening is largely ignored in practice. In lessons that focus on the right answers, students are seldom given an opportunity to think about their listening processes or to develop the necessary strategies and skills. Listening lessons are often nothing more than obtaining information to answer questions. The teacher often decides what to listen to, how to listen, and when to listen. To effectively help L2 listeners improve their listening comprehension, teachers need to acknowledge the role metacognitive knowledge plays in facilitating comprehension and the need to sensitize students to it by involving them in more process-based listening activities.

Based on our experience in this study, we are convinced even more that metacognitive instruction should be a key part of developing learners' listening. In order to do this, two new activities have since been included in our listening course curriculum. These are the use of listening diaries and a group listening project.

Our Chinese students are asked to keep listening diaries as a way of making a deliberate effort to increase their exposure to L2 listening, reflect on the listening process, and promote strategy use. Adapting Goh's (1997) procedure for keeping listening diaries, each week students will report on one situation in which they listen to English outside of the classroom. They then submit a summary and personal response of what they listen to, explain the strategies they use to comprehend, and include plans for future listening.

The group listening project aims to make the students more metacognitively conscious of the listening process through involvement and collaboration. It serves to enhance the three types of metacognitive knowledge: task, strategy, and person. To carry out the project, students work in groups of four to develop either a video or radio programme and devise listening activities to present the programme to the class. While developing the programme and activities, students have to consider what kinds of listening material might motivate their fellow students and what kinds of activities might enhance listening. We hope our research will encourage other language teachers in Asia to carry out their own classroom-based research (either by replicating this present study or developing their own method) that can identify effective listening tasks for developing their learners' listening competence.

Xuelin Liu teaches at the National Institute of Education in Singapore.
Christine C. M. Goh also teaches at the National Institute of Education in Singapore.

Appendix A: A Guide for Self-Directing Listening

Name:

Passage title:

Date:

BEFORE LISTENING

Goal Definition

What is my purpose for listening to this recording?

Action Plan

What is the best way to achieve my goal?

What do I already know about this topic?

What information can I expect to hear?

What words can I expect to hear?

What difficulties can I expect?

What can I do to cope with these difficulties?

AFTER LISTENING

Evaluation

How much have I understood?

What were the difficulties? Were they what I had expected?

Were my strategies effective? Is there anything else I should do the next time I listen?

Source: Adapted with permission of the Regional Language Centre, Singapore, from Goh (2002)

Appendix B: Strategies Used and Problems Identified in Phase 1

Type of Strategy	Strategy Use in the Interviews	Strategy Use in the Classroom
Social-Affective	**Cooperation** · Ask for information in a polite way · Ask for examples and repetition · Ask for explanation · Tell people to write down unfamiliar words · Ask people to slow down · Use paraphrase to verify interpretation **Confidence building** · Tell oneself not to be shy · Tell oneself not to be afraid · Try to relax	**Cooperation** · Ask the teacher to play recordings again to check comprehension **Confidence building** · Try to relax
Metacognitive	**Prelistening preparation** · Preview questions · Predict what people will say **Directed attention** · Concentrate hard **Selective attention** · Pay attention to key words · Be aware of body language, eye contact, and gestures **Comprehension monitoring** · Listen to recorded interviews · Check comprehension by repeating	**Prelistening preparation** · Read questions before listening to get main ideas · Try to remember questions · Use questions to predict the contents **Directed attention** · Try to concentrate · Follow the contents · Skip difficult information and continue listening

Type of Strategy	Strategy Use in the Interviews	Strategy Use in the Classroom
Metacognitive (continued)		**Selective attention** · Focus on key words · Listen carefully for main ideas · Follow information relevant to questions about the contents · Pay attention to structure · Focus on the beginning part of a text **Comprehension monitoring** · Check answers by recalling what is heard · Draw on prior experience to check understanding
Cognitive		**Prediction** · Predict the contents of a text **Elaboration** · Use background knowledge to interpret new information **Visualization** · Try to imagine a picture of the speaker or words heard **Contextualization** · Place information in a meaningful context
Perceived Problems	· Feeling shy and nervous · Lack of fluency · Lack of confidence · Afraid to ask for repetition · Have problem with abbreviations · Cannot understand Singapore English · Fast speed · Limited vocabulary	· Miss upcoming information when thinking about word meaning · Limited vocabulary · Cannot get details when the speed is too fast · Cannot segment streams of speech · Unable to understand structure · Cannot concentrate all the time · Forget what is heard · Cannot recognize words known

Appendix C: A Comparison of Strategies Used in Two Types of Classroom Listening Tasks

Type of Strategy	Strategies Used in the Classroom (Phase 1)	Strategies Used in Self-Directing Listening (Phase 2)
Cognitive	**Prediction** · Predict the contents of a text **Elaboration** · Use background knowledge to interpret new information **Visualization** · Try to imagine a picture of the speaker or words heard **Contextualization** · Place information in a meaningful context	**Prediction** · Predict contents before listening · Predict continuations **Elaboration** · Use personal experience/examples · Use knowledge about the subject matter **Visualization** · Imagine a picture or a scene on hearing words **Contextualization** · Put information in a context · Relate information to personal knowledge · Relate one part of a text to another **Making inferences** · Use context clues to infer meaning of unknown words · Use information understood to guess the unknown parts · Use language knowledge to guess missing information · Guess the missing information using prior knowledge
Social-Affective	**Confidence building** · Try to relax **Cooperation** · Ask the teacher to play recordings again to check comprehension	**Confidence building** · Relax · Overcome nervousness · Be confident · Think positively · Encourage self **Cooperation** · Discuss with others · Share information with each other · Ask others for help

Type of Strategy	Strategies Used in the Classroom (Phase 1)	Strategies Used in Self-Directing Listening (Phase 2)
Meta-cognitive	**Prelistening preparation** · Read questions before listening to get main ideas · Try to remember questions · Use questions to predict contents **Selective attention** · Focus on key words · Listen carefully for main ideas · Follow information relevant to questions about contents · Pay attention to structure · Focus on the beginning part of the text **Directed attention** · Try to concentrate · Follow contents · Skip difficult information and continue listening **Comprehension monitoring** · Check answers by recalling what is heard · Draw on prior experience to check understanding	**Prelistening preparation** · Learn some background information about a topic by reading · Brainstorm ideas and related information · Discuss with classmates related information · Try to predict contents by previewing the prelistening questions **Selective attention** · Focus on main points · Ignore new words · Skip details · Pay more attention to structure · Focus on topic sentences · Focus first on gist and then on details · Pay attention to signal words · Pay attention to the beginning and ending · Pay more attention to key words · Pay attention to different types of questions · Focus on specific parts of texts · Do not take detailed notes **Directed attention** · Concentrate during listening · Think hard · Stick to main ideas without worrying about missed information · Continue to listen despite new words · Listen carefully · Concentrate to listen for gist and details **Comprehension monitoring** · Check understanding during listening · Check understanding using prior knowledge · Use examples to check comprehension · Check comprehension with context · Use logic to check comprehension **Use of strategies** · Use appropriate listening strategies · Share strategies with classmates · Ask the teacher for effective strategies

Type of Strategy	Strategies Used in the Classroom (Phase 1)	Strategies Used in Self-Directing Listening (Phase 2)
Meta-cognitive (continued)		**Take notes** · Take notes while listening · Write down key words · Use symbols and abbreviations **Practice** · Practice listening to different types of material · Have more listening practice · Create opportunities to listen to English · Listen to English regularly **Vocabulary words** · Prepare new words before listening · Look up new words after listening · Increase vocabulary words

From Chalkboard to Lectern to Chalkboard: The Journey of an Applied Linguistics Lecturer (*Vietnam*)

Stephen H. Moore

Issue

This chapter is concerned with my transformation from English language teacher to applied linguistics lecturer in a Southeast Asian context. Having taught general English and English for specific purposes (ESP) in Cambodia, Japan, Thailand, and Vietnam in the 1990s, by 2001 I found myself facing the challenges of teaching various applied linguistics and TESOL courses to postgraduate students in Australia and overseas. This chapter explores these two different but related roles by examining more closely my experience in just one country, Vietnam, where there seems to be an insatiable demand to learn English and ever increasing numbers entering the profession to teach it. My English teaching experience in Vietnam involved ESP teaching in Hanoi and Ha Long from 1994 to 1995 as a consultant to the Asian Institute of Technology Center in Vietnam. The main focus of this chapter, however, relates to my experience as an applied linguistics lecturer in Ho Chi Minh City (HCMC) from 2001 to 2003 as a consultant to the University of Canberra's offshore MA TESOL program (in collaboration with HCMC University of Education).

This postgraduate degree evolved from a postgraduate diploma set up in 1998. It has an annual intake of about 30 students who are English teaching professionals with bachelor's degrees and are generally based in or around HCMC. Applicants are screened in September and October, and a new cohort begins the program in January each year. During the period on which I am reporting, the MA program had 12 units, which were taught in three blocks of intensive study beginning each January and June or July. The degree took approximately 18 months to complete. Four subjects were taught in each block, and each subject was taught over about 30 contact hours (6 hours per day for 5 days). The students' ages ranged from mid-20s to mid-40s, and the gender mix was typically about 20 males and 10 females. The lecturers were either staff at the School of Languages and International Education at the University of Canberra or specialists hired as lecturer consultants.

The key issues discussed in this chapter relate to the teacher reorientation from helping students learn English to helping students process content, a reorientation that is mirrored in the altered learner roles themselves. Although there is a rich supply of literature from which English language teachers can draw ideas on teaching methodology, there is very little to guide the applied linguistics lecturer in this regard. In fact, in my experience as both a tertiary-level student and lecturer, it seems that the accepted norm is for lecturers to be left to deliver the content in whatever manner they choose (notwithstanding their often limited training as content teachers). When applied linguistics lecturers are also former English teachers, it can be quite unsettling for them to try to avoid or ignore the learners' language problems and focus just on the course content. No doubt it must be equally frustrating for their students to find language concerns hitherto addressed in class being marginalised in lectures. I have documented here my attempt to begin to reconcile these views.

My main motivation for this analysis has been to clarify my experiences in the Vietnamese context to enable my teaching and lecturing to improve. Being a good teacher is something that I value a great deal, so knowing what action I can take to help realise my teaching potential is an important outcome. Beyond my own personal interests, however, I hope that this chapter will interest other teacher educators confronted by the particular challenges of teaching students who are nonnative English speakers. Given the strong demand for well-qualified English teachers in Vietnam and neighbouring Asian countries, it seems likely that these issues will remain relevant and important for many years to come.

Background Literature

Although it is not uncommon for English language teachers to progress to TESOL lecturer status, I have found that published accounts of the transformational issues are rare in the academic literature of teacher education. Many books can provide assistance in English language teaching methodology (e.g., Larsen-Freeman, 1986; Nunan, 2000; Ur, 1991), and many more are formatted as teacher handbooks (e.g., topics such as teaching business English or using newspapers in the classroom). However, a thorough review of the literature reveals that there are no publications dealing exclusively with the issue of how to teach applied linguistics (e.g., second language acquisition, testing and evaluation, or discourse analysis) at the tertiary level. What is available in the language education literature is concerned with related issues such as how to teach language across the curriculum in primary and secondary schools (e.g., Mohan, 1986), the different discourses of applied linguists and language teachers (Kramsch, 1995), and critiques of standard teacher training methods (Holliday, 2005). Looking at teaching methodology in the higher education sector, there are again dozens of publications dealing with generic lecturing and teaching (e.g., Edwards, Smith, & Webb, 2001; Forsyth, 2003; Fry, Ketteridge, & Marshall, 1999; Hativah, 2001), and some dealing with discipline-specific lecturing and teaching (e.g., Hativah & Marincovich, 1995). But I have found none dealing with lecturing and teaching the discipline of applied linguistics.

Wallace (1991) suggested that there are three models of professional education commonly practised: (1) the craft model, in which the learner studies with a master; (2) the applied science model, in which the "findings of scientific knowledge and experimentation are conveyed to the trainee by those who are experts in the relevant areas" (p. 9); and (3) the reflective model, which "gives due weight both to experience and to the scientific basis of the profession" (p. 17). Although Wallace (a language teacher educator himself) did not specifically address the discipline of applied linguistics, an applied linguistics lecturer would most likely be teaching within the second or third paradigms, given the impracticality of the first model in dealing with the number of students typically taught in any given course. My personal teaching dilemma might even be explained as relating to the transition from the applied science model to the reflective one.

Richards (1996) shed a bit of light on the issue of teaching applied linguistics as he surveyed content and process issues in second language teacher education. He suggested that there are just five content areas to be covered: (1) general teaching skills, (2) language proficiency, (3) subject matter knowledge, (4) pedagogical reasoning and decision making, and (5) personal theory of teaching. Richards then went on to provide a taxonomy of instructional approaches that are relevant to these content areas, such as information-oriented approaches (lecturing), proficiency-focused activities, and observation of teaching in different settings. Citing the trends in second language teacher education noted in Richards and Nunan (1990), he suggested, in effect, that applied linguistics needs to be made relevant to teacher training and that top-down lecturing should be replaced by bottom-up learning experiences such as project work and data collection and analysis.

Although there is a paucity of guidance to assist the lecturing methodology of subject-specific applied linguistics content, what little is available can still be helpful. For example, the series *Language Teaching: A Scheme for Teacher*

Education (Oxford University Press) is a good source of tasks for some applied linguistics subjects (e.g., discourse studies), which at least implies a task-based methodology. Indeed, one writer, Kennett (2004), went so far as to suggest there is only one methodology for delivering content of any kind: input, task, and output. I would argue, however, that at least two other possible models are available for teaching applied linguistics, although the feasibility of each is open to debate. First, there is the learner-centered problem-based learning model, in which a problem is generated, discussed, and solved through further investigation. Such an approach, though attractive in many ways (and aligned with the trends cited in Richards & Nunan, 1990) would not be suitable to the limited time available in intensive teaching scenarios. The second possibility would be to teach the content through bilingual delivery (e.g., first language texts or interpreters). The feasibility of a bilingual approach would depend very much on the resources of the particular program and would conceivably call into question the credibility of teachers needing such a degree of support in their supposed field of expertise.

What emerges clearly from this review of the literature is that applied linguistics as a field has so far not seemed to merit any significant investigation of how best to teach it (or its typical subdisciplines). Such research, when done, will nevertheless be of great interest to many in the field. In the meantime, an applied linguistics lecturer seems to have a great deal of latitude in terms of how he or she lectures. This flexibility can be liberating for a gifted teacher but very challenging for the novice lecturer—especially one who clings to a distinction between the roles of lecturer and teacher.

Procedures

The basic lecturing style that I prepared and delivered for teaching applied linguistics content subjects consisted of oral presentation followed by tasks (usually undertaken in small groups or individually) followed by class feedback. The length of this cycle varied, but I tried not to speak for more than 20 minutes at a time and to limit the cycle to less than 60 minutes. Sometimes tasks and feedback were configured differently (e.g., through pair work or groups reporting back to the whole class). There was nothing particularly innovative about this approach, and it was one that my colleagues from the University of Canberra also used. It was a tried and trusted methodology. Nevertheless, this was my first appointment as a lecturer, and teaching 30 hours of content in 1 week was a new experience for me. I felt under constant pressure to perform to a high standard, given the perceived high status of my position. A summary of the units I taught, my preparations, and mechanisms for recording feedback are set out in the appendix at the end of this chapter.

I shall now provide a chronological account of the five occasions on which I lectured in HCMC from 2001 to 2003, as set out in Table 1. Within this account I will provide an ongoing analysis of issues, responses, results, and reflections as they occurred to me at the time. Procedurally, this series of cycles mirrors an action research model of planning, action, observation, and reflection. In this sense, the research is replicable by any teacher dealing with similar circumstances. I hope this approach will contribute to a better understanding of the evolution of my teaching and my attempts at improving it. I shall then add further comments derived from my more recent reflections on these matters.

SENSING A PROBLEM

Linguistics was the first unit I lectured on during my first visit to HCMC University of Education, and the prescribed text was *An Introduction to Language* by Fromkin, Blair, and Collins (1999). I had been advised that most students in Cohort 1 had already studied linguistics in their undergraduate degrees and that I should expect them to have a basic foundation already in place. My plan, therefore, was to cover a lot of ground quickly and, being sensitive to learners' needs, spend more time on areas that might not have been covered or well-understood in previous studies. The reality was that five 6-hour days in succession covering the length, breadth, and some considerable depth of linguistics was extremely demanding and exhausting for me and most of my students. As the week wore on, I became more aware of the English limitations of the learners with a non-English-speaking background (NESB). (It is worth noting here that three of the four cohorts of students I taught at HCMC from 2001 to 2003 had two native speakers of English enrolled. This created an interesting dynamic but also a considerable challenge to pitch my English at a level that would

Table 1. Summary of Applied Linguistics Units Taught From 2001 to 2003

Lecture Date	Subject Content	Year Cohort Started	Cohort No.
January 2001	· Linguistics · Discourse Studies	2001 2000	1 0
July 2001	· Language Change	2001	1
January 2002	· Language Acquisition · Discourse Studies	2002 2001	2 1
July 2002	· Language Change · Technology in Language Teaching	2002 2002	2 2
July 2003	· Language Change · Discourse Studies	2003 2003	3 3

accommodate the full range of English-speaking proficiency in the class). I began to realise that many of the NESB learners were not keeping up with readings, and participation in classroom tasks was often unenthusiastic. However, being primarily concerned with getting through the syllabus, I was reluctant to alter my teaching style to accommodate the language learning needs of NESB students. By the end of the week, it was clear to me that their English proficiency was limiting their ability to learn the content of linguistics.[1]

Achieving my goal of presenting the whole syllabus was, in the end, of little satisfaction. I began to contemplate how I might have done better if I had known at the beginning of the course what I knew by the end of it (i.e., students' actual knowledge of linguistics, their interests, and their English ability). In such an intensive teaching situation, I had very little free time in which to make any major modifications to the methods or materials I had prepared. Indeed, once the teaching week started, the pressure to cover the content was overwhelmingly the driving force. As my concern still focused mostly on my delivery of content rather than its reception by my students, I began to record some notes to myself about the challenges of teaching this particular subject. Regrettably I did not have a student evaluation form to administer to the learners and thus was left in the dark concerning the views of Cohort 1 students. Therefore, my sense of the English proficiency limitations of this group was left unresolved.

The week after I lectured to the newer Cohort 1 students in the Linguistics unit, I taught the Discourse Studies unit to the Cohort 0 students, who were near completion. This experience was significantly different: There were no native English speakers in the cohort; the general level of English was higher (there were half a dozen learners with exceptionally good English); and the students seemed more interested in the subject content. The content of this unit was more of a mix of different sources, including some of my own research, than the content of the Linguistics unit, which closely followed the textbook. English language issues seemed less pressing with this group, and I felt that perhaps between these two cohorts, I had seen the range of student ability that I would be dealing with on these teaching assignments.

Again, however, I was more concerned with my own ability to lecture than with the students' ability to learn from my lectures. I dutifully made more notes about the subject content and my lecturing style so that I could improve my future teaching of this unit should the opportunity present itself. As for obtaining student feedback on my lecturing, I again overlooked the value of this information, perhaps because I knew I would not be teaching those learners again.

RESPONDING TO THE PROBLEM THROUGH DIGRESSION

Following those experiences, I was asked to teach Language Change in July 2001 to Cohort 1 (the same cohort I had taught Linguistics to in January). I was eager to do a better job with this group than previously, but I was teaching a content unit new to me as well. The Language Change unit, in fact, struck me as an odd unit to have in a TESOL degree. However, in many ways it could be seen as an extension of the Linguistics unit, which is how I presented it to the learners.

To make the unit more palatable to my Vietnamese students, I took a risk in devoting some time to considering how the Vietnamese language had changed over the years. My reasoning was that if the learners could appreciate how their own native language had changed over the generations, then they might be more interested in the changes in English. In the event, most students did seem to be very engaged when discussing in English how Vietnamese had changed since their childhood. Moreover, by allowing them to work with Vietnamese, I had defused to some extent the issue of their English proficiency. When we came to focus on changes in English, I tried to stress the sort of language change that has an impact on the learning of English (e.g., the issue of English spellings being a poor guide to English pronunciation) and therefore of more obvious value to these learners as English teachers.

The overall result was that I was happier with my lecturing of this content to Cohort 1 than I had been with lecturing them in Linguistics 6 months previously. Still, I was lulled into believing that they too were satisfied with my teaching, and again I overlooked the need for a formal student evaluation procedure.

RESPONDING TO THE PROBLEM THROUGH DENIAL

In January 2002 I taught Cohort 1 for a third and final time. This time I would be teaching them Discourse Studies, the unit that I had first taught a year before, to Cohort 0, and that I thought had gone rather well. Therefore, I felt confident that my lectures would have a polished feel about them and that the students would learn fairly easily. Although reteaching the same unit does present a good opportunity to adjust teaching methodology, having lecture notes already prepared can also act against major innovations. In the event, the lecturing followed the typical cycles, and the learners were more or less engaged with the materials.

Yet again, I failed to elicit a proper formal student evaluation of my teaching of the unit. I felt that I had got the measure of content teaching from my previous encounters with this group, and the proof was that Cohort 1 students were performing as well on my units as they were on my colleagues' units. Basically, I was complacent and effectively in denial that there was a serious issue of English language proficiency hindering my students' ability to learn the content as I was presenting it.

A LECTURING INNOVATION AND AN UNEXPECTED WAKE-UP CALL

In January 2002 I also taught the Applied Linguistics (language acquisition) unit to a new group of students, Cohort 2. Again, the content of this unit was new to me as a lecturer. Nevertheless, I felt more comfortable with this material than with the broader, or pure, linguistics topics, and therefore I approached the unit with more confidence. In designing the materials for this course I aimed to assist students with their learning by using handouts that were meant to act as scaffolding prompts for note making. The handout would typically have a topic heading followed by various bullet-point subheadings. I also displayed transparencies of the handouts using an overhead projector so that learners could see which points I was talking about. My lecturing style in this case was to talk to the bullet points and expect students to listen attentively and then make their own notes (much as my classmates and I had done throughout our tertiary-level studies).

Alas, this proved a controversial methodology. Rather than appreciate that I was giving them something more than I gave Cohorts 0 and 1, some learners complained that they wanted the handouts a day in advance. (I presume they wanted to familiarise themselves with the vocabulary and get a sense of the shape of the lectures.) I was reluctant to give an advantage to students who would have time to read the notes in advance. Therefore, I found it preferable, in a sense, that everyone was equally disadvantaged.

Another sore point about this innovation came to my attention several weeks after the lecturing block. Apparently some students complained to the program managers that they were unhappy with my lecturing methodology in this unit. More specifically, they were unhappy with my jumping between handouts, overhead transparencies, and references to extracts from the two course texts. The texts, *Issues in Applied Linguistics* by McCarthy (2001) and *How Languages Are Learned* by Lightbown and Spada (1999), are both highly readable accounts of key issues in language acquisition. However, it seemed that the students did not appreciate the readability factor and, in spite of having their own copies in front of them, felt that I was proceeding too quickly.

These criticisms left me feeling quite frustrated that all my hard work in preparing the lectures and doing my best to present them in an interesting and efficient way had not counted for much. Again, I seemed to be hitting an invisible wall of language ability. I felt that possibly the majority of learners were finding it difficult to process the English needed to understand and make the most of the lectures. The embarrassment of hearing critical student feedback through channels beyond the classroom finally spurred me to design a formal student evaluation instrument modeled on one that I had used successfully on the University of Canberra campus. From that point on I used the new form for my lectures at HCMC.

RESPONDING TO THE WAKE-UP CALL

The criticisms of my teaching by Cohort 2 were something that I could not ignore. In July 2002 I was due to face this same cohort for the Language Change and Technology in Language Teaching units. I was prepared to meet the students halfway: I would try to make the lectures more accessible, but I would expect them to inform me immediately if they were unhappy with my methodology. I told the students at the beginning of the first unit that I was aware of difficulties some had suffered in my previous class and would try to avoid repeating them this time. I indicated at the start of the week that students would have a formal written student evaluation form to complete at the conclusion of the week's lectures. I also made a mental note to seek feedback midway through the week about how well the learners were coping with the lectures.

Results

I taught the Language Change unit as I had done previously, except I slowed down the pace to allow learners more time to process the lecture content. (The content, accordingly, had to be reduced in breadth or depth of coverage.) Table 2 summarises the ratings of 27 students who, in completing the student evaluation form, responded to the following question: "All things considered, how would you rate the teaching of this lecturer in this subject?"

These ratings suggest that apart from one discontented learner, the rest of the cohort members were mostly quite satisfied with the lecturing of this content subject. I was somewhat relieved but also determined to improve future ratings.

The Technology in Language Teaching unit was easily the most TESOL-like subject that I taught at HCMC. The content was very familiar to virtually all students, and the areas that were new to some students (e.g., using the Internet in computer labs) still seemed of considerable interest to them. Another advantage was that I could demonstrate and model how to teach in this unit, whereas

Table 2. Student Evaluation for Language Change 2002

Rating	No. of Students
Excellent	1
Very good	16
Good	4
Satisfactory	5
Not quite satisfactory	—
Poor	1
Very poor	—
Total	**27**

the other applied linguistics units focused more on knowledge and conceptual understanding. For this unit, student ratings of the overall teaching of this subject are set out in Table 3.

These results were actually heartening to me because they showed that my lecturing of applied linguistics subjects was actually relatively good. Naturally, however, I was disappointed that I seemed to have done less well in the domain of the practical training of English teachers. A deeper analysis of the student feedback for this TESOL unit revealed that many students were disappointed at not being given hands- on instruction in how to use video cameras, computer labs, and the Internet for classroom teaching.[2]

The fifth and final visit I made to HCMC as a consultant lecturer was a year later, in July 2003, when I taught a new group of students, Cohort 3, the Language Change and Discourse Studies units. Even though I would be lecturing each unit for the third time, I approached the task warily. I had some confidence that I knew the content, but I also had some anxiety that many students' limited English abilities would hinder their access to the course content. In the event, I kept the lecture pace as slow as I could manage, and I relied on the evaluation forms to indicate how students found my teaching of the units. The respondents' ratings of the overall lecture quality in these subjects are set out in Table 4.

There would appear to be just one learner in each course unhappy with the lecturing but otherwise a fairly positive evaluation from the rest of the cohort. Unfortunately, the student evaluation form I used did not shed much light on English language processing difficulties, because it focused on nonlanguage issues.

Table 3. Student Evaluation for Technology in Language Teaching 2002

Rating	No. of Students
Excellent	—
Very good	7
Good	3
Satisfactory	2
Not quite satisfactory	4
Poor	—
Very Poor	—
Total	**16**

Table 4. Student Evaluations 2003

Rating	Discourse Studies	Language Change
Excellent	1	2
Very good	5	8
Good	8	5
Satisfactory	3	1
Not quite satisfactory	—	1
Poor	1	—
Very Poor	—	—
Totals	**18**	**17**

Reflection

Now, from a *post facto* position, I would like to present reflections that have been more deeply considered with the passage of time. My purpose here is to develop a better understanding of the learning difficulties experienced by many of the students who sat through my lectures. Also, having identified those difficulties, I want to articulate action memos that will help me realise my reflections as future actions.

Throughout the period from December 2000 to December 2003 I was engaged with either designing or adapting lecture materials for five different applied linguistics units, delivering the lectures, marking assignments for these units, and corresponding by e-mail with many (but not all) students. Although my concerns about my own ability to deliver the lectures dominated my thoughts during these three years, I did use certain techniques or practices aimed at helping students—especially the NESB ones—to learn:

- Course outlines (including core texts and supplementary readings) were provided well before the course commencement date.

- Class handouts were provided for most sessions.

- A glossary of key terms was provided for many of the units.

- The pace of lectures was gradually slowed over the 3 years, usually by concentrating on less material but covering it in more depth.

- Where possible, amplification was used to help with my voice projection.

- Marking criteria were provided with course assignments.

Beyond these admittedly standard measures, I have persistently felt that there must have been more that I could have done to facilitate the learning of content by my students. In this regard I am particularly mindful of the largely invisible yet palpable role played by English language proficiency. To reiterate, the formal and informal feedback I received from native-English-speaking students indicated that they had no difficulty in following my lectures. The feedback I received from NESB students similarly did not explicitly identify English proficiency issues as a concern of theirs, and the formal student evaluation instruments did not specifically address this potential issue.[3] How then could I have lectured differently to be more inclusive of the NESB students and their language needs? I shall now discuss various plans of action that, had I taken them, would have provided an improved context for content learning.

ACTION: MAKING THE CASE FOR LINGUISTICS IN TESOL

As someone who has since completed a PhD in linguistics, I see almost any form of linguistics training (applied or pure) as of potentially great relevance to teachers of English as a second language and English as a foreign language. From personal experience I have also noted how some teachers seem to be disinclined to see the value of anything that does not directly affect what they do in their English classrooms. Given the added difficulty of a language barrier in HCMC and the possibility that a significant number of students would question the value of the applied linguistics units I was teaching, I wonder if I sufficiently tried to cultivate an appreciation for the applied linguistics courses' relevance to more practical TESOL subjects. In any future teaching of these units, I plan to nurture such an appreciation at the beginning.

ACTION: THE EFFECTIVE USE OF DISCOURSE MARKERS IN LECTURES

Slowing the pace of my lecture delivery and amplifying my voice were two important concessions made to help my students follow the lectures more easily. In addition, I should have more systematically refined my lecture hall English by speaking in a less conversational style and in a more organised fashion with consistent use of discourse markers. For example, I missed many opportunities when I might have said something such as, "There are four important ways in which languages change. First, there is. . . . Second, we must consider. . . . Third. . . . And, fourth. . . . " Similarly, cause and effect relationships should be presented unambiguously through easily understood conjunctions. For example, "we know that languages live because. . . . " I think most of my students were quite capable of taking useful notes if they had been more attuned to the structure of my lecture presentations. Without such structure, it would be easy to see how students might have perceived the lectures as a mass of tangled and disorganised information.

ACTION: AVOID READING ALOUD

I often gave in to the temptation to read aloud certain passages of written text that seemed to succinctly sum up a particular point I wanted to make in my lectures. Prominent among my reasons for doing so was to encourage students to actually read the same passages in their own time. I was, in effect, trying to balance the importance of the texts with the reality that many students were, through work, family, and other commitments, simply not finding the time to read them. Some students were highly critical of this classroom practice, and I wonder if their objections were perhaps accentuated by their difficulties in understanding the English. After all, written English is much more lexically dense than spoken English and, accordingly, is more cognitively demanding to process than typical spoken language. I would have done better to orally paraphrase the extracts and limit the number used in any given lecture.

ACTION: RESTRICTING THE USE OF METALANGUAGE

There is a vast amount of linguistic metalanguage that can be used and misused in lectures, and how it is to be treated is an important issue in a TESOL degree. Notably, students who desire more precision in their expression will be attracted to more explicit and specialised jargon. Indeed, this was the case in the phonology component of the Linguistics unit, where students sometimes used terms such as *lenition, syncope,* and *aphaeresis.* Furthermore, students have the sense that using metalanguage is a kind of identity badge that a "real" language specialist wears. On balance, I believe that it is important to restrict the use of metalanguage to a degree of delicacy that offers good, but not excessively demanding, coverage. I do not think that a lecturer teaching predominantly NESB students should have to deal with some of the very fine distinctions that are evident in specialist subdisciplines of linguistics (phonetics, phonology, grammar, etc.). Instead of jargon, teachers can use clear English descriptions to discuss the important concepts.

ACTION: DIGRESSING TO EAP ISSUES WHEN STRATEGICALLY WARRANTED

It is often the case that tertiary-bound language learners do not appreciate the importance of skills in English for academic purposes (EAP) until they are actually faced with the demands of real lectures or real assignments. Given this typical scenario, it makes sense to allow for some limited digressions in lectures to deal with EAP-type issues when it seems clear that the particular issue is of relevance to many of the learners. Advice concerning academic referencing is a good example of an area that came to life for the HCMC students, but it should have been dealt with in earlier courses. The cost/benefit analysis of such a digression is clear: The sooner the students understand more clearly what is expected of them in academic writing, the sooner their writing improves (and the less time the lecturer has to spend struggling to understand their written assignments).

Two further matters warrant mention with regard to helping NESB students cope better in their applied linguistics courses, but these relate to matters beyond the classroom experience: assignment marking and ongoing correspondence.

ACTION: INCLUDING CLARITY OF ENGLISH IN THE MARKING CRITERIA

Keeping the playing field fair for native English speakers and NESB students at the same time is a challenge when setting assignments. The issue of language ability can bring profound challenges to written and oral assignments. However, native speakers too can have difficulty expressing themselves in English. The issue of how to deal with English proficiency in assessing assignments can be settled either by letting it cut across all grading criteria or by setting up a separate criterion exclusively for clarity of English and restricting its impact (as far as consciously possible) to that one place. It is important for the NESB learners to see that their language skills per se will not preclude them from potentially achieving a very good result for demonstrated understanding of a subject.

ACTION: LANGUAGE SUPPORT IN CONJUNCTION WITH OTHER CORRESPONDENCE

Inevitably, an intensively taught course will leave many students with questions that arise long after the lecturer has departed. It is important, therefore, to have a channel (e.g., e-mail or fax) for students to make contact with the lecturer to enable such matters to be clarified. There is no reason why such correspondence cannot include issues related to language matters, although the lecturer must take care to offer such support ethically and equitably. Certain issues are bound to recur (e.g., academic referencing), and help offered to one student often can be recycled when the same issue arises with another student.

In this chapter, I have tried to clarify some of the important and complex issues that are present in the interface between language and content learning and teaching. To understand them better requires good channels of feedback between teacher and learners (e.g., through using well-designed student evaluation forms). To be able to act on the issues to facilitate and improve student learning requires a commitment on the part of the teacher to continually and critically reflect on the quality of his or her teaching.

Throughout my intensive lecturing of applied linguistics in HCMC, I often perceived a sense that all was not well in my classroom. The precise difficulty, however, was largely unarticulated and difficult to pin down. Upon reflection of the sort that I have documented in this chapter, the main issue now seems more clearly associated with language and the demands of tertiary-level academic studies in English. What I was perceiving was, I believe, the constant tension between the learners' implicit expectations and need for English support on the one hand, and the lecturer's view of his or her role and the appropriate level of English support for postgraduate students on the other. Softening my stubborn insistence on a distinction between lecturing and teaching was a revelation to me—a coming of age as a lecturer—and one with great benefits in furthering the interests of the learners. Indeed, it has helped me to see that the most appropriate methodology for teaching applied linguistics to NESB students must be the one that best suits the students' ability to learn.

Stephen H. Moore teaches at Macquarie University in Australia.

Notes

1. Personal communication with the native-English-speaking students indicated that they had no difficulties in following my lectures. Indeed, this turned out to be the case for all the native English speakers I taught in HCMC, thus suggesting to me the importance of the role of English in my NESB students' learning difficulties.

2. There were several reasons that these needs could not be met. First, the necessary equipment was not available. Second, because many of the learners taught in resource-poor environments, it seemed inappropriate to build too much of the course around technology that was not available to them. It was deemed to be better to focus on older and simpler technologies and how to exploit them to their best effect.

3. The most common English language concerns that came to my notice seemed to relate either to explaining vocabulary (i.e., applied linguistics terminology) and related concepts or, more surprisingly, explaining the assignment rubrics. This latter concern was often obsessive for every cohort, and it worried me in its implications about students' English ability. If they truly had such difficulties in understanding fairly straightforward instructions, how could they possibly cope with the demands of understanding applied linguistics?

Appendix: Summary of Lecture Preparation, Innovation, and Feedback

Date	Subject	Preparation Required	Source Materials	Significant Innovation	Main Feedback Mechanism
Jan. 2001	Linguistics	From scratch	Mainly one textbook	—	Informal notes made by lecturer
Jan. 2001	Discourse Studies	From scratch	Two texts plus supplementary materials	Presented related personal research	Informal notes made by lecturer
July 2001	Language Change	Some materials provided	One text plus supplementary materials	Included Vietnamese language changes	Informal notes made by lecturer
Jan. 2002	Language Acquisition	From scratch	Mainly two texts	Handouts with scaffolded headings	Informal notes made by lecturer
Jan. 2002	Discourse Studies	Revising materials already taught previously	As used previously	—	Informal notes made by lecturer
July 2002	Language Change	Revising materials already taught previously	As used previously	—	Student evaluation forms
July 2002	Technology in Language Teaching	Some materials provided	One text plus supplementary materials	—	Student evaluation forms
July 2003	Language Change	Revising materials already taught previously	As used previously	—	Student evaluation forms
July 2003	Discourse Studies	Revising materials already taught previously	As used previously	—	Student evaluation forms

"I Want to Study TOEFL!" Finding the Balance Between Test Focus and Language Learning in Curriculum Revision (*Japan*)

Patrick Rosenkjar

Issue

In Japan, university entrance examinations represent a major rite of passage for young people, controlling their access to life chances, remunerative employment, and social prestige. Every March during the examination season, hundreds of thousands of young Japanese undergo what Japanese society terms *shiken jigoku* or "examination hell" (Brown & Yamashita, 1995a, 1995b). As White (1987) notes, "The whole country seems to be watching, coaching, and waiting for the results. The press features photographs of mothers waiting outside examination sites, and stories of crises and tragedies" (p. 142). The system has spawned a myriad of private after-class schools (*juku*) attended by elementary through high school students and cram schools (*yobiko*) to prepare high school students and graduates for university entrance exams. This intense focus on entrance examination performance continues even under today's greatly changed educational and demographic conditions, in which a place in some university exists for any Japanese high school graduate who wants one (Ministry of Education, Culture, Sports, Science, & Technology, 2005). The examination system inevitably leads to a national preoccupation with exam preparation and test scores, sometimes to the exclusion of knowledge useful in itself.

The Japanese cultural emphasis on one-off exams that function as gatekeepers to higher educational opportunities strongly influences the attitudes of students in the Academic Preparation Program (the APP) of Temple University, Japan Campus. The Japan campus is a branch of Temple University in Philadelphia, offering university-level instruction through the medium of English. The APP is an intensive pre-undergraduate program aimed at preparing students with the academic English ability and study skills needed for success in undergraduate work. A short description of the APP curriculum is included here, and a more extensive one may be found at the Temple University, Japan Campus (n.d.) Web site.

One of the main criteria for promotion through and out of the APP is proficiency as measured by the Test of English as a Foreign Language (TOEFL). Therefore, unfortunately but understandably, Japanese APP students tend to equate the TOEFL with the university entrance exams. Not recognizing that the TOEFL is a general test of academic English proficiency that is not specifically related to the content of any program (Brown, 1995, 1996), APP students often focus on passing the TOEFL while ignoring or downplaying the development of actual academic skills needed for survival after entrance into undergraduate study. Thus, a large challenge for APP curriculum planners has been working out how to structure the program to emphasize essential English and academic skill development while incorporating the direct TOEFL study that students say they want.

This chapter reports on research undertaken to inform a comprehensive curriculum revision project in the APP that I initiated shortly after being appointed the new director of the program in September 2003. One of the major issues arising in that project was the mismatch between students' desires to, in their words, "study TOEFL" and curriculum planners' desires to provide the proper balance between language- and skill-focused activities. Curriculum planners wanted to foster the acquisition of academic English and study skills, on the one hand, and provide direct TOEFL instruction to meet the felt needs of APP students, on the other.

Although APP curriculum planners were aware that second language acquisition (SLA) theory strongly suggests that acquisition results from an overall meaning-focused context with some focus on form (see, for example, Doughty & Williams, 1998; Ellis, 2003; Lee, 2000), they still found it necessary to attend to students' expressed wish for traditional focus on grammatical forms and explicit test-taking strategies in TOEFL preparation classes. To resolve this dilemma, planners tried to expand the direct focus on form in the APP curriculum while incorporating it into skill-building and communicative activities believed to be useful for acquisition. Even though some of these activities were provided in courses other than explicit TOEFL preparation classes, they were labeled as TOEFL-related because they served to develop skills that would be useful for the test.

In this chapter, I explain the curriculum of the APP; the revision project; and how teachers, students, and other stakeholders were consulted and reacted at several stages in the process. I also include some reflections on how current changes in the TOEFL may help resolve the problem of pressure to teach to the test by making the test itself more closely related to the communicative needs of students taking English for academic purposes (EAP).

Background Literature

Writers on curriculum development (Brown, 1995; Graves, 1996; Richards, 2001) agree on the necessity of gathering a large amount of data about the context of instruction, student needs, and course purposes. They also agree that major stakeholders include faculty and students themselves and that the best curricular decisions result from incorporating input from these groups. Brown (1995) and Richards (2001) provide an extensive discussion of the types of information that can potentially be gathered. Brown (2001) further offers specific guidelines for designing questionnaires to yield the maximum amount of useful data. The project reported in this chapter incorporated many of these writers' suggestions on the process of curriculum development.

Many APP students seem to hold the belief that the most effective method of learning a second language is through explicit teaching of grammatical forms followed by practice sentences, in other words, through a traditional structural syllabus. Such a view of SLA would account for the emphasis they put on direct grammar teaching and TOEFL exercises. However, this view is at odds with current SLA theory, which holds that an overall focus on meaningful interaction, combined with some focus on form, provides the optimal conditions for acquisition.

Therefore, a second area that informed the APP's curriculum development project was the growing literature on the role of form- and meaning-focused activities in language classrooms. The issues involved here are summarized very succinctly in the introduction to a study by Ellis, Basturkmen, and Loewen (2001). Ellis and colleagues accepted the need for focus on meaning, but they explained why it is also necessary to focus on form, discuss how to do so, and define focus on form. Doughty and Williams (1998) provide a book-length discussion of those and related issues. In a similar vein, Williams (1995) discusses the need for a focus on form to be embedded in a meaning-focused syllabus. In a fairly accessible way, she sets forth the rationale for form-focused instruction while rejecting a return to the traditional grammatical syllabus. She also offers some possible strategies for focusing on form and lists some of the unanswered questions about focus on form. Ellis (2003) and Lee (2000) include focus on form as an integral part of larger treatments of task-based teaching, and Nassaji and Fotos (2004) summarize the implications of current research on grammar teaching for communicative language classrooms. The consensus of these researchers and of many others in SLA is that communicative language teachers "in focusing on meaning and the overall success of communication . . . have overlooked the issue of accuracy" (Williams, 1995, p. 13).

Therefore, there is widespread agreement that a focus on meaning along with a focus on form is essential for acquisition. The question for communicative language teaching proponents now seems to be not whether to focus on form, but what is the most effective method for doing so. APP curriculum developers and APP students were deeply divided on this last issue.

Procedures

The APP has been in existence in Japan since 1982. In the 1980s, it was divided into six proficiency levels organized in a traditional skills-based structure with listening/speaking and reading/writing courses, and with the upper levels also including content courses. By the time I became the program director in fall 2003, the APP had only three levels (Program 1, Program 2, and Program 3) as a consequence of earlier streamlining.

THE STARTING POINT

For almost 20 years, a prominent and distinctive feature of the program's curricular approach had been emphasis on learning English through study of some academic content area. Content-based instruction relies on the belief derived from communicative language teaching in the 1980s that learners acquire a second language by doing academic course work through the medium of that language. Such an approach seems particularly appropriate for an EAP program. Brinton, Snow, and Wesche (1989) and Mohan (1986) provided early arguments in favor of content-based language teaching. Part of the point of the APP content courses is that students acquire language by using it for communication. Another part of the rationale is that such courses approximate the experience of study that EAP students will face when they graduate from the APP and matriculate into credit-bearing university courses.

A second major feature of the APP was reading-based writing courses. Eisterhold (1990) emphasized the need to integrate reading with writing, although she avoids making any recommendations for specific forms of pedagogy. In the APP, this type of course highlighted text-responsible writing on the assumption that the need for EAP students to be responsible for ideas found in source texts fosters language growth and general intellectual development (Leki & Carson, 1997).

Thus, the APP's writing courses asked students to engage with the ideas contained in reading texts and interact with peers about those ideas in order

---

to produce writing that shows awareness of the content of the texts that they have read. Methodologically, the process writing approach greatly influenced the types of writing assignments APP students received, with a great emphasis on fluency development, discourse structure, and a large volume of writing from the very beginning and gradually increasing attention to grammatical accuracy at later stages. So the reading-based writing courses asked students to produce journals, free-writes, summaries of readings, and multiple drafts of formal essays. There is a vast amount of pedagogical literature on second language writing, much of which is synthesized in Casanave (2004). Consideration of most of the issues Casanave presents underlay the APP's approach to the teaching of writing.

The old APP also offered traditional TOEFL preparation courses focusing on test-taking strategies and practice activities for the three sections of the TOEFL. This type of course had long been controversial among some APP teachers who felt that it did not contribute to the development of English language knowledge or useful skills. However, it was a long-established element of the program that offered what students said they wanted, probably as a consequence of their intense focus on tests.

Although APP students at all three levels took courses in reading-based writing, content, and TOEFL preparation, only Program 1 students had an additional 6 hours per week of listening/speaking. There did not seem to be any special reason for the lack of listening/speaking courses at the upper levels, except for the perception that Program 2 and Program 3 courses were so demanding that students would have little time for additional classes.

Table 1 shows the allocation of class time by course type and student level in the old course lineup that was in place before the curriculum revision project began.

Table 1. Class Hours and Structure of the APP Through Spring 2004 Before Curriculum Revision

Course Type	Program 1 TOEFL Scores up to 439	Program 2 TOEFL Scores 440–469	Program 3 TOEFL Scores 470–499
Listening/Speaking	6 hrs/wk	0 hrs/wk	0 hrs/wk
Reading-Based Writing	6 hrs/wk	6 hrs/wk	6 hrs/wk
Content	6 hrs/wk	6 hrs/wk	6 hrs/wk
TOEFL Preparation	4.5 hrs/wk	4.5 hrs/wk	4.5 hrs/wk
Total	22.5 hrs/wk	16.5 hrs/wk	16.5 hrs/wk

CURRICULUM REVISION

I initiated the curriculum revision project in spring 2004 after determining that we needed to increase class hours and time on task to accelerate student progress through the program. To begin the process, I notified faculty and staff members—via an electronic mailing list set up for the APP—of the intention to increase student class hours, at the same time asking them to brainstorm the best ways to use the additional class time. The resulting individual responses were distributed by the list to the entire group so that all would have the chance to comment on the ideas proposed. This elicited a large number of ideas from the responding faculty and staff in several rounds of discussion.

To discover students' views on the matter, I visited each APP class to introduce myself as the new director, to invite students to communicate with me, and to explain and distribute a survey about possible curriculum changes. The survey contained three questions, which asked students to

1. State the ideal number of hours (3, 4.5, or 6 hours per week) for each of three existing APP courses.

2. Rank seven possible additional courses (derived from the faculty and staff suggestions) in order of importance (grammar, TOEFL vocabulary/reading, listening/speaking, computer skills, reading fluency, language lab, and independent study lab) and provide the ideal number of weekly hours for each.

3. Provide any other comments or suggestions they wished to make.

Student responses were carefully tallied. In addition, in my own reading-based writing class, I assigned students to write an essay giving their suggestions for the new curriculum. After considering the input from faculty, administrative staff, and students, I devised and circulated for comments by faculty and staff an initial proposal incorporating many of the suggestions that had been made, along with my own ideas. Even though this plan did not include all the ideas proposed, I tried to ensure that all suggestions were considered and that all contributors felt that their views had been given a fair hearing.

The amended plan then went through another round of review as APP members reacted to it. Thus, from the outset, teaching and nonteaching employees of the APP as well as APP students were involved in the process. One important and striking point at this stage was that the resulting proposal contained many worthwhile points that I would not have thought of on my own.

In addition to more class hours and new course types, the emergent plan for the new curriculum broke the lowest proficiency level into two: a basic and an advanced section. This division resulted in four APP levels, instead of three. Because many Program 2 and Program 3 students had requested courses in listening/speaking, these were added to their weekly schedules. I also produced a set of listening/speaking course guidelines for APP faculty that listed general course goals and more specific microskills. The guidelines provided a rubric for translating microskills into lesson objectives and an annotated bibliography of professional readings related to the design of syllabi and lesson plans for listening/speaking courses. Several faculty members had urged systematic instruction in vocabulary and reading skills, and I agreed that these were points of weakness in the curriculum. Therefore, new courses devoted to these areas were added. Students had also requested more form-focused, explicit grammar instruction, and some faculty members had strongly supported stand-alone grammar courses as well. Limitations on the available weekly instructional time and my preference to contextualize grammar teaching within the content of other courses led me to decide to combine grammar with both the reading-based writing and the vocabulary courses. Finally, the new grammar/vocabulary course and the new reading laboratory course were labeled TOEFL-related. The skills covered in those courses were directly relevant to the test, and it seemed wise to point this out to students.

In addition to explicit grammar instruction, the grammar/vocabulary course aimed for systematic development of high-frequency vocabulary items in line with the suggestions of Nation (1990, 2001) and others. It also aimed to teach strategies by which students could individually build their English vocabularies. The TOEFL reading laboratory course aimed for systematic and sustained development of reading skills through timed readings (Spargo, 1989, 2001) by focused skill-based activities on short reading passages (Jamestown, 1999, 2000), work with SRA Reading Labs kits (McGraw-Hill, n.d.), and extensive reading (Day & Bamford, 1998).

To conserve program resources while avoiding any increase in tuition for the additional hours, the plan also envisioned offering both the TOEFL reading laboratory and the TOEFL practice classes to larger-than-normal groups of students working on individually paced activities supervised by advanced graduate students in the MEd program in TESOL. The graduate students themselves would be under the mentorship of professional full-time APP master teachers and, ultimately, of me.

To explain to continuing students how the curriculum would change, I visited classes and presented sample summer schedules reflecting the changes, along with a worksheet on them. In effect, the newly revised curriculum was the content of a lesson taught to the students by lecture and a task sheet asking them to read and draw some inferences from the sample schedules. The task sheet is included as Appendix A.

Table 2 shows the structure of the revised curriculum that was put into effect in the summer 2004 term.

The next step was to assess student reactions to the changes. At midterm in

Table 2. Class Hours and Structure of the APP After the Initial Curriculum Revision

Course Type	Program 1 Basic TOEFL Scores up to 409	Program 1 Advanced TOEFL Scores 410–439	Program 2 TOEFL Scores 440–469	Program 3 TOEFL Scores 470–499
Listening/Speaking	6 hrs/wk	3 hrs/wk	3 hrs/wk	3 hrs/wk
Reading-Based Grammar/Writing	6 hrs/wk	6 hrs/wk	6 hrs/wk	6 hrs/wk
Content	0 hrs/wk	6 hrs/wk	6 hrs/wk	6 hrs/wk
Grammar/Vocabulary for TOEFL	3 hrs/wk	3 hrs/wk	3 hrs/wk	3 hrs/wk
TOEFL Practice (Taught by MEd Students)	3 hrs/wk	3 hrs/wk	3 hrs/wk	3 hrs/wk
TOEFL Reading Laboratory (Taught by MEd Students)	6 hrs/wk	3 hrs/wk	3 hrs/wk	3 hrs/wk
Total	24 hrs/wk	24 hrs/wk	24 hrs/wk	24 hrs/wk

the summer 2004 semester, after having had some 6 weeks of experience with the new curriculum, students were asked to comment on it. I used a bilingual questionnaire administered in every APP class, reproduced here in English only as Appendix B. Questions 3, 4, and 5 of this questionnaire were based on a Likert scale so that quantitative analyses of the answers could be performed by means of a computer spreadsheet program. Questions 7 through 10 were open ended, and students were invited to write whatever they wished in response. Where necessary, bilingual staff members translated the responses into English. Categories of responses were then tallied and ranked by frequency. Thus, students were again consulted, in both quantitative and qualitative ways, to determine their views on how the new curriculum was working.

Results

The results of the questionnaire were mildly encouraging because the overall rating of the APP on Question 3 ("Are you generally satisfied with the APP?") averaged 4.53 on the 7-point scale. Most individual courses scored higher, with both the reading-based grammar/writing and content courses being especially highly evaluated. However, two exceptions were the grammar/vocabulary for TOEFL and TOEFL reading laboratory courses. The reason for the dissatisfaction with the grammar/vocabulary course seemed to be that the students did not see the rationale for combining these two distinct areas of language study. Students also objected to the large class size in the TOEFL practice class and in the TOEFL reading laboratory. In addition, with regard to the TOEFL reading laboratory, they frequently objected to the individually paced work and to spending time reading in class, which they believed could have been done at home.

In view of the student responses to the questionnaire, several points were obvious. First, the high ratings for the reading-based grammar/writing and content courses indicated that these courses were working well and needed no major overhaul. In effect, students were reporting that they recognized that they were successfully learning through courses primarily based on meaning-focused input and output. Therefore, both content-based instruction and reading-based writing were retained as cornerstones of the APP curriculum. However, it was also clear that further changes with regard to several of the other courses were needed, and APP curriculum planners thus redesigned the course lineup for fall 2004 as indicated in Table 3. Vocabulary study was incorporated with reading fluency development, and grammar was combined with the TOEFL course (although, of course, writing and content teachers continued to be free to address grammar and vocabulary issues as they arose in their classes).

Moreover, the new plan put TOEFL work of the relevant type in each of three courses: listening/speaking (with 1 hour per week of TOEFL listening practice), vocabulary/reading fluency (with 2 hours per week of TOEFL reading practice), and TOEFL grammar practice (with 3 hours per week of TOEFL grammar

Table 3. Class Hours and Revised Structure of the APP After Student Feedback on the Initial Curriculum Revision

Course Type	Program 1 Basic TOEFL Scores up to 409	Program 1 Advanced TOEFL Scores 410–439	Program 2 TOEFL Scores 440–469	Program 3 TOEFL Scores 470–499
Listening/Speaking	3 hrs/wk	3 hrs/wk	3 hrs/wk	3 hrs/wk
Reading-Based Writing	6 hrs/wk	6 hrs/wk	6 hrs/wk	6 hrs/wk
Content	6 hrs/wk	6 hrs/wk	6 hrs/wk	6 hrs/wk
Vocabulary/Reading Fluency	6 hrs/wk	6 hrs/wk	6 hrs/wk	6 hrs/wk
TOEFL Grammar Practice	3 hrs/wk	3 hrs/wk	3 hrs/wk	3 hrs/wk
Total	24 hrs/wk	24 hrs/wk	24 hrs/wk	24 hrs/wk

study). Thus, the total time devoted to direct TOEFL study was increased by about 3 hours per week. The TOEFL courses and direct TOEFL instruction in other courses remained important aspects of the program, but the challenge has continued to be teaching useful academic and language skills while catering to the student emphasis on form-focused TOEFL instruction.

To provide feedback to students on the questionnaire, I again visited each class with a letter reporting the results and announcing a second revision of the course lineup. During this visit, I explained each point in the letter and solicited questions and comments. My letter as program director to the students is reproduced here as Appendix C.

Reflection

Any project of curriculum revision is ongoing and requires research to discover the viewpoints of all concerned at multiple stages. The specific curriculum revision reported here relied on collaboration of all faculty and administrators of the APP and consulted APP students in several ways and at all critical points. Thus, this research underlines the importance of systematic inclusion of all stakeholders' views in the curriculum revision process. Although the APP's yearlong curriculum revision project began with general questions, one specific focus quickly became apparent as a deep concern of students and instructors. Thus, even though I did not initiate the process with that issue at the forefront, I was reminded of its importance when I solicited students' and teachers' views on curriculum change. Flexibility in response to the concerns that emerge as stakeholders are consulted is a keystone of successful curriculum revision, and this project underscored that fact.

That major substantive issue was, of course, the intense preoccupation of APP students with explicit grammar and TOEFL study, which they see as essential for their academic progress. APP students seem to see no contradiction between their desire for a greater emphasis on form-focused instruction and their very high rating of meaning-focused approaches such as the content and reading-based writing courses. It is likely that this issue is also important for other students in Asia, and indeed around the world, who plan to matriculate in English-medium universities. What is certain is that test anxiety and preference for explicit focus on forms loom large in the minds of the Japanese students in the APP. Although faculty members who are informed about SLA may not agree with the intensive formal instruction that the students demand, emphasis on explicit grammar and TOEFL study is a fact of life in Japan that cannot be ignored. This is probably a consequence of the role of university entrance tests in Japanese society. The result is that instruction based on test preparation and focused on explicit grammar provides face validity for the program's curriculum in APP students' eyes.

Therefore, we had to find creative ways to integrate explicit grammar and TOEFL study with the learning of language skills actually useful for academic work. Moreover, we had to ensure that students recognized that they were getting work relevant to their needs even if it was not in a TOEFL practice course. It may be that we were at least partially successful in better preparing our students. One indicator of that success is the fact that promotion and graduation rates have gone up since the implementation of the new curriculum.

Nevertheless, the tension between studying for TOEFL and learning useful skills remains. With the introduction of the new Internet-based TOEFL that is coming soon to Japan, the APP will undoubtedly need to revise its curriculum again. The new TOEFL appears to have much greater validity as a measure of academic proficiency because it tests all four language skills and requires students to combine modalities in responding to questions. For example, examinees must read a passage, listen to a lecture on a related topic, and then make an oral presentation or write an essay in response to a question (Educational Testing Service, 2005). Essentially, the new TOEFL replicates the combination of language skills for communicating ideas that academic work typically requires of students.

This has far-reaching implications for the design of the APP curriculum and of EAP courses and curricula generally, and could potentially go a long way in the direction of making teaching to the test much more closely related to real-life academic skills. In this way, students' desires for direct TOEFL study and teachers' desires for course content related to academic needs may be satisfied simultaneously. If so, when APP students say, "I want to study TOEFL," the program's curriculum can directly and obviously respond while also satisfying teachers and administrators that the TOEFL-related courses contribute to the development of the communicative skills we know are essential for academic purposes.

Patrick Rosenkjar is Director of the Academic Preparation Program at Temple University, Japan Campus.

Appendix A: Worksheet on the New APP Curriculum and Questionnaire (Distributed to Students Near the End of the Spring 2004 Term)

Directions: Look at the sample summer schedules for the APP, and answer the following questions with your partner.

1. Find and name three new classes for P2 and P3.

2. For each of the classes you listed in question #1, answer the following questions:

   a. How many hours per week do these classes meet?

   b. Which new class(es) will help you to understand lectures better?

   c. Which new class(es) will help you to read faster and understand more?

   d. Which new class(es) will help you to express yourself more clearly in writing essays?

   e. Which new class(es) will help you to learn to feel more comfortable in asking questions in class?

   f. Which new class(es) will give you more practice taking TOEFL exams?

   g. Which new class(es) will help you to improve your understanding of TOEFL grammar?

   h. Which new class(es) will help you to improve your TOEFL listening skills?

   i. Which new class(es) will help you to improve your TOEFL reading skills?

3. Please answer the following questions by looking at all six classes you will be taking next term.

   a. How will P1 be different from P2 and P3?

   b. How will P1 next term be different from P1 this term?

   c. Which class(es) will help you to improve your vocabulary?

   d. Which class(es) will help you to improve your TOEFL score?

4. Which content courses would you be interested in taking?

   a. American History

   b. Psychology

   c. Art

   d. American Studies

   e. Japanese History

   f. Human Behavior

   g. Other_____

Appendix B: Survey of APP Students About the APP Curriculum (Administered Shortly After the Midpoint of the Summer 2004 Term)

Please tell us your thoughts about the APP curriculum and studying in the APP in order to help us respond better to your needs as students. You may write either in English or in Japanese. Do not write your name on this questionnaire; all answers will be anonymous.

1. Your class/section: _____ (example: P1Basic; P1 Advanced A; P2B; P3C)

2. You have been in the APP for _____ semesters, including the current semester.

3. On a scale of 1 (least) to 7 (most), rate your general satisfaction with the APP.

   My satisfaction level with APP is   1   2   3   4   5   6   7

4. On a scale of 1 (least useful) to 7 (most useful), rate each of your courses with respect to its usefulness for learning English.

   Listening/Speaking   1   2   3   4   5   6   7

   Grammar/Vocabulary   1   2   3   4   5   6   7

   Reading-Based Grammar/Writing   1   2   3   4   5   6   7

Content		1	2	3	4	5	6	7
TOEFL Reading Lab		1	2	3	4	5	6	7
TOEFL Practice		1	2	3	4	5	6	7

5. Write in the first blank how many hours of homework per week you actually do for each of your courses. Then check a), b), or c) to show your opinion about whether this is the right amount of homework for each course.

Listening/Speaking = _____ hours =
    a) ___ too little b)___ just right c)___ too much

Grammar/Vocabulary = _____ hours =
    a) ___ too little b)___ just right c)___ too much

Reading-Based Grammar/Writing = _____ hours =
    a) ___ too little b)___ just right c)___ too much

Content = _____ hours =
    a) ___ too little b)___ just right c)___ too much

TOEFL Reading Lab = _____ hours =
    a) ___ too little b)___ just right c)___ too much

TOEFL Practice = _____ hours =
    a) ___ too little b)___ just right c)___ too much

6. Do you have a part-time job? Circle one answer: Yes/No.

If "Yes," how many hours per week do you work at it? _____ hours/week.

7. Use this space to write any comments you would like to make about each of your courses:

Listening/Speaking:

Grammar/Vocabulary:

Reading-Based Grammar/Writing:

Content:

TOEFL Reading Lab:

TOEFL Practice:

8. In your opinion, what is the biggest problem with the APP curriculum?

9. In your opinion, what is the biggest positive point about the APP curriculum?

10. What other comments would you like to make about the APP that have not been covered in any of the previous questions?

Appendix C: APP Director's Letter to Students Reporting Questionnaire Results (Distributed to Students at the End of the Summer 2004 Term)

To all APP students:

This letter is to report to you the results of the questionnaire that you filled out a few weeks ago and to thank you for your candid comments about study in the APP. I read all the questionnaires very carefully and really appreciated hearing your views.

Some of the major points that emerged from your comments were

1. You all do a lot of homework, but the great majority of you believe that the amount of homework in each class is "just right."

2. You want more direct study of TOEFL.

3. You think the TOEFL classes are not interesting, but necessary.

4. Many of you do not see the value of some of the classes that are currently being offered.

5. You rate the APP at 4.53 on a scale of 1 to 7 (slightly above average, but I hope to make the APP very much above average).

6. You consistently rate the Reading-Based Writing and Content courses as the ones in which you learn the most English. (Both received average scores of a little less than 6.0 on the 7-point scale.)

7. You want more English to be used by teachers and other students.

I thank you sincerely for sharing your reactions and feelings about the APP with me. I wish to take this chance to tell you about some changes that the APP will make starting in the fall semester. These changes are the direct response to your concerns as they appear in the questionnaire:

1. The total amount of homework will not change.

2. All sections of the TOEFL class at each level will use the same textbook. This should make the TOEFL classes at each level more similar to each other.

3. Groups will no longer be combined into one class for TOEFL study. Instead, each group will have its own TOEFL class, just like its own Content or Reading-Based Writing class.

4. The Listening/Speaking classes will all have one hour per week of direct TOEFL listening practice. This will be connected with the academic and social listening goals of the course.

5. The Grammar/Vocabulary class and the Reading Lab class will not be taught again. Instead, there will be a new class called Vocabulary/Reading Fluency. This new class will meet for 6 hours per week, and 1½ to 2 of those hours will be spent on direct study of the TOEFL reading section. Each of the new Vocabulary/Reading Fluency classes will also only be one group of students; we will not combine two groups into one class.

6. The Vocabulary/Reading Fluency class will aim at helping you to learn new words, read faster, and develop the reading skills needed for success at the reading section of the TOEFL and for success at general academic reading.

7. So, the total amount of time spent on direct TOEFL study will be increased to 5½ to 6 hours per week. There will also be at least 3 to 5 hours per week spent on activities that are indirectly, but closely, related to TOEFL practice.

8. Classes will be taught only in English (with the exception of occasional explanation of difficult points in Japanese).

9. All teachers and students will be encouraged to use English as much as possible on the TUJ campus.

10. More teachers will be native speakers of English.

The new curriculum will look like this:

Reading-Based Writing	=	6 hours per week
Content	=	6 hours per week
Vocabulary/Reading Fluency	=	6 hours per week
Listening/Speaking	=	3 hours per week
Grammar/TOEFL Practice	=	3 hours per week
Total hours	=	24 hours per week (the same as now)

From my viewpoint, the challenge of designing an appropriate curriculum is to give enough focus to TOEFL study while still emphasizing the English knowledge and skills you will need as CLA students. I believe that it is possible to integrate the study of useful skills with direct TOEFL practice, and the new class lineup will do so in both the Listening/Speaking and Vocabulary/Reading Fluency classes.

Thank you again for your honest feedback. It has helped us to redesign the curriculum to meet your needs better. I look forward to learning from you again next semester on how you feel about these changes.

Learning English well enough to do university study is a very big job, but I think that the changes in the APP that I have described here will help you to succeed at it. Please let me know how this works for you. Good luck with your studies and work hard!

Sincerely,

Patrick Rosenkjar, EdD
Professor of English Language Education
Assistant Dean for English Language Education
Director, Academic Preparation Program

Bridging the Classroom Perception Gap: Comparing Learners' and Teachers' Understandings of What Is Learned (*Japan*)

Timothy Stewart

Issue

How many times have you heard yourself and your colleagues say something like "Great lesson" or "That lesson bombed"? Reflection on the reasons for perceived success or failure in the classroom will often consist of brief hallway exchanges amongst colleagues. As teachers, we tend to assume that the way we look at a task will be the way learners look at it. However, "there is evidence that while we as teachers are focusing on one thing, learners are focusing on something else" (Nunan, 1989a, p. 20). That is, "learners may have learned little from the teaching points and a lot from everything else that happened in the lesson" (Allwright, 2005, p. 14). Therefore, because learners often have alternative ideas about what was important in a lesson, do we not have a responsibility as teachers to try to learn more about the impressions our students develop about our lessons?

The issue of inviting learner views on lessons holds particular relevance for Asian contexts in which learners expect their teachers to have firm control over classroom events (e.g., Ballard, 1996; LoCastro, 1996; Wadden, 1993). In Japan the education system is highly centralized, and teachers often lament about their inability to stray from the curriculum laid out by the Tokyo-based Ministry of Education. The expectation in Japanese classrooms is that lessons should be teacher centered with minimal input from students about course content or learning objectives.

For 2 years I team taught an integrated language content course called Issues in Cross-Cultural Communication with a specialist in that field. The course used task-based learning to prepare Japanese university students for a semester of studying abroad in English speaking countries. Tasks developed for the course (see Appendix A) aimed to build academic skills students would need while studying abroad. Prior to teaching this course, I had been seriously pondering the following questions: How could we find out what our learners think about lessons? How far might students' perceptions of learning tasks converge and diverge with our own? I thought that if we knew more, we might be able to use this information to improve our course planning and instruction. In essence, my partner and I felt that by listening to our learners, we could make the learning experience better for them as well as more rewarding for ourselves. With that in mind, I argue in this chapter for a multifaceted approach to task evaluation as a way to match teacher and learner impressions of task appropriateness.

Background Literature

It seems self-evident that teachers and students do not view classroom events through the same lens. But is there really a gap between how teachers and their learners view classroom activity? Three studies conducted in different countries with learners at different proficiency levels might shed light on this issue. First, Slimani's (1989) study on uptake in an Algerian university found that learners' reporting on what they learned in lessons differed from what she observed and recorded. A second study for consideration was done by Block (1996). He focused his study on similarities and differences between teacher and learner perceptions of learning purpose. Block observed a lesson for MBA students in a Spanish university. He found that learners did not find importance in what the teacher considered to be the focus of the lesson. Also, the activity that the learners thought was the most valuable was viewed as insignificant by the teacher. Finally, in a nationwide survey conducted in South Africa, teachers were asked about teaching and learning (Barkhuizen, 1998). Teachers responded by expressing what they surmised were the feelings and thoughts of their learners. The teachers were surprised to learn that the impressions of their students frequently differed from their own thoughts and feelings. These studies show the potential problems raised by the perception gap between teachers and the learners in their classrooms. The fact is that because classroom communication remains in teacher control, students often struggle to understand the patterns of communication presented (Johnson, 1995).

Because "differences in teachers' and students' perceptions of the classroom context can lead to different interpretations of and participation in classroom activities" (Johnson, 1995, p. 5), this gap in perceptions should be of more universal concern to educators. Although teachers might have control over classroom communication, students influence classroom events perhaps as much as they are influenced by them. "Most teachers admit that the success of any classroom event depends on how students perceive and respond to it" (Johnson, p. 40). Nunan (1989b) claims that "the orientations of the learner will constitute a hidden agenda and will largely dictate what is learned" (p. 180). In other words, what is learned is largely "determined by how learners perceive the usefulness of classroom events" (Kumaravadivelu, 2003, p. 78).

The course that is the focus of my study was cotaught by me, a TESOL specialist, together with a professor of cross-cultural studies. We were equal partners and as such jointly created materials, taught, and determined grades. The course was self-contained, and we worked simultaneously, meaning we traded off the lead and supporting teaching roles (see Stewart, Sagliano, & Sagliano, 2002, for more details on this team teaching approach). Through our collaboration, a model for assessing tasks evolved.

My partner and I planned the course around a series of tasks (see Appendix A), headed by two research projects. As we negotiated the course objectives, the framework for assessing course tasks emerged. What my teaching partner and I searched for was a way to explore and then match teacher and learner impressions of task appropriateness. After reading Barkhuizen's (1998) article, I suggested using learning log journals for this exploration (Genesee & Upshur, 1996). Based on discussion and consultation with other colleagues, we decided to ask the 22 students in the course to write their impressions of course tasks, with a set of question prompts to guide them. To match teacher and learner perceptions, both teachers also wrote learning log entries using identical prompts. Care was taken to avoid perpetuating a teacher-centered view of learning that often results when reflection is done by teachers only (McDonough, 1994).

To help define learning tasks, I turned to Ellis (2003), whose work suggested several essential features of language learning tasks. To Ellis, classroom activities that focus on grammatical structures are mechanical exercises, not tasks. That is, to be defined as tasks, activities need to communicate some new information in situations where meanings are unpredictable. Tasks evaluated in the course were primarily focused on meaning and required "learners to process language pragmatically in order to achieve an outcome" (Ellis, p. 16). Details of the two major research projects are outlined in Appendix A.

Procedures

While writing learning log entries over one term, my partner and I began to visualize a multilayered process of evaluation. Each layer added a deeper level of understanding of the perceptions teachers and learners have about tasks. The approach eventually encompassed the following layers:

1. In-class student learning logs

2. In-class teacher learning logs

3. Summaries of learning log entries

4. Teacher reflections on Layers 1–3

5. Course evaluation questionnaire data

6. Course development decisions

At the start, I had visualized only the learning logs, Layers 1 and 2. Logs were completed in class at the end of a selected task. This took about 10 minutes of class time.

Layer 3 evolved after the course when I saw the necessity of coding all student entries and summarizing the teacher evaluations. The coding of this data was done in about 2 hours. Once the data set was coded, the next step was interpretation.

My coteacher and I decided upon a reflection stage in which we compared the teacher and student learning log data. This began with teachers writing individual reflections on the data in Layers 1–3. After reading each other's reflections, we discussed them. During the discussion phase in Layer 4, we made tentative decisions about course changes. Altogether, this layer of written reflection and discussion took about 2 hours.

Later the idea of adding Layer 5 came to me so we could compare our tabulated course-end questionnaire data with the student learning log evaluations of tasks. This step took less than 2 hours.

Finally, we reflected on the possible meanings of all of this information, discussed our observations, and made decisions about course development. Layer 6 took about 2 hours.

Because evaluations were written during lessons, the entire approach took less than 8 additional hours. I did not see this as being much extra time to spend on course development, because it provided my coteacher and me data on which to make informed decisions.

The following steps outline the procedures in detail for teachers interested in experimenting with this approach. Many of these steps are illustrated in the next section.

SELECTING TASKS FOR EVALUATION

- Be clear on your purpose for evaluation (i.e., assess appropriateness of new tasks).

- Based on the purpose, decide which tasks should be evaluated.

FINDING PARTNERS FOR REFLECTION

- If you are not team teaching, try to find a colleague to discuss the course with. Consider approaching someone who teaches another section of the same course, a master teacher assigned to mentor your professional development process, or a trusted colleague.

WRITING THE PROMPTS

- Decide whether or not to involve students in this process.

- Be sure to model log entries before the first evaluative reflection. (See sample prompts in Appendix B.)

COMPLETING IN-CLASS STUDENT LOGS (LAYER 1)

- Stress that this exercise is for course development and not to grade learner understanding or mastery of material.

- Number the logs and distribute one to each student.

- Print copies of the prompts, write them on a board/poster, or project them onto a screen/wall during each evaluation.

- Have students write the date and task name each time.

COMPLETING IN-CLASS TEACHER LOGS (LAYER 2)

- Do not read other logs before completing your own.

- Complete log entries at the same time the students do theirs.

SUMMARIZING THE LEARNING LOGS (LAYER 3)

- Read all logs, and categorize main points about learning generated by tasks.

- Create a chart for each task with main points and corresponding log number.

REFLECTING (LAYER 4)

- Read summaries of student and teacher learning logs. Write reflections on issues that present themselves.

- Discuss these reflections with colleagues and make tentative decisions.

REVIEWING ADDITIONAL INFORMATION (LAYER 5)

- Collect additional information such as evaluations of teaching, end-of-course evaluations, or transcripts of classroom interaction.

- Analyze this information.

MAKING FINAL DECISIONS (LAYER 6)

- Reflect on additional information in relation to tentative decisions.

- Finalize decisions on task and course development.

Results

In this section, the layers of the approach are explained with accompanying samples related to the final research project. The final research project was one of two research projects integrated into the course (see task descriptions in Appendix A). Learners designed their projects using a model research project outline as a guide. Topics for these projects were ranked by each student from amongst those brainstormed together in class, and we grouped students according to these rankings.

The primary goal was to prepare students for doing independent research during their semester abroad. Throughout the process, we maintained an integrated model of language instruction and addressed reading, writing, and speaking skills at various intervals. We emphasized the language of comparison-contrast, chart/table reading, and oral research presentation.

LAYER 1. IN-CLASS STUDENT LOGS

The student learning logs were one-way journals, so they were not overly time consuming. The prompts (see Appendix B) focused learner entries on task evaluation yet were open ended. The logs formed records of learner needs as expressed by learners themselves, as shown in Figure 1. To prevent confounding effects, we avoided reading student logs until our own entries were complete.

Task #4: Final Research Project   **6/26/2002**

1. Were you absent for part of this task?

   No.

2. What did you learn from this task?

   I learned how to collect the data. There are some ways to collect the data. Observation, interview, questionnaire and. . . .

3. How much did you learn from this task? (Circle one)

   very little   very much

   1   2   (3)   4

4. Explain your reasons for the above rating.

   I learned many things from this task. For example, we learned hypothesis. I think it is useful because I have to write senior thesis. When I write senior thesis, I have to make good hypothesis. Research project is good practice for senior thesis. However, I knew that collecting the data is difficult. . . .

Excerpts of Student #20 journal written in class 6/26/02.

Figure 1. Sample in-class student journal entry.

LAYER 2. TEACHER LOGS

All participants evaluated course tasks using identical question prompts. While writing journal entries, my impressions of the process ranged from satisfaction to self-doubt. The timing and freedom of the reflection process allowed me to capture my thoughts on tasks (see Figure 2 for an example), which was satisfying. However, I often felt that what I had to say was fairly self-evident and need not be recorded. I now believe that without a record fresh from the moment, it is all but impossible to reconstruct accurate impressions of a learning task.

My rating for this project was a 3. My main reasons were that students appeared very engaged by the project and had produced a lot of written material. One concern was about the ability of learners to analyze their data and relate it to the broader area of cross-cultural issues. The other drawback I saw was the use of Japanese in some groups. This concern was magnified for me because of the amount of time the task took to complete.

LAYER 3. SUMMARIES OF LEARNING LOGS

At the end of the course my coteacher and I did a content analysis of the logs (see Figure 3). Learning log content suggested categories of data that generalized the ideas found in the entries. The coding process of analyzing qualitative data

Name: Teacher A   Date: June 26, 2002   Task: Final Research Project

Journal entry #4—excerpt

2. It seems to me that the students are beginning to learn how to put a research project together and complete it. They generated the topics for research with some examples coming from us. We formed the working groups based on their choice of topic. . . . They then went into the field and collected data and brought it back for analysis. So they should have learned something about developing a research idea into a plan with specific questions and definitions, and collecting and analysing data.

3. *[Teacher's answer was 3 on 1–4 scale.]* I think that much learning was generated by this task.

4. The fact that most of the students could come up with reasonable hypotheses and definitions of key terms without much assistance from us indicates success. Another indicator is the fact that they all were able to organize their research and findings for analysis. The harder part will be whether they can explain how their data relates to their hypothesis and then make conclusions drawing on course concepts to make their analysis meaningful. . . .

Figure 2. Sample teacher learning log entry.

gave it a quantitative dimension. After coding, teacher and learner data were more readily comparable. This information allowed us to identify what our learners saw as the main strengths and weaknesses of particular tasks. Thus, we were able to determine the patterns of responses and the salient issues needing reflection (see Figure 4).

The class rated the final research project task highly for an average of 3.5 out of a possible 4. There were three significant areas of learning mentioned by seven or more students in their logs. Most students said that they learned something about the process of doing research. Students also wrote that they learned

What Students Said They Learned (Edited to Top Five)	Journal No.
1. I learned how to do research.	4, 5, 7, 8, 9, 11, 12, 13, 14, 17, 19, 20, 21
2. I learned new information about our chosen research topic.	1, 3, 4, 7, 12, 15, 16, 17, 18, 19, 22
3. I learned about contemporary Japanese culture.	2, 4, 6, 10, 15, 18, 21
4. I enjoyed/saw importance of group work.	4, 13, 14
5. I think this project is useful preparation for study abroad or other classes.	11, 20, 22

Figure 3. Sample summary of student journal comments about final research project [June 26, 2002].

Teacher A	Teacher B
Student learning: — Difficulty of doing research and analysis. — Developing a research idea into a plan with specific questions and definitions, and collecting and analysing data.	Student learning: — I think they learned how to think and communicate systematically. Beginning with inkling, a question, or a guess (hypothesis), they went about seeking information to confirm or disconfirm their guesses. — Perhaps this activity is too oblique for students. — Should consider replacing it.
Rating: 3.5	Rating: 3
Reasons for rating: — Majority of students able to write reasonable hypotheses. — All were able to organize their research and findings for analysis. — Analysis remained weak. — Better students forced to carry some of weaker ones.	Reasons for rating: — Learned about research method in a passing sort of way (going through motions). — Dissatisfied with their ability to make inferences about their data. — The learning outcomes achieved did not measure up to the length of time it took to do the project.

Figure 4. Sample summary of teacher journal comments on final research project [June 26, 2002].

content information about their research topic. Learning about contemporary Japanese culture was the third most significant area of learning mentioned. The only negative comments about the task came from two students who stated that doing this type of research was new for them and difficult to understand at first. The significance of these comments became clearer to me when I realized that they were written by two of the top students in the class. If the meaning of the project proved difficult for them to grasp, then it stood to reason that others felt similarly.

My partner was very critical of the task in her evaluation. She concluded that "It's time to drop this activity." She felt that many learners "just went through the motions" and did not reflect on the meaning of the task. That is, they were not able to see how differences between their chosen sites for research (i.e., hotel vs. traditional inn) might reflect larger and deeper differences or changes in the society at large. Reading this, I saw that we continued to question how transparent the connection is for our students between the research tasks and our expectations as far as course content.

LAYER 4. TEACHER REFLECTIONS ON LAYERS 1–3

After reading the summaries of teacher and student learning logs, we each wrote further detailed reflections (see Figure 5). The act of committing thoughts to paper is an integral part of the process. We exchanged our written reflections and considered them for a day or so before meeting. In this meeting, we continued the process of reflection through discussion. These focused conversations led to tentative decisions about the future shape of the course. As the data were interpreted and reinterpreted several times, there is a genuine research process here far beyond the norm of intuitive reflection.

LAYER 5. COURSE EVALUATION DATA

Our end-of-course questionnaire, distributed in the final class, was an anonymous survey that asked students for a 1 to 4 rating on each task listed in the categories of enjoyment, English learning, and content learning. An example of the tabulated data is shown in Table 1. A comments space was provided under each task. Also, at the end of the survey we asked for "suggestions for improving the course" as well as the question, "What are the most useful/important things that you learned?" The students' suggestions for improving the course were the following:

- Do more simulations.

- Research project needs more time to collect data.

Final Research Project, October 2002

Teacher A:
My partner's ratings of the research-related tasks in the course indicate her frustration with the projects in terms of length and outcomes. In reading our journals it doesn't seem that either one of us is content that the outcomes have been equal to the time and effort expended. For example, I stated in my journal reflection that conclusions drawn were not well-connected to the course. I felt that we did a better job at this last year. This point, of course, gets back to our shared concern over devising a theoretical framework for the course that is as useful and meaningful as it is transparent to the students.

Teacher B:
Again the length of these projects is something that concerns both of us. My impression is that we need to focus more directly on aspects of Japanese culture using sources from books and the Internet as research material. As so many students mentioned again learning about how to do research, it indicates that we should include some research project. At least three mentioned how they enjoyed the group work involved. Developing much shorter research projects and/or including more checkpoints along the way could better ensure that some students don't do the lion's share of the work.

Figure 5. Sample of teacher reflections on data.

- Newspaper summary is good.

- Give more directions before tasks.

The tabulation and interpretation of the questionnaire data was purposely left until after the journal evaluations had been summarized and initially reflected on, as described in Layer 4. At the end of a course, students may be better able to see the purpose of tasks and how tasks link. This kind of data is very useful in a supplementary role, but I stress that end-of-course surveys are no substitute for data collected during or immediately after tasks.

LAYER 6. COURSE DEVELOPMENT DECISIONS

We held further reflection discussions to consider additional data. We talked about the tentative plans for course development made in Layer 4 in relation to the end-of-course questionnaire data. We also discussed how the journal summary information from Layer 3 related to this new information. At that point, my partner and I felt prepared to finalize decisions. These are explained in the Reflection section.

Reflection

Reflection on the learning log data led my partner and me to two major course decisions: changes to the theoretical underpinnings of the course and a more pronounced emphasis on language practice.

THEORETICAL FOUNDATION

The major decision was to de-emphasize the theoretical framework and work with more practical material at the beginning of the course. The change was to begin the course with a series of cross-cultural simulation tasks. After the first simulation, I saw that it was not possible to front-load all of the simulations and hope learners would understand them with much depth. Hence, it became necessary to preteach concepts before introducing more simulations. We introduced the concepts along with some simple cross-cultural simulations in an attempt to make them more transparent.

Table 1. Sample of 2002 End-of-Course Questionnaire Data

Task	Enjoyment	English Learning	Content Learning
Model Research Project	3.0	3.7	3.9
Final Research Project	3.4	3.9	3.8

Note: Overall average 3.6 on 4.0 scale

Our teacher evaluations were positive about the beginning activities on perception and stereotypes. At that time, I voiced tentatively that the new approach might be more effective, and my coteacher stated her belief that the approach seemed more accessible than that taken in 2001. As I read our later journal entries, however, enthusiasm tempered somewhat.

The students on average rated the task as a 3, the same as my rating, but significantly lower than my partner's 4. I missed a key culminating class, so that could explain my lower rating. My partner had witnessed more of how learners had synthesized material.

Over two teachings of the course, we continued to debate about what theory, how much theory, and how to teach the theoretical concepts to our learners. A further example of this can be seen in the evaluations of the Shaka-Shaka and Dagang simulation (see Appendix A). Learners gave this an average rating of 3.6. I rated it as a 3, and my partner gave it a 3.5. The two teacher evaluations emphasized our concern that students did not exhibit an understanding of the simulation beyond the surface level. I laid blame for such superficial learning on lack of time. On reflection it seemed to me that the theoretical concepts were not reviewed enough before the simulations. Comments in student journals bolstered this assessment, because at least three students mentioned their disappointment with the Shaka-Shaka Dagang debriefing presentations: "They were nearly all the same."

MORE EXPLICIT TEACHING OF LANGUAGE

Noticing what is not said in reflective learning logs can be as important as recording what is said. I was struck by the sparseness of comments describing language learning. There were some, but we and our students seemed to have been very much focused on process and content, not language. For me, this raised questions regarding the nature of language and content learning in discipline-based courses. The course tasks were all designed to focus on meaning, although language skills were taught throughout. The content, the procedural needs of the tasks, and student performance together dictated the focus for language instruction. I noted our approach to language instruction embedded in context, meaning, and process as a good one, yet I felt that more discrete and explicit language instruction was needed.

I naturally raised this concern with my coteacher, and we made a decision to give language objectives greater prominence in the course. In addition to introducing a writing correction guide for peer editing, we planned to do much more reading practice with short readings about Japan and the countries students would travel to for study abroad. We planned additional readings about current news in countries that students planned to visit for study-abroad programs. The students then presented news summaries to others who were planning to go to that particular country. These activities are adaptations of the watch-and-report news presentations described in Appendix A.

We both rated the task as a perfect 4, and it got the second highest rating from students on the end-of-course survey. The goal was to improve this popular task by focusing the content on study-abroad country information and having individuals present to small groups of students planning to study in those countries, rather than to the entire class. One of my hopes was that this would encourage more discussion questions.

POTENTIAL ADAPTATIONS

My hope is that other teachers might adapt these procedures to suit their teaching situations. The entire process took about 8 hours of time outside class. It produced a written record that facilitated decision making and created a dynamic understanding about task appropriateness. However, it is inconceivable that teachers would engage in this type of evaluation for *all* tasks in every course. Because burnout is a serious concern (Allwright, 2005), teachers should be selective when choosing tasks for evaluation.

The procedures could be adapted in different ways. Breen's (1989) task-in-process evaluation is challenging but appealing. Rather than evaluating many tasks throughout a course, key tasks could be isolated and evaluated more thoroughly according to Breen's framework. Moreover, videotaping key activities for analysis seems sensible when evaluating extended tasks in particular. Evaluations of fewer tasks could involve transcribing interactions as well to add depth in understanding how tasks work in process (Farrell, 2004; Kumaravadivelu, 1991; Slimani, 1989). Nunan's (1989a) checklist for evaluating tasks is too extensive for reflective journals but certainly could be used in the final layer of the process to guide discussions about tasks. An interview layer might be considered, but learners might feel awkward being interviewed by course instructors about course tasks. An alternative is to have other teachers conduct the interviews. My advice is that teachers avoid adding too many layers and making evaluation too much of a chore. It is best to design evaluative tools that fit the particular situation.

BENEFITS OF THIS TYPE OF CLASSROOM RESEARCH

Through this process, my partner and I learned more than we had expected about ourselves as teachers, our learners' expectations, and our course. During the early stages of the process of writing and reading log entries, we both had the impression that there really was not much in these learning logs for reflection. As we systematically analyzed the entries, however, it became clear that there was indeed much that we could learn.

Barkhuizen's (1998) advice to teachers is to "continuously explore their classes, particularly their learners' perceptions" of them (p. 104). Mismatches will occur, so teachers should work to identify and manage them. The multi-layered approach to task and course evaluation detailed in this chapter is one of a range of possibilities. Kumaravadivelu (2003) details a number of activities teachers can use to try to minimize perceptual mismatches with their students. Student perceptions can make or break a lesson. Therefore, learner perspectives need to be made a part of the lesson planning process. When teachers and learners collaborate to facilitate learning, the experience of second language education can become more enjoyable and valuable for all participants.

Tim Stewart teaches at Kumamoto University in Japan.

Appendix A: Task Descriptions

1. **Perception, Stereotypes, and Values.** (2 weeks) Students listed stereotypes they knew about people from the United States, Canada, and Japan, and later asked natives of those countries to comment on them. Note taking from a lecture on perception followed. There was a small-group discussion on sources and countermeasures for stereotyping. Following this was a reading on values. Individuals' responses were shared on the board with the rest of the class to show diversity of opinion even among people from the same culture (debunking the myth of Japanese homogeneity).

2. **Shaka-Shaka and Dagang Simulation.** (2 days) This task was an adaptation of the cross-cultural simulation BaFa BaFa, designed by R. Garry Shirts. Students were divided into two equal groups. Each group was taught rules for a simple culture. Pairs of students then entered the "foreign" culture. This simulated the experience of interacting with a new culture. Debriefing took place for an extended period.

3. **Model Research Project.** (4 weeks) This project began by using elements of culture to compare Japan 100 years ago and Japan today. Students went individually to either a franchise or nonfranchise restaurant and filled in data onto worksheets. Later, in the classroom, pairs who went to the same category of restaurant compiled and compared their data. Next, they compared this data with that of a pair who went to a different category of restaurant. Data were then analyzed in a series of steps leading to a final presentation including comments on Japanese culture as seen through these restaurants.

4. **Final Research Project.** (5 weeks) This project was based on the model research project but was designed by the learners. Students selected from amongst possible research sites brainstormed in class. They wrote their

top three ranked sites on a paper (e.g., *ryokan* vs. hotel, MIC vs. Miyazaki University, kindergarten vs. day care centre). The teachers then grouped students using these rankings. In groups of four, students listed questions they had about these places and created categories and data collection tools to study their questions. Once collected, the data were analyzed and written up.

5. **Watch and Report News Presentations.** (10+ weeks) Individual student presentations of current news to the whole class. Following the watch-and-report model demonstrated by teachers, students searched for news articles related to cross-cultural issues. They then summarized articles and made brief presentations of the main points. Classmates took notes and asked questions.

6. **Study-Abroad Preparation Tasks.** (4 days) This task began with a question-and-answer session with 3rd-year students who had experienced study abroad a year earlier. In the next class, we did various activities with a cross-cultural video for students going to study in the United States. The instructor gave a short lecture on symptoms of culture shock, and together we brainstormed possible solutions. Next, students prepared short explanations of aspects of Japanese culture, and we did a carousel speaking activity, mixing students into different groups several times. Finally, we watched video skits made by a previous year's senior students that gave advice about study abroad.

Appendix B: Sample Journal Prompts

Date: _____Task name: _____

1. Were you absent for part of this task?

    YES

    NO

2. What did you learn from this task?

3. How much did you learn from this task? (Circle one)

    very little   very much

    1   2   3   4

4. Explain your reasons for the above rating.

CHAPTER 12

Does Project-Based Learning Work in Asia? (*China*)

Wang Ge

Issue

As an instructional approach in Western countries, project-based learning (PBL) has been acclaimed by many language teachers and researchers because it contextualizes learning by presenting students with problems to solve or questions to answer (Lee, 2005; Moss & Van Duzer, 1998). However, in many Asian countries, classroom observations have indicated that PBL may not be as effective as some Western language teachers expect. In the real Asian language classroom, students often switch to their mother tongue, and the problem of getting them to respond in English is particularly difficult during PBL (Tsui, 1996). In China, for example, pedagogical conflicts have often been reported when implementing PBL with Chinese students and expatriate teachers. The conflicts seem to stem from differences between the Western approach to teaching and Asian students' learning styles. Li (1999) describes the conflicts as follows:

> The discourse of participation was strongly resisted by Chinese students, and teaching by native speakers often failed to achieve the desired results. In spite of the "good" intentions on the part of both native teachers and Chinese

---

Note: This is an expansion and revision of a presentation given at the 4th International Conference on ELT in Beijing, China, 2004.

students, there existed a vast gulf in their perceptions of what constituted "good" teaching and learning, of what appropriate roles they were fitted in, and what they expected of each other. (Abstract section, para. 2)

Some Western scholars complain that Chinese learners have neither the written and oral skills of analysis and reflection, nor the independence of thought and study that are required in Western universities, especially for implementing PBL (Ballard & Clanchy, 1991). Based on this assumption, Chinese students are often categorized as "passive rote learners, whose logic follows a strange spiral pattern and who are products of a static, unchanging, traditional society" (Pennycook, 1998, p. 162).

For Chinese teachers of English, even those with a great interest in PBL, another challenge is finding suitable materials and ways to encourage and maximize students' use of the target language. Considering these potential hurdles, I decided to investigate whether PBL would work in my class in China and what modifications might be necessary to suit the Chinese context. I also wanted to find out what the key obstacles to carrying out PBL in China might be and how I might solve these problems.

This chapter reports the findings of a qualitative study conducted from April to October 2003 at a tertiary institution in southwest China. The participating students were my English major sophomores. Three connected projects, all based on the hot topic of severe acute respiratory syndrome (SARS), a virus that was spreading in China at the time, were introduced to my intensive English language reading class in the second academic semester.

Background Literature

A previous analysis of PBL by Moss and Van Duzer (1998) defined it as "an instructional approach that contextualizes learning by presenting learners with problems to solve or products to develop" (para.1). Different from the general top-down approach in a teacher-centered classroom, the attractiveness of PBL lies in the long-term learning activities that are interdisciplinary, student centered, and integrated with real-world issues and practices. PBL, which is also known as problem-based teaching, authentic learning, and anchored instruction, has its intellectual roots in the Socratic method dating back to early Greek philosophy and draws on cognitive psychology and pedagogy. It is based on purposeful learning (Dewey, 1938), social interaction (Vygotsky, 1978a), and discovery learning (Bruner, 1996). According to constructivists, people construct knowledge on the basis of their experiences. Therefore, students need opportunities in the classroom to learn through experience and experimentation.

PBL has won favor among Western teachers because of the following advantages over top-down teaching:

- It can motivate students by engaging them in their own learning. PBL provides opportunities for students to pursue their own interests and questions and to make decisions about how they will find answers and solve problems.

- It also provides opportunities for interdisciplinary learning. Students apply and integrate the content of different subject areas at authentic moments in the production process instead of in isolation or in an artificial setting.

- It makes learning relevant and useful to students by establishing connections to life outside the classroom, addressing real-world concerns, and developing marketable skills.

- It provides many different opportunities for teachers to build relationships with students. Teachers may fill the varied roles of coach, facilitator, and colearner. (San Mateo County Office of Education, n.d.)

In terms of language pedagogy, Fried-Booth (2002) defined project work as "student-centred and driven by the need to create an end-product" (p. 6). He argued that "the route to the end-product brings opportunities for students to develop their confidence and independence and to work together in a real-world environment by collaborating on a task" (p. 6). Lee (2005) interpreted PBL as "an instructional approach that contextualizes learning by presenting students with problems to solve and questions to answer" (p. 21). He argued that PBL can open up valuable opportunities to integrate content knowledge with language learning. Beckett and Slater (2005) agreed, asserting that "project-based instruction is a valuable way to promote the simultaneous acquisition of language, content, and skills, provided that students in academic [English language] classes can see the value of learning through projects, which the literature notes has not consistently been the case" (p. 108).

Researchers have observed that the hot issue–based language project (HBLP) can be an effective task-based strategy in foreign language teaching. This experience-oriented approach puts more emphasis on the process of interaction and exploration than on assimilation and passive intake. In this sense, English as a foreign language (EFL) learners are no longer "defective native speakers" (Liddicoat, Crozet, & Lo Bianco, 2000, p. 181) but users of the language (Firth & Wagner, 1997) for the purpose of communication in various social contexts.

In comparison with traditional teacher-centered rote learning in Asian countries, HBLP offers the following benefits that Nunan (2005) noted:

- An infusion of more student-centered learning to diversify a teacher-centered approach.

- More use of authentic experiences and materials to allow students to construct their own meaning.

- Opportunities for personal and active accomplishment, including promoting a greater sense of language ownership.

- Increased student participation when task teaching is well planned and implemented with sensitivity to the overall local context as well as to students' learning styles, learning and communicative strategies, personalities, and multiple intelligences.

- Clearer lesson goals tied to the success of task completion.

- Opportunities for ongoing assessment and "wash-back" benefits for the teacher and learner.

Based on the existing research, I would argue that HBLP could serve the following purposes in an EFL context:

- Enhance students' practical abilities to communicate in the target language

- Develop student-centered learning, emphasizing participation

- Cultivate a range of learning strategies and study skills

- Cultivate a creative spirit in language learning

- Develop skills in intercultural communication and increase cultural awareness

- Use multiple teaching modes and models that cater to more students' learning styles

Procedures

In early spring 2003, an unexpected plague known as SARS broke out in China. It was first found in Canton and then discovered in most provinces of China. During the plague, SARS made media headlines in China as well as around the world. Therefore, it became a hot topic on college campuses. Given this situation, I developed a series of projects concerning this topic as assignments for my intensive reading class. Because SARS was the hottest topic at the time and everyone in China, including tertiary students, had to face it, I thought it would make a good topic for discussion in the language classroom and help my students develop awareness toward epidemic diseases.

I assigned three projects related to the different phases of the SARS plague—the beginning of the outbreak, the peak time, and the post-outbreak period, as shown in Table 1.

In terms of the pedagogical outcomes of the assignments, I expected these

Table 1. Project Descriptions

Project	Content
Project 1 (April 2003)	**Group discussion:** How to keep away from SARS
Project 2 (mid-May 2003)	**Written report:** My view on SARS
Project 3 (October 2003)	**Writing task:** Li Ming, one of your roommates and a close friend, is a SARS virus carrier who has been recovered for months. However, some of your roommates still refuse to talk to him, and some have even asked him to move out of the dorm. As the head of the dorm, what would you do to solve the problem?

projects to maximize students' attention to accuracy, fluency, and complexity (see Figure 1).

The projects were designed to achieve different linguistic or communicative tasks in light of the students' cognitive competence and second language (L2) proficiency. Based on the rich information sources from newspapers and the Internet, I believed that tertiary students could carry out the projects under my guidance and through cooperative learning in my classroom. To achieve this purpose, I assigned in-class and after-class reading and research tasks to ensure that students were adequately prepared for their classroom work. The process is outlined in Figure 2.

Figure 2 describes a framework of HBLP that I developed. I assumed that linguistic and communicative competence could be developed by working on

Target:	Second-year English major students of Southwest Forestry College, a tertiary institution in Southwest China
Goals:	1. Build vocabulary on communicable diseases. 2. Present personal views on SARS. 3. Develop linguistic and communicative competence. 4. Build up problem-solving competence in real life.
Input:	News report on SARS from the English language newspaper China Daily and the Internet
Activities:	1. Read or listen to related articles during and after class. 2. Discuss ways to prevent SARS, and offer personal comment. 3. End product: Solve relevant problems.
Teacher role:	Monitor and facilitator
Learner role:	Conversational and discussion partner, presenter, and researcher
Setting:	1. Group work, discussion, presentation 2. After-class research and writing

Figure 1. Profile of plan and goals for SARS projects.

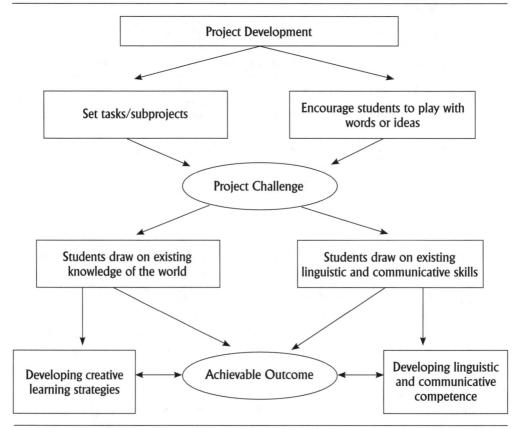

Figure 2. A framework for the hot issue−based language project.

carefully designed tasks based on hot issues such as SARS. Drawing on their existing knowledge of the world and their L2 proficiency, students were expected to fulfill the project assignments and in the process develop creative learning strategies and improve their linguistic and communicative competence. The framework outlined in Figure 2 contains four stages:

1. Brainstorming questions (warm-up)

2. Task setting (with language assistance and research method instruction)

3. Project implementation (interaction between teacher and students)

4. Product report

As for the first stage, I posed the following questions to the students before introducing the projects on SARS to my class:

- What are the hot topics on campus?

- Have you heard the term SARS? If so, what is the full name of SARS?

- What are the symptoms of SARS?

- What causes SARS?

- Who is at high risk?

The previously mentioned questions aimed to arouse my students' interest and encourage them to collect data and exchange views on the given topic. The questions were built on a schema of easy-to-difficult sequence and called for students' investigation and negotiation. To make sure that students could find the answers to these questions fairly easily, I suggested some channels for gathering information:

- The Internet (Google or other search engines)

- Newspapers and magazines

- TV news and radio broadcasting

- Handbooks or posters issued by medical agencies

After the students had researched the idea, I gave the following instructions for the second stage:

As you mentioned, SARS is the hottest topic on the campus. I know all of you are quite concerned about this epidemic, for there are increasing reports on the toll and new suspected cases. In fact, I am very scared as you are, but we have to figure out something to get others alert and take some protective measures. As Shakespeare says, "to be or not to be, that is the question." In the following weeks, I hope we can work together on a project on SARS for the following objectives. . . .

Apart from enough input to warm up and the necessary explanations for the projects, I also provided language assistance to ensure the success of the projects. For example, I introduced some technical terms in advance:

Acute	Blood test	Breathing difficulty	Chest fluoroscopy
Chest pain	Chills	Contiguous	Disinfection
Dry cough	Epidemics	High fever	Inflammation
Masks	Nauseous	Poor appetite	Rash and diarrhea
Respiratory	Short of breath	Sore throat	Suspected case
Symptoms	Syndrome	Traces of blood	

The background knowledge, clear instructions, and language assistance are critical at the beginning of the project, because support at this stage will help build up students' confidence and lead to a smooth transition to the next stage.

In the third stage, students were encouraged to ask questions and discuss the problems they encountered with me and their fellow students. I acted, in this circumstance, not only as a project observer but also a coach and facilitator who was always ready to give a hand. For example, for the groups who had difficulty in collecting data or starting a discussion, I usually offered some tips and talked with them as a participant throughout the project.

The product report was the final stage of the projects. The results were displayed in a number of ways. For example, oral presentations were employed for Project 1, and written products were required for Projects 2 and 3. To make sure that the presentations were comprehensible and each member of a group was involved, students who were talkative were recommended by other group members as presenters, and those who were less free with words but rich in thought were appointed to draft the reports.

Results

PROJECT 1

In group discussions, each group presented suggestions to answer the question of how to keep away from SARS. Those suggestions are highlighted in Table 2.

PROJECT 2

In terms of Project 2, one of my students offered a very impressive and positive understanding of SARS as follows:

> It touched me so much when a friend told me that there was a new interpretation for SARS as sacrifice, appreciate, reflect, and support. As can be seen, medical professionals have *sacrificed* so much, even their lives, to save the patients and contain the disease. We should *appreciate* what others have done

Table 2. Suggestions Presented for Project 1

Group No.	How to Keep Away From SARS
G1	Develop good personal habits (e.g., wash hands and face often).
G2	Do not spit and cough in public.
G3	Drink concoction of traditional Chinese medicine.
G4	Do not eat wild animals.
G5	Wear surgical masks.
G6	Do not share dishware with others.
G7	Do sports often.

for us and also *appreciate* our lives. SARS gives us an opportunity to *reflect* on our unhealthy living styles and also a chance for the government to *reflect* on the way it operates . . . and now as responsible citizens, we should *support* the national effort to combat the epidemic—SARS.

PROJECT 3

What made me most excited were the comments from my students for Project 3, in which the students had to provide a written piece that would outline how to help their fictitious roommate Li Ming. Here are some excerpts from students' work on the project:

Student 1—First, I would talk with other roommates and ask their attitude about it. I would let them know that SARS is not so horrible and we can take some actions to prevent it effectively. Second, I would talk with Li Ming and help him to overcome his blue mood and encourage him to solve all problems he will meet. I would let him know that all our roommates welcome him to return to the dorm. Maybe a welcome back home party would be held to bridge the gap between us.

Student 2—I would arrange a meeting at our dorm soon in order to help Li Ming and other roommates. The most efficient way is to encourage them to be in one another's shoes.

Student 3—We should treat him equally and let him feel a warm heart in the world. As we are classmates, we can't let him stay alone. As friends we should look after one another. I have another experience. I used to have a roommate with Hepatitis-B virus. But we treated her as usual except that we took some protective measures. As a result, she (virus-carrier) was happy and confident and we also learned something to prevent the disease. It's a good example. We should treat him (Li Ming) in the same way, don't you agree?

Feedback from the three projects indicated that HBLP was a success in my class, because students satisfactorily achieved most of the linguistic and communicative tasks, as I had hoped. In my view, HBLP was an effective language teaching and learning approach for my large classes. Although these classes had students with mixed language abilities, each student could contribute different talents and creativity to solving problems. My students experienced such problem-solving skills as discussion, debate, social interaction, information searches, and justification of their opinions. They also developed such cognitive skills as posing questions, developing a work plan, collecting and analyzing data, and drawing conclusions from the data. Above all, and of most importance for a language teacher in China, my students' linguistic and communicative competence developed substantially.

Also of note from my experience with PBL is the possibility of further developing my students' analytic and speculative learning strategies. The students had to study the problem at hand in great detail, and they had to interact in my classroom in English with each other and with me. In my classroom, I like to emphasize the process of learning rather than the product of learning, and PBL was an excellent tool to help me achieve this end. Most students are now in favor of teamwork, because it makes the advantages of group learning more clear to them. Therefore, they are now more willing to engage in pair and group work in my English language classes. After one semester's training in PBL, most of my students have learned how to survey a topic, find the main idea, conduct a discussion within a group, and present their arguments in public—and all this in English. At the same time, they have developed certain social and collaborative skills such as working as a team, solving problems, and learning how to see more than one side of a discussion.

Reflection

When using a PBL approach to language teaching, the teacher should note that it is often difficult for students to access suitable materials that are compatible with their cognitive competence and L2 proficiency. In terms of suitable materials, Hwang (2005) advises us to "select appropriate authentic materials that are pegged to learners' levels and interests" (Section 5, para. 11). Day (2004) also suggests that "teachers should use materials that are appropriate for the linguistic abilities of their students" (p. 110). Based on these views, I suggest that language teachers who want to implement PBL in China should design projects that are easily managed in terms of their students' L2 competence, general interest, and curriculum requirements. However, I still continue to struggle with and reflect on the following questions:

- When and how should a language project be introduced?

- Is it possible to manipulate project characteristics and classroom situations?

- How do you fill the gaps between the original project-as-work plan and the actual project in process?

- What are the pedagogical goals of the projects—accuracy oriented, fluency oriented, or complexity oriented?

- How can we achieve the intended pedagogical objectives without undermining students' personal preferences in language learning?

- How can we maximize the use of the target language in an EFL classroom?

To develop a workable language project, the following questions should be considered by the project designers:

- Is the project carefully selected for lexical and syntactic appropriateness?

- Is the content familiar or interesting to the participants?

- Is the outcome predictable, and what options can be taken to mend the problems in the process of the project implementation?

- Are the pedagogical goals of the project clear enough for both the project designer and the participants? For example, is the content form focused or meaning focused? Are relevance and rationale carefully and clearly explained to the participants? What are the end objectives of the project—linguistic competence or communicative competence?

One way of answering these questions is for language teachers in China and other Asian contexts to implement the same type of PBL project that I have outlined in this chapter, see what develops, and then analyze the results. On reflection, the thorniest issue when implementing PBL may be the skills of the teacher. Because many language teachers in China lack experience with and training for PBL, they can often get frustrated with the shortage of appropriate materials, evaluation criteria, and the additional workload involved in the role change from instructor to facilitator. This can be a huge cultural leap for teachers used to closely directing their students' education. Furthermore, the test-oriented teaching in China often creates problems with implementing such a PBL-based language project successfully. As Lee (2005) observed

> Although students are aware that PBL is likely to result in less boring and less conventional English lessons, the need to get good examination results may override the desire for more interesting learning experience. Hence, students may adopt a resistant and recalcitrant attitude towards PBL. (p. 24)

Consequently, I would argue that English language teaching (ELT) in China must be reevaluated and focus on the students' communicative performance rather than on testing achievements tied to reading and grammatical knowledge. Accordingly, a curriculum based on developing communicative competence should be designed in line with the local context. We teachers must also learn to trust our students in managing and manipulating project work. If Chinese English language teachers always believe the cultural generalization that their students are passive learners, teachers may then accordingly "react and respond in ways that reinforce the generalizations, in effect making them true" (Curtis, 1999, p. 13). For example, there is still a belief in China that language learning is a collection of discrete facts to be learned, memorized, and repeated without meaning, and as a result, rote learning is emphasized and even preferred. Li Jiongying (2005) sums up the cultural tendency in the following way:

> In Chinese culture, memory strategies, or mnemonics, have been traditionally attached great importance to by both instructors and learners in Chinese formal education, and are viewed as one of the most important factors in making good achievements on tests of various kinds. (p. 144)

I also suggest that systematic training in project design, implementation, and assessment should be introduced to Chinese language teachers. First of all, an "I can do it" belief must be established among these teachers, so they can develop confidence in managing and manipulating project work in their classes. In terms of other problems with PBL, such as the source of project materials, the development of computer networks can help. For example, the Internet, as a medium of local and global communication, can help language teachers provide easy access to the information and materials necessary for the project work.

Based on my experience, I believe that PBL can make language learning more interesting and relevant for my students because it can provide a "link between outside classroom reality and inside-classroom pedagogy" (Littlewood, 2004, p. 324). The findings indicate that the language teacher, both as a project designer and practitioner, is in a strategic position to monitor students' participation and set the tone and pace of students' involvement. Furthermore, HBLP contributes to the development of learner autonomy and encourages language learners to reflect on problems in the real world. As Fried-Booth (2002) put it, "Project work pushed forward the boundaries by bringing students into direct contact with authentic language and learning experiences not usually available within the four walls of an ELT classroom using textbooks" (p. 6).

To ensure the success of project work in Asia, I think the first action for language teachers and students is to change our stereotyped concept of language teaching and learning. Hyun and Finch (1998) have pointed out that "our view of language learning is affected by the general methodology, so that we tend to see language as a collection of discrete facts to be learned, memorized, and repeated without meaning" (p. 70). Based on this tendency, many L2 students in Asian countries favor the traditional learning style of rote learning. As educators, it is important to arouse our awareness by reflecting on our personal conceptions of language learning, because these conceptions will influence our approaches to teaching and learning.

My successful use of PBL suggests that project work should not be reserved only for Western learners. It can be applied in Asian L2 learning contexts if it is properly conducted. PBL challenged my students and me a great deal because of the culture of teaching and learning in China. However, when we responded to it, I grew along with my students. As a result, the increased awareness and knowledge I gained from my research may in turn encourage me to try further new approaches, techniques, tasks, and activities. For example, when bird flu broke out in China in 2005, I asked my students to create posters and handbooks to inform and warn other students.

Wang Ge teaches at Southwest Forestry College, China.

CHAPTER 13

How Does Course Content Affect Students' Willingness to Communicate in the L2? (*China*)

Jennifer Weathers

Issue

Learning a second or foreign language involves not only acquiring knowledge about the language but also developing the skills to use it effectively. Few teachers or researchers would deny that in order to develop these skills, particularly in speaking, it is essential for learners to actually use the target language (Hu, 2002; MacIntyre & Charos, 1996; Tsui, 1996). This realization has led to an increased focus on communicative competence in the last several decades and has prompted teachers around the world to adopt methodologies based on communicative language teaching (CLT) principles.

But "communication is more than a means of facilitating language learning, it is an important goal in itself" (MacIntyre & Charos, 1996, p. 3). Although the importance of communication is generally accepted by teachers and students alike, learners often still seem reluctant or unwilling to communicate using the second language (L2) (Nimmannit, 1998; Tsui, 1996). Many researchers and teachers have also noticed that this reticence is particularly common among Chinese and other Asian students (Nimmannit, 1998; Tsui, 1996; Wen & Clement, 2003).

As a foreign English teacher at a medium-sized university in northeast China, I encountered various degrees of reticence among students in my oral

English classes. For the most part, the freshmen English major students seemed more than willing—eager, even—to make use of both in- and out-of-class opportunities to develop their oral skills. However, I also taught one class of sophomores in a special 5-year English program who were generally much less communicative.

These students did not pass the college entrance examination but would receive the same diploma as their 4-year counterparts after studying 5 years at an increased tuition rate. Unlike the students in the regular classes who mostly came from poor, rural villages throughout China, the 5-year students were all from middle-class communities in the city or province where the university is located. Many of their families have *guanxi*, or connections, through which they will find jobs after graduation.

Perhaps as a result of their family backgrounds, many of the students in this class seemed apathetic toward studying. For example, the attendance in this class was quite poor compared to that of the regular classes: In the second semester, there were 25 absences from these 17 sophomore students over 14 weeks. On the other hand, there were only 14 absences from a total of 72 students in the three freshmen classes. In addition, 6 of the 17 students failed to turn in more than half of the homework assignments. Although the information was of little consolation, I was told that these issues with attendance and homework extended beyond my class.

In general, the proficiency levels of the students in this class were also lower than those of the regular English major students. Although a few students could not understand a word I said or express a single thought in English, several others were easily at an intermediate level in their oral proficiency. This disparity added to the challenge of teaching this class. Similarly, several students were always quick to respond, and many others never volunteered to answer. Perhaps the eagerness of the few left little time or incentive for the silent majority to pay attention and was at least partially to blame for their lack of involvement.

Throughout the year, I attempted to help these students become more proficient speakers of English by providing as many opportunities as possible for them to use the language. Still, many were reluctant to speak. As I contemplated this issue, three possibilities seemed most plausible: issues of ability, anxiety, or attitude. Maybe some students were unable to respond because they could not comprehend the instructions and questions or because they did not know how to perform the assigned tasks. For other students, the issue might have been one of fear or anxiety; perhaps they were afraid of being ridiculed for making mistakes or resented for showing off. Finally, a lack of interest or motivation might have affected some of the students. According to Oxford and Shearin (1994), "motivation determines the extent of active, personal involvement in L2 learning" and is generally considered to be one of the main factors determining language learning success (p. 12).

Background Literature

Although many of the possible explanations previously offered appear to be specific to this particular group of students in this particular context, several Chinese cultural and educational values may also help explain the students' reticence. First, Chinese culture is quite collectivistic. Wang, Brislin, Wang, Williams, and Chao (2000) explain that "collectivists are more likely to view their participation in groups as the basic unit of their self-image" (p. 30). In China, a student's self-image and identity are highly dependent on his or her relationships with classmates; as a result, he or she may feel uncomfortable standing out from the group to answer questions or express his or her ideas (Nimmannit, 1998). Similarly, although a very competent student may be able to respond correctly with little effort, he or she may fear resentment from peers for showing off (Tsui, 1996). The Chinese value of modesty, then, may prevent proficient students from displaying their abilities. On the other hand, less adept students may also avoid speaking out for fear of making mistakes and losing face. The cultural value of face protection likely makes Chinese students exceptionally "sensitive to the judgement of the public upon their language behaviours" (Wen & Clement, 2003, p. 20) and hesitant to take such risks in the classroom.

Educational traditions may also contribute to the problem of reticence in the classroom. Typical Chinese learning strategies such as reception, memorization and reproduction, and mastery (Hu, 2002) seem to encourage learners to be more passive than many teachers today would like. The first strategy, reception, illustrates the roles that teachers and students have traditionally filled. The teacher is the expert whose job is to deliver knowledge; the students are receivers, empty vessels to be filled (Hu, 2002; Pratt, 1992). In this type of teacher-centered classroom there would be little opportunity for students to share their own ideas. Although this traditional methodology has gradually been fading away, the underlying cultural values remain (Wen & Clement, 2003).

In addition, "education has traditionally been viewed more as a process of accumulating knowledge than as a practical process of constructing and using knowledge for immediate purposes" (Hu, 2002, p. 97). The Chinese educational system teaches students to value knowledge for knowledge's sake, encouraging them to memorize the material taught and reproduce it perfectly on demand (Hu, 2002). They are not, however, asked to apply the information immediately, which is one of the main tenets of CLT. Students unaccustomed to these new expectations, then, may find it difficult to take such an active role in the classroom.

Finally, in China "learning is never considered to be complete until full mastery is achieved" (Hu, 2002, p. 101). Because these students typically had spent much of their time and effort meticulously learning the "laws" of English, they may have become overly concerned with correctness (Wen & Clement,

2003). As a result, they may have been afraid to speak out until certain they could respond flawlessly, thereby missing out on many opportunities to test their hypotheses and further develop their competence.

Procedures

My real concern as I began preparing to teach this class for a second semester was "How can I get the students in this class to speak more English?" In the beginning, I planned to make three different kinds of changes that I hoped would increase the students' levels of participation—changes to the content of the lessons, to the groupings, and to the types of activities. However, as the end of the first cycle drew near, I still had many questions and hypotheses about how content could be manipulated to encourage students' active involvement in class. As a result, I decided to narrow my focus and continue experimenting with different kinds of content for the second and third cycles. My research question then became "How does course content affect students' willingness to communicate in the target language?"

CYCLE 1

After a long winter break spanning both Christmas and China's Spring Festival, I decided to begin the second semester with a lesson about holidays. I intended to ask students to discuss Chinese festivals first and then teach them about some U.S. holidays as well. However, the students were extraordinarily engaged as they debated which Chinese festivals were most important and discovered ways to explain to their foreign teacher why and how they celebrate each. We never got to U.S. holidays that day. After the class, as I pondered the students' unusual activity, it occurred to me that they may have been more responsive because they were discussing a topic with which they were all intimately acquainted.

Schema theory holds that the meaning of any text is not contained within the text itself but rather is retrieved or constructed through interaction with a reader's background knowledge (Carrell, 1984). The theory plays an important role in most models of reading comprehension and explains the results of many studies indicating that comprehension is better when content is familiar (Carrell, 1987; Johnson, 1981; Nelson, 1987). Although generally applied to the receptive skills and used to explain the accuracy or quality of comprehension, perhaps schema theory could also be applied to the productive skills and used to explain the quantity of language produced. In fact, a study by Zuengler (1993) confirms this hypothesis. She found that when interlocutors were unequally knowledgeable about the topic of conversation, the relative expert produced more words. Content knowledge, then, appears to contribute to conversational involvement and may explain the level of participation in my class that day.

As a result of this research and experience, I decided that for the first phase of my investigation I would continue to provide topics for discussion that centered on Chinese culture. I hoped that the students would find the opportunities to teach me about China both interesting and engaging and would be more willing to communicate as a result. However, I first wanted to teach a lesson on U.S. holidays so that students would have the two parallel classes to compare later. The next three lessons each began with and focused on Chinese culture, although I did continue to include some information about U.S. culture after the students' schemata were activated. The themes of these lessons were traveling, cooking, and eating out.

During this initial stage of my research, I tried many methods of collecting data. After the first lesson of the term, I began keeping a teaching journal to help me record and process my observations and reflections. I also planned to survey and interview the students in the class after each cycle to discover their reactions to the changes and their perceptions of their and their classmates' levels of participation. In addition to this second-order information, though, I also wanted to collect some first-order data.

During the 3rd week of the term, I began tape-recording each lesson. I planned to count the number of utterances each student contributed to the class discussions and perhaps time the length of each student's speech. However, after recording two classes, I discovered that the sound quality was too poor to identify the speakers or hear their comments clearly. The following week, I tried tape-recording several small-group discussions instead, hoping that the sound quality would be better with the recorders nearer to the speakers. Unfortunately, the sound quality was even worse because the room was relatively noisy with four groups conversing concurrently. In addition, I observed that many of the students seemed uncomfortable or distracted by the recorders. For example, the most active member of one group wrote down some notes on a paper and passed it around so that each student could read from the paper and contribute to the discussion. This behavior, however, was atypical, and the data collected was deemed invalid. Concluding that it was more important to preserve the natural classroom atmosphere, I decided to discontinue recording the classroom interactions.

In the 3rd week I also invited a friend, Ying (all names have been changed), to begin observing the class. Equipped with a seating chart and a key of marks to use for different types of utterances (e.g., asking a question, volunteering an answer, or answering a direct question), she began tallying each time each student spoke during whole-class discussions. She was also asked to observe the small-group interactions, although she did not record data for these. After the class, Ying expressed difficulty in accurately recording each student's participation because she was sitting behind the students and because often several students answered simultaneously during whole-class discussions. Throughout the rest of the term, Ying continued to observe the class. I did not ask her to take notes after the first 2 weeks, but we often discussed our impressions of the lessons and the students' responses to them.

Because obtaining first-order data through recordings and observations was largely unsuccessful, I proceeded with collecting second-order data. In addition to my own perceptions chronicled in my teaching journal, I triangulated the data by consulting Ying and the students themselves. In addition, I utilized methodological triangulation by collecting information from the students through surveys and interviews. At the end of the final week of the first cycle, I invited three students to come to my apartment for interviews. During the following week's lesson, I conducted a survey with the entire class.

CYCLE 2

In general, I felt that the discussions we had about Chinese culture were rather authentic, because there was a real purpose for the students to use English. However, as I watched them discussing the cultural topics in small groups before sharing their ideas with me, I realized that those tasks were actually quite artificial and unnatural because they all already knew the answers. As a result, for the second phase of my research, I decided to choose more relevant topics that would allow the students to interact more meaningfully with one another instead of simply preparing ideas to share with me.

Many experts have asserted that choosing topics and tasks that relate to students' interests will likely increase their motivation and willingness to communicate in the L2 (Dornyei, 1994; Nimmannit, 1998). Therefore, I decided to focus my next five lessons on the theme of relationships. In addition to being a familiar topic, I believed that discussing friendship and dating would be intrinsically interesting for this particularly sociable class of students.

During this phase of my investigation, I continued to record my observations and perceptions in my teaching journal and discuss the students' participation with my observer. I also interviewed one of my original interviewees again and administered another survey with the students in the class.

CYCLE 3

As I began the second cycle, I expected the discussions about everyday topics such as friendship and dating to be more relevant because the students probably already talked about them in Chinese. Afterwards, however, I realized that the conversations were still not very realistic: Why should they talk about these things in English when they are all Chinese? Therefore, for my third and final cycle, I decided to turn to authentic materials to provide the content for the lessons, hoping it would be more natural for students to discuss Western materials in English. I also supposed that the students would find the materials interesting and would be more willing to communicate in the target language as a result. Dornyei (1994) and Shumin (1997) both recommend utilizing authentic materials such as recordings, films, and texts to increase students' desire and willingness to communicate. Therefore, I decided to experiment with literature, music, and films for the three lessons that remained.

Before the first class, I asked the students to read Kate Chopin's (1894) "The Story of an Hour" and answer several comprehension questions for homework so that they would be prepared to discuss elements such as characters, setting, and themes during our time together. In the class, I had students discuss several questions with a small group and find references in the text that supported their opinions. I hoped that by having the text in front of them even some of the least participatory students would be able and willing to read a sentence or two to contribute to the discussion. I then asked each group to share their answers with the class so they could compare their opinions and interpretations.

Several problems with this lesson quickly emerged. First, it was fairly obvious that a few students had not read the story. However, because I was not sure, I allowed them to remain in the classroom. As a result of being unprepared, they often talked together in Chinese instead of paying attention to the lesson, which was quite distracting to the students who were actively discussing the story. Even the students who appeared prepared, though, seemed to be talking in Chinese more than English. When I approached a group and asked a direct question, they were able to answer insightfully, but perhaps the deep content was difficult for them to discuss in their second language. Finally, at the end of the class when I asked, "Did you like the story?" most responded that they did. However, several expressed dissatisfaction with the story because as single young men and women they could not easily relate to its theme of the potentially oppressive nature of marriage.

The 2nd week I chose two songs to use in class as a basis for discussions about advice and self-esteem. The students first listened to the song "Everybody's Free (To Wear Sunscreen)" (Schmich, 1997, track 5) and filled in the missing words on their handout of the lyrics. They were then asked to discuss several questions about the song's themes. Unfortunately, many of the students felt the need to look up all the words they did not know before commencing their discussions, which took a good deal of time with this long song. After a brief discussion of the first song, I played Christina Aguilera's "Beautiful" (Perry, 2001, track 11) as the students read along on their second handout. This song was shorter and easier for the students to understand, but they still spent some time looking up words before proceeding with the next discussion.

In retrospect, I should have asked the students to read the lyrics at home before coming to class so that our limited time together could have been spent talking instead of reading. Or, rather than asking students to interact with the lyrics of songs, I could have had them discuss the sound of various styles of music. For example, they could have described the feeling of the songs and the instruments they heard, or guessed what the songs might be about and what kind of people might listen to each.

Two weeks before the third and final lesson of Cycle 3, I invited the students to come in groups of four or five to my apartment to watch a movie together. Even after several groups called to reschedule, only 11 of the 17 students came. I chose a different movie for each group so that in class the students could describe and compare the various films.

For the class discussion, after a brief introduction of movie genres I asked the six students who had not come to watch the movies to leave because they would have had nothing to contribute to the remainder of the class. I then asked each movie group to discuss their film's characters, plot, and theme. I warned them that each student would need to be able to describe the events of the movie because after a few minutes they would form new groups and would have to explain their film to several students who had watched different movies. When the new groups formed, the students enthusiastically began describing the films in great detail. In fact, I had to ask them to tell only the most important parts so the other students would have time to share as well!

This discussion was the most exciting of the entire semester, probably because the students really enjoyed the movies and were eager to discuss them. Still, there were a few complications. First, not all of the students needed to speak in the new groups. Because five students had watched one movie, four the second, and only two the last, there were two or three representatives from two of the movies in each of the new groups. In addition, several groups were reluctant to split and join other students. Because they usually work with the same part-ners or groups, they seemed somewhat uncomfortable with other, less familiar classmates.

The following week, after the class's written exam, I gave each student a course evaluation survey. I also invited the three students who completed their surveys most conscientiously to come for interviews later in the week.

Results

CYCLE 1

On the Cycle 1 survey, I first asked students to compare discussing Chinese and U.S. culture. A majority of the students (69%) indicated that they found Chinese culture easier to talk about; the remaining students found them equally easy. Only a few students found either Chinese or U.S. culture more interest-ing; a majority (63%) were equally interested in both (see Table 1). Most of the students (69%) perceived that they and their classmates were talking more this term than the first term; I agreed. When I asked them to explain why they

---

Table 1. Cycle 1 Survey Results (*n* = 16)

Area of Comparison	Chinese Culture	Equal	American Culture
Easier to talk about	11	5	0
More interesting	2	10	4

were talking more, several themes emerged in these 11 students' responses: Five mentioned an increased ability or vocabulary; two mentioned being less anxious; and eight mentioned positive attitudes toward English or the class.

The same themes emerged in the interviews when I asked why some students were talking more than others. One interviewee, Beth (personal communication, April 3, 2005), admitted that she did not speak much because she felt shy and afraid of making mistakes. She speculated that other students talked more for several reasons: Their English was better, they liked to speak, and they liked "showing themselves." Another student, Angela (personal communication, April 4, 2005), said she felt that the most talkative students were not necessarily better at English but rather just liked speaking English. Audrey (personal communication, April 8, 2005), one of the more active students, repeatedly mentioned several things that she thought prevented her classmates from speaking: Their English levels were very low, their vocabularies were insufficient, they did not like English, and they were not interested in the topics. She seemed to feel very strongly that the biggest cause of their unwillingness to communicate was their dislike for the subject. She explained, "They choose study English, um, maybe their parents order them to choose. But, they really don't like. You know, if they don't like something, they will not pay attention to."

Although certain students remained less talkative than others, I agreed that the students in general were more willing to communicate than they had been the first term. I believed that this increase was due in part to the changes in the content.

CYCLE 2

Attendance was poor during the second cycle and may have affected the survey results: Students who missed several classes may have selected answers that seemed logical but were not necessarily based on actual experiences. Perhaps because of this, there were several notable discrepancies between the students' and my impressions of their involvement during this second phase of research. First, a majority of the students (71%) indicated that they had more to say about everyday topics than about cultural topics (see Table 2). In her interview, Audrey (personal communication, May 13, 2005) agreed, explaining that her classmates could not talk as much or express their ideas about the difficult cultural topics in English. Conversely, my perception was that the students had

Table 2. Cycle 2 Survey Results (*n* = 14)

Area of Preference	Cultural Topics	Equal	Everyday Topics
More to say	0	4	10
More interesting	1	7	5
More useful	3	8	3

actually been contributing more during the cultural discussions, especially when asked to explain something about China to me.

In addition, five students found everyday topics more interesting, and about half of the students thought the cultural and everyday topics were equally interesting (see Table 2). However, when asked which activity from the previous 5 weeks had been their favorite, the most common response was a simulated wedding ceremony we had performed, which was much more of a cultural activity.

CYCLE 3

Of those who turned in the final course evaluation surveys, more than 90% agreed that they had more to say about a topic when they prepared something ahead of time, and they claimed that they would be willing to prepare something before every class. However, because several students failed to read the story or watch a movie, I was somewhat skeptical that they would actually follow through with that. In addition, Audrey (personal communication, June 17, 2005) admitted that her classmates, rather than completing assignments on their own, often asked if they could copy her homework before class began. Feeling obliged, Audrey generally consented.

When asked to compare the three types of content used throughout the semester, more students preferred talking about the everyday topics; in addition, they found them most interesting and easiest to talk about (see Table 3). The comments from the interviews explained these results. When I asked Audrey what kinds of topics she thought would appeal to her classmates, she said, "the topic about something that's close to us. . . . I think they will interest in it. If

Table 3. Cycle 3 Survey Results (*n* = 14)

Area of Preference	Cultural Topics	Everyday Topics	Authentic Materials
Liked most	3	9	2
Most interesting	4	10	0
Easiest to talk about	2	8	4

the topic is, um, uh, difficult and far to us, they will not enjoy." Lydia (personal communication, June 16, 2005) also said that the everyday topics were easiest, "because the things, the topic is very near in our life. So I think, we can a lot of ideas about the everyday topic."

Finally, when comparing the widespread use of discussions during the second semester with the first term's reliance on a more functional textbook, 79% of the students said they preferred the discussions, and 73% agreed that the discussions helped them to talk more than using the book. When asked why, four students mentioned that the discussions were more interesting. Beth, for example, wrote, "Because in this term we discuss questions both are we interested, it can make we have more words to talk." These responses seemed to confirm the important role that interest plays in students' willingness to communicate.

Reflection

One of my main purposes for conducting teacher research was to solve problems in my classroom. However, after nearly 4 months of questioning, applying changes, and monitoring results, I am still not satisfied with the level of participation in this 5-year English major class. Overall, I believe that the students did talk more this term than they did during the first term, but countless factors could have contributed to this change. Regarding the course's content, the students' willingness to communicate in the L2 appeared to be directly related to their interest in the subject matter. However, a lack of interest in English itself may have contributed to some students' lack of motivation and, as a result, their reticence.

Scovel (2001) writes, "Of all the affective (emotional) factors discussed over the years by both teachers and SLA [second language acquisition] researchers, by far the most predominant is . . . motivation" (p. 121). Motivation has received this abundance of attention because it is generally believed to be one of the most important variables affecting students' success in learning a second or foreign language (Dornyei, 1994; Oxford & Shearin, 1994). Several dichotomies have been proposed to explain different types of motivation, and research has attempted to discover the effects of each. However, most experts today agree that "it is the overall amount, not necessarily the type, of motivation that counts most in SLA" (Scovel, 2001, p. 125). In addition, Oxford and Shearin as well as Scovel have noted that kinds and degrees of motivation can and do change over time, implying that motivation can be changed as well. Researchers have tested numerous hypotheses about means of increasing students' motivation and offer a myriad of suggestions for classroom teachers. Oxford and Shearin, for example, described five implications of their motivational model, and Dornyei listed 30 strategies with which teachers could experiment.

However, before considering what other kinds of changes might positively influence this class's motivation and willingness to communicate, I wanted to revisit the challenges of this particular teaching context by examining both my and the students' own perceptions of the problem. First, at all three of our meetings, Audrey (personal communication, April 8, 2005; May 13, 2005; June 17, 2005) identified her classmates' dislike of English as the major source of their unwillingness to communicate. Another student, Lydia (personal communication, June 16, 2005), drew a connection between enjoying a subject and learning it well: "I think everyone, if we are very enjoy it we can learn it more and more." My conversation with Dawn (personal communication, June 16, 2005) revealed a similar belief. "I think, first things, the people must, must interest in English," she said. But when asked if there was anything that teachers could do to make English more interesting for students, Dawn replied flatly, "no." These students all seemed to agree that a lack of intrinsic motivation was affecting at least some of their classmates.

Extrinsic motivation also appeared to be lacking for the students in this class. First, scoring poorly on exams and failing classes did not hinder their ability to progress to the next class or grade. Graduation was basically guaranteed, regardless of performance. Audrey (personal communication, June 17, 2005) explained, "All students in our class, after the university, they all can get a diploma, so they think study hard is not very important." I then asked about the effects of students' studies on finding jobs, to which Audrey replied, "Maybe their parents has a method." Dawn (personal communication, June 16, 2005) had a similar explanation: "Some people's family have many money, so they don't very like study. His father and mother will help him find job." But, I wondered, if the underlying problem is a lack of motivation, what is the next step toward remedying the situation?

As a result of my observations and analyses of the data collected through this process of teacher research, I now have a deeper understanding of the issue of reticence in this class, and understanding the problem is perhaps the first step toward finding a solution. However, rather than continuing to make changes to individual courses or instructors' approaches, I believe that the real change needs to occur at the institutional level. The following proposal would require the collaboration of several teachers and administrators over an extended period of time; however, I believe the time and effort invested would be worth the cost.

First, instead of allowing students to progress and graduate regardless of their efforts and achievements, a 1- or 2-year probationary period should be established for the students in this program. Measures of each student's progress in each of the four skill areas should be taken into account and various sources of information consulted, (e.g., class participation, grades, scores on examinations). At the end of the probationary period, if a student is determined to have made considerable effort and progress, he or she should be integrated into one of the regular, 4-year English major classes. However, if his or her performance fails to meet the school's standards, the student should be asked to leave the university.

Traditionally, students in the 5-year classes have been labeled as bad students from the beginning and have, not surprisingly, learned to accept that role. Although they are generally less diligent and proficient than their peers, the students' haste to self-criticize was disconcerting. Dawn (personal communication, June 16, 2005), for example, commented, "My class, every people study English not very well." Lydia (personal communication, June 16, 2005) made a similar remark: "I think in our class, our study is not very well. And maybe sometimes we are very lazy." This poor self-image and lack of confidence may have detrimental effects on the students' future studies because "language learners may very well be self-fulfilling prophets when it comes to SLA" (Scovel, 2001, p. 124). By proving their abilities and integrating with the regular classes, these students might finally be able to elude the stereotype of inadequacy.

Motivated by the forthcoming consequences of their actions, these students would be bound to make progress in their language learning endeavors, which would likely increase their motivation to continue studying. This motivation, then, would stimulate further progress, and the cycle would continue. Of course, these envisioned results are merely speculative at this point. But by implementing these changes and systematically observing the effects, greater insight into this issue could be achieved.

Jennifer Weathers teaches English as a second language in a private language school in Cincinnati, Ohio.

References

Albertson, L. R. (1998). *A cognitive behavioral intervention study: Assessing the effects of strategy instruction on story writing.* Unpublished doctoral dissertation, University of Washington.

Allwright, D. (2005). From teaching points to learning opportunities and beyond. *TESOL Quarterly, 39*(1), 9–31.

Almarza, G. G. (1996). Student foreign language teacher's knowledge growth. In D. Freeman & J. C. Richards (Eds.), *Teacher learning in language teaching* (pp. 50–78). Cambridge: Cambridge University Press.

Anderson, J. R. (1983). *The architecture of cognition.* Harvard: Harvard University Press.

Aoki, N., & Smith, R. (1999). Learner autonomy in cultural context: The case of Japan. In D. Crabbe & S. Cotterall (Eds.), *Learner autonomy in language learning: Defining the field and effecting change* (pp. 19–27). Frankfurt: Peter Lang.

Ballard, B. (1996). Through language to learning: Preparing overseas students for study in Western universities. In H. Coleman (Ed.), *Society and the language classroom* (pp. 148–168). Cambridge: Cambridge University Press.

Ballard, B., & Clanchy, J. (1991). *Teaching students from overseas: A brief guide for lecturers and supervisors.* Melbourne: Longman Cheshire.

Barkhuizen, G. P. (1998). Discovering learners' perceptions of ESL classroom teaching/learning activities in a South African context. *TESOL Quarterly, 32*(1), 85–108.

Bazerman, C. (2004). Speech acts, genres, and activity systems: How texts organize activity and people. In C. Bazerman & P. Prior (Eds.), *What writing does and how it does it: An introduction to analyzing texts and textual practices* (pp. 309–339). Mahwah, NJ: Lawrence Erlbaum.

BBC. (n.d.) BBC World Service Learning English magazine radio programme. Retrieved May 2, 2006, from http://www.bbc.co.uk/worldservice /learningenglish/radio/index.shtml

Beckett, G. H., & Slater, T. (2005). The project framework: A tool for language, content, and skills integration. *ELT Journal, 59*(2), 108–116.

Benson, P. (2001). *Teaching and researching autonomy in language learning*. Essex: Longman.

Benson, P. (2005). (Auto)biography and learner diversity. In P. Benson & D. Nunan (Eds.), *Learner's stories: Difference and diversity in language learning* (pp. 4–21). Cambridge: Cambridge University Press.

Benson, P., Chik, A., & Lim, H. (2003). Becoming autonomous in an Asian context. In D. Palefreyman & R. Smith (Eds.), *Learner autonomy across cultures: Language education perspectives*. London: Palgrave Macmillan.

Block, D. (1996). A window on the classroom: Classroom events viewed from different angles. In K. M. Bailey & D. Nunan (Eds.), *Voices from the language classroom: Qualitative research in second language education* (pp. 168–194). Cambridge: Cambridge University Press.

Bloor, T., & Bloor, M. (2004). *The functional analysis of English* (2nd ed.). London: Arnold.

Braddock, R., Roberts, P., Zheng, C., & Guzman, T. (1995). *Survey on skill development in intercultural teaching of international students*. Sydney: Macquarie University, Asia Pacific Research Institute.

Breen, M. (1989). The evaluation cycle for language learning. In R. K. Johnson (Ed.), *The second language curriculum* (pp. 187–206). Cambridge: Cambridge University Press.

Brinton, D. M., Snow, M. A., & Wesche, M. B. (1989). *Content-based second language instruction*. New York: Newbury House.

Brown, A. (1999). *Singapore English in a nutshell: An alphabetical description of its features*. Singapore: Federal.

Brown, G. (1990). *Listening to spoken English* (2nd ed.). London: Longman.

Brown, J. D. (1995). *The elements of language curriculum: A systematic approach to program development*. Boston: Heinle & Heinle.

Brown, J. D. (1996). *Testing in language programs*. Upper Saddle River, NJ: Prentice Hall Regents.

Brown, J. D. (2001). *Using surveys in language programs*. Cambridge: Cambridge University Press.

Brown, J. D., & Yamashita, S. O. (1995a). English language entrance examinations at Japanese universities: 1993 and 1994. In J. D. Brown & S.O. Yamashita (Eds.), *Language testing in Japan* (pp. 86–100). Tokyo: The Japan Association for Language Teaching.

Brown, J. D., & Yamashita, S. O. (1995b). English language entrance examinations at Japanese universities: What do we know about them? *JALT Journal,* 17(1), 7–30.

Bruner, J. (1996). *The culture of education.* Cambridge, MA: Harvard University Press.

Carrell, P. L. (1984). Schema theory and ESL reading: Classroom implications and applications. *Modern Language Journal,* 68(4), 332–343.

Carrell, P. L. (1987). Content and formal schemata in ESL reading. *TESOL Quarterly,* 21(3), 461–481.

Casanave, C. P. (2004). *Controversies in second language writing: Dilemmas and decisions in research and instruction.* Ann Arbor: University of Michigan Press.

Cheng, K. M. (1996, November). *Excellence in education: Is it culture-free?* Keynote paper presented at the annual conference of the Educational Research Association, Singapore.

Cheng, X. (2000). Asian students' reticence revisited. *System,* 28(3), 435–446.

Cheng, X. (2002). Chinese EFL students' cultures of learning. In C. Lee & W. Littlewood (Eds.), *Culture, communication, and language pedagogy* (pp. 103–116). Hong Kong, SAR, China: Hong Kong Baptist University Press.

Chinokul, S. (2004, September–December). A comparative study of the process of learning to teach English as a foreign language via reflective teaching. *Journal of Research Methodology,* 17(3), 321–339.

Chopin, K. (1894). The story of an hour. Retrieved May 2, 2005, from http://www .vcu.edu/engweb/webtexts/hour/

Christie, F., & Misson, R. (1998). Framing the issues in literacy education. In F. Christie & R. Misson (Eds.), *Literacy and schooling* (pp. 1–17). London: Routledge.

Cleverley, J. (1991). *The schooling of China: Tradition and modernity in Chinese education.* North Sydney, Australia: Allen & Unwin.

Cortazzi, M., & Jin, L. (1996). Cultures of learning: Language classrooms in China. In H. Coleman (Ed.), *Society and the language classroom* (pp. 169–206). Cambridge: Cambridge University Press.

Cotterall, S. (1995). Developing a course strategy for learner autonomy. *ELT Journal,* 49(3), 219–227.

Cotterall, S., & Reinders, H. (2001). Fortress or bridge? Learners' perceptions and practice in self-access language learning. *Tesolanz,* 8, 23–38.

Curtis, A. (1999). What EFL teachers learn from action research. *Proceedings of the 1998 Korea TESOL Conference, Korea,* 13–14.

Day, R. R. (2004). A critical look at authentic materials. *Journal of Asia TEFL,* 1(1), 101–114.

Day, R. R., & Bamford, J. (1998). *Extensive reading in the second language classroom.* Cambridge: Cambridge University Press.

Dewey, J. (1938). *Experience and education.* New York: Macmillan.

Dickinson, L. (1992). *Learner autonomy 2: Learner training for language learning.* Dublin: Authentik.

Dooley, K. (2001). Re-envisioning teacher preparation: Lessons from China. *Journal of Education for Teaching,* 27(3), 241–251.

Doughty, C., & Williams, J. (Eds.). (1998). *Focus on form in classroom second language acquisition*. Cambridge: Cambridge University Press.

Dornyei, Z. (1994). Motivation and motivating in the foreign language classroom. *Modern Language Journal, 78*, 273–284.

Educational, Inspirational and Devotional Tools for Catholic Educators, Catechists, Parents, and Students. (n.d.). Reflection journal activities [Online resource]. Retrieved May 1, 2006, from http://www.catholic-forum.com/churches /cathteach/outcomes_rubric_reflection_journal.html

Educational Testing Service. (2005). *TOEFL iBT tips: How to prepare for the next generation TOEFL test and communicate with confidence*. Princeton, NJ: Author.

Edwards, H., Smith, B., & Webb, G. (Eds.). (2001). *Lecturing: Case studies, experience, and practice*. London: Kogan Page.

Eisterhold, J. C. (1990). Reading-writing connections: Toward a description for second language learners. In B. Kroll (Ed.), *Second language writing: Research insights for the classroom* (pp. 88–101). Cambridge: Cambridge University Press.

Ellis, R. (2003). *Task-based language learning and teaching*. Oxford: Oxford University Press.

Ellis, R., Basturkmen, H., & Loewen, S. (2001). Preemptive focus on form in the ESL classroom. *TESOL Quarterly, 35*(3), 407–432.

Farrell, T. S. C. (2004). *Reflecting on classroom communication in Asia*. Singapore: Longman.

Ferris, D., & Tagg, T. (1996). Academic listening/speaking tasks for ESL students: Problems, suggestions, and implications. *TESOL Quarterly, 30*(2), 297–320.

Firth, A., & Wagner, J. (1997). On discourse, communication, and (some) fundamental concepts in SLA research. *Modern Language Journal, 81*(3), 285–300.

Fischer, F., Bruhn, J., Grasel, C., & Mandl, H. (2002). Fostering collaborative knowledge construction with visualization tools. *Learning and Instruction, 12*(2), 213–232.

Flavell, J. H. (1979). Metacognition and cognitive monitoring: A new area of cognitive developmental inquiry. *American Psychologist, 34*(10), 906–911.

Flower, L., & Hayes, J. R. (1981). A cognitive process theory of writing. *College Composition and Communication*, 365–387.

Flowerdew, J. (Ed.). (1994). *Academic listening, research perspectives*. Cambridge: Cambridge University Press.

Flowerdew, J., & Miller, L. (1995). On the notion of culture in L2 lectures. *TESOL Quarterly, 29*(2), 345–373.

Forsyth, D. (2003). *The professor's guide to teaching: Psychological principles and practices*. Washington, DC: American Psychological Association.

Freedman, A. (1994). "Do as I say": The relationship between teaching and learning new genres. In A. Freedman & P. Medway (Eds.), *Genre and the new rhetoric* (pp. 191–210). London: Taylor and Francis.

Freeman, D. (1998). How to see: The challenges of integrating teaching and research in your own classroom. *The English Connection, 2,* 6–8.

Fried-Booth, D. L. (2002). Introduction. *Resource books for teachers: Project work.* Oxford: Oxford University Press. Retrieved December 12, 2005, from http://www.oup.com/pdf/elt/catalogue/0-19-437225-1-a.pdf

Fromkin, V., Blair, D., & Collins, P. (1999). *An introduction to language* (4th ed.). Sydney: Harcourt.

Fry, H., Ketteridge, S., & Marshall, S. (Eds.). (1999). *A handbook for teaching and learning in higher education: Enhancing academic practice.* London: Kogan Page.

Gardner, D., & Miller, L. (1999). *Establishing self-access: From theory to practice.* Cambridge: Cambridge University Press.

Garrott, J. R. (1995). Chinese cultural values: New angles, added insights. *International Journal of Intercultural Relations, 19*(2), 211–225.

Genesee, F., & Upshur, J. A. (1996). *Classroom-based evaluation in second language education.* New York: Cambridge University Press.

Ghaye, A., & Ghaye, K. (1998). *Teaching and learning through critical reflective practice.* London: David Fulton.

Goh, C. C. M. (1997). Metacognitive awareness and second language listeners. *ELT Journal, 51*(4), 391–397.

Goh, C. C. M. (1998). How learners with different listening abilities use comprehension strategies and tactics. *Language Teaching Research, 2*(2), 124–147.

Goh, C. C. M. (2002). *Teaching listening in the language classroom.* Singapore: SEAMEO Regional Language Centre.

Gorman, G. E., & Clayton, P. (1997). *Qualitative research for the information professional: A practical handbook* (1st ed.). London: Library Association Publishing.

Gorsuch, G. (1998). *Yakudoku* in EFL instruction in two Japanese high school classrooms: An exploratory study. *JALT Journal, 20*(1), 6–32.

Graves, K. (1996). A framework of course development processes. In K. Graves (Ed.), *Teachers as course developers* (pp. 12–38). Cambridge: Cambridge University Press.

Gupta, A. F. (1994). *The step-tongue: Children's English in Singapore.* Clevedon, England: Multilingual Matters.

Haste, H. (1987). Growing into rules. In J. Bruner & H. Haste (Eds.), *Making sense: The child's construction of the world* (pp. 163–195). London: Methuen.

Hativah, N. (2001). *Teaching for effective learning in higher education.* Boston: Kluwer.

Hativah, N., & Marincovich, M. (Eds.). (1995). *Disciplinary differences in teaching and learning: Implications for practice.* San Francisco: Jossey-Bass.

Hato, Y. (2005). Problems with top-down goal setting in second language education: A case study of the "Action Plan to Cultivate 'Japanese with English Abilities.'" *JALT Journal, 27*(1), 33–52.

Hayes, J. R. (1996). A new framework for understanding cognition and affect in writing. In C. M. Levy & S. Ransdell (Eds.), *The science of writing: Theories, methods, individual differences, and applications* (pp. 1–27). Mahwah, NJ: Lawrence Erlbaum.

Hinkel, E. (2002). *Second language writers' text: Linguistic and rhetorical features.* Mahwah, NJ: Lawrence Erlbaum.

Ho, J., & Crookall, D. (1995). Breaking with Chinese cultural traditions: Learner autonomy in English language teaching. *System, 32*(2), 235–244.

Holec, H. (1985). *Autonomy in foreign language learning.* Oxford: Pergamon.

Holec, H. (1987). The learner as manager: Managing learning or managing to learn? In A. Wenden & J. Rubin (Eds.), *Learner strategies in language learning* (pp. 145–157). Hertfordshire: Prentice Hall.

Holliday, A. (2005). *The struggle to teach English as an international language.* Oxford: Oxford University Press.

Hollingsworth, S. (1989). Prior beliefs and cognitive change in learning to teach. *American Educational Research Journal, 26,* 160–189.

Horton, P. B., McConny, A. A., Gallo, M., Woods, A. L., & Hamelin, O. (1993). An investigation of the effectiveness of concept mapping as an instructional tool. *Science Education, 77*(1), 95–111.

Horwitz, E. K. (1988). The beliefs about language learning of beginning university foreign language students. *Modern Language Journal, 72,* 283–294.

Hu, G. (2002). Potential cultural resistance to pedagogical imports: The case of communicative language teaching in China. *Language, Culture and Curriculum, 15*(2), 93–105. Retrieved July 9, 2005, from http://www.multilingual-matters .net/lcc/015/0093/lcc0150093.pdf

Hu, J. (2004). *The report for employment of graduates.* Beijing, China: China Compilation and Translation Press.

Hurd, S. (1998). Too carefully led or too carelessly left alone? *Language Learning Journal, 17,* 70–74.

Hwang, C. C. (2005, March). Effective education through popular authentic materials. *Asian EFL Journal.* Retrieved March 8, 2005, from http://www.asian-efl-journal.com/march_05_ch.php

Hyun, T. D., & Finch, A. (1998). *Task-based teaching in a traditional setting: Understanding the students.* Proceedings of the 1997 Korea TESOL Conference, Kyoung-ju, South Korea, 69–76.

Jamestown Publishing. (1999). *Six-way paragraphs.* Lincolnwood, IL: Author.

Jamestown Publishing. (2000). *Six-way paragraphs in the content areas.* Lincolnwood, IL: Author.

Johnson, K. (1992). The relationship between teachers' beliefs and practices during literacy instruction for nonnative speakers of English. *Journal of Reading Behavior, 24,* 83–108.

Johnson, K. E. (1995). *Understanding communication in second language classrooms.* New York: Cambridge University Press.

Johnson, K. E. (1999). *Understanding language teaching: Reasoning in action.* Boston: Heinle & Heinle.

Johnson, K. E., & Golombek, P. R. (2002). *Teachers' narrative inquiry as professional development*. Cambridge: Cambridge University Press.

Johnson, P. (1981). Effects on reading comprehension of language complexity and cultural background of a text. *TESOL Quarterly, 15*(2), 169–181.

Jones, J. (1995). Self-access and culture. *ELT Journal, 40*(3), 228–234.

Joram, E., & Gabriele, A. J. (1998). Preservice teachers' prior beliefs: Transforming obstacles into opportunities. *Teaching & Teacher Education, 14*(2), 175–191.

Kagan, D. M. (1990). Ways of evaluating teacher cognition: Inferences concerning the Goldilocks principle. *Review of Educational Research, 60*, 419–469.

Kagan, D. M. (1992). Implications of research on teacher belief. *Educational Psychologist, 27*, 65–90.

Kang, L. (2003). Chinese children's changing family and school environments. *Journal of Family and Economic Issues, 24*(4), 381–395.

Kennett, P. (2004). Trainer training across the curriculum. In D. Hayes (Ed.), *Trainer development: Principles and practice from language teacher training*. Melbourne: Language Australia.

Kern, R. (2000). *Literacy and language teaching*. Oxford: Oxford University Press.

Khanh, D. T. K., & An, N. T. H. (2005). Teachers' attitudes to classroom research in Vietnam. *Teacher's Edition, 18*, 4–7.

Knowles, M. (1975). *Self-directed learning: A guide for learners and teachers*. New York: Association Press.

Kohonen, V. (1991). *Foreign language learning as learner education*. Paper presented at University of Helsinki, Finland.

Kramsch, C. (1995). The applied linguist and foreign language teacher: Can they talk to each other? In G. Cook & B. Seidlhofer (Eds.), *Principle and practice in applied linguistics: Studies in honour of H. G. Widdowson* (pp. 43–56). Oxford: Oxford University Press.

Kumaravadivelu, B. (1991). Language-learning tasks: Teacher intention and learner interpretation. *ELT Journal, 45*(2), 98–107.

Kumaravadivelu, B. (2003). *Beyond methods*. New Haven, CT: Yale University Press.

Larsen-Freeman, D. (1986). *Techniques and principles in language teaching*. Oxford: Oxford University Press.

Lee, I. (2005). The implementation of project-based learning: A study in two Hong Kong secondary English classrooms. *Journal of Asia TEFL, 2*(1), 21–54.

Lee, J. F. (2000). *Tasks and communicating in language classrooms*. Boston: McGraw-Hill Higher Education.

Leki, I., & Carson, J. (1997). "Completely different worlds": EAP and the writing experiences of ESL students in university courses. *TESOL Quarterly, 31*(1), 39–69.

Li, J. Y. (2005). An empirical study on learning strategies of tertiary-level EFL learners in China. *Journal of Asia TEFL, 2*(1), 131–154.

Li, M. S. (1999, July). *Discourse and culture of learning—Communication challenges*. Paper presented at 1999 joint conference of Australian Association for Research in Education and New Zealand Association for Research in

Education, Melbourne. Retrieved May 20, 2004, from http://www.aare.edu .au/99pap/lim99015.htm

Liddicoat, A. J., Crozet, C., & Lo Bianco, J. (2000). Striving for the third place: Consequences and implications. In J. Lo Bianco, A. J. Liddicoat, & C. Crozet (Eds.), *Striving for the third place: Intercultural competence through education* (pp. 181–187). Melbourne: The National Languages and Literacy Institute of Australia.

Lightbown, P., & Spada, N. (1999). *How languages are learned* (2nd ed.). Oxford: Oxford University Press.

Little, D. (1991). *Learner autonomy 1: Definitions, issues, and problems.* Dublin: Authentik.

Little, D. (1995a). Learner autonomy: A theoretical construct and its practical application. *Die Neueren Sprachen, 93*(5), 430–442.

Little, D. (1995b). Learning as dialogue: The dependence of learner autonomy on teacher autonomy. *System, 23*(2), 175–181.

Littlejohn, A. (1985). Learner choice in language study. *ELT Journal, 39*(4), 253–61.

Littlewood, W. (1999). Defining and developing autonomy in East Asian contexts. *Applied Linguistics, 20*(1), 71–94.

Littlewood, W. (2000). Do Asian students really want to listen and obey? *ELT Journal, 54*(1), 31–35.

Littlewood, W. (2001). Students' attitudes towards classroom language learning. *Language Teaching Research, 5*(1), 3–28.

Littlewood, W. (2004). The task-based approach: Some questions and suggestions. *ELT Journal, 58*(4), 319–326.

Liu, N., & Littlewood, W. (1997). Why do many students appear reluctant to participate in classroom learning discourse? *System, 25*(3), 371–384.

Lo, R. (2001).The role of class teachers in a key secondary school in Shanghai. *Pastoral Care in Education, 19*(1), 20–27.

LoCastro, V. (1996). English language education in Japan. In H. Coleman (Ed.), *Society and the language classroom* (pp. 40–58). Cambridge: Cambridge University Press.

Lortie, D. (1975). *Schoolteacher.* Chicago: University of Chicago Press.

MacIntyre, P. D., & Charos, C. (1996). Personality, attitudes, and affect as predictors of second language communication. *Journal of Language and Social Psychology, 15*(1), 3–26.

Mariani, L. (1997). Teacher support and teacher challenge in promoting learner autonomy. *Perspectives, 23*(2). Available: http://www.iatefl.org.pl/tdal/n6luciano .htm

Martin, J. R. (1996). Evaluating disruption: Symbolising theme in junior secondary narrative. In R. Hasan & G. Williams (Eds.), *Literacy and society* (pp. 125–171). London: Longman.

McCarthy, M. (2001). *Issues in applied linguistics.* Cambridge: Cambridge University Press.

McDonough, J. (1994). A teacher looks at teachers' diaries. *ELT Journal, 48*(1), 57–65.

McGraw-Hill. (n.d.). *SRA reading labs.* DeSoto, TX: Author.

McKay, S. (2000). An investigation of five Japanese English teachers' reflections on their U.S. MA TESOL practicum experience. *JALT Journal, 22*(1), 46–68.

Medgyes, P. (1992). Native or nonnative: Who's worth more? *ELT Journal, 46*(4), 340–349.

Meijer, P. C., Verloop, N., & Beijaard, D. (1999). Exploring language teachers' practical knowledge about teaching reading comprehension. *Teaching and Teacher Education, 15*, 59–84.

Mendelsohn, D. (1995). Applying learning strategies in the second/foreign language listening comprehension lesson. In D. Mendelsohn & J. Rubin (Eds.), *A guide for the teaching of second language listening* (pp. 132–150). San Diego, CA: Dominie Press.

Mergendoller, R., & Sacks, C. (1994). Concerning the relationship between teachers' theoretical orientations toward reading and their concept maps. *Teaching & Teacher Education, 10*(6), 589–599.

Miller, L. (1999). Self-access learning in primary and secondary schools: The Malaysian experience and the Hong Kong potential. In B. Morrison (Ed.), *Experiments and evaluation in self-access language learning* (pp. 61–72). Hong Kong: HASALD.

Ministry of Education, Culture, Sports, Science, & Technology. (2005). *Statistical abstract (Education, culture, sports, science, and technology).* Tokyo: Author.

Mohan, B. (1986). *Language and content.* Reading, MA: Addison-Wesley.

Morine-Dershimer, G. (1993). Tracing conceptual change in preservice teachers. *Teaching & Teacher Education, 9*(1), 15–26.

Moss, D., & Van Duzer, C. (1998). Project-based learning for adult English language learners. ERIC Digest. Retrieved December 12, 2005, from http://www.ericdigests.org/1999-4/project.htm

Nassaji, H., & Fotos, S. (2004). Current developments in research on the teaching of grammar. *Annual Review of Applied Linguistics, 24*, 126–145.

Nation, I. S. P. (1990). *Teaching and learning vocabulary.* Boston: Newbury.

Nation, I. S. P. (2001). *Learning vocabulary in another language.* Cambridge: Cambridge University Press.

Nelson, G. L. (1987). Culture's role in reading comprehension: A schema theoretical approach. *Journal of Reading, 30*(5), 424–429.

Nguyen, D. C. (2000). Seminar with students' self-study nowadays. *Dai Hoc va Giao Duc Chuyen Nghiep* [Review of Higher and Vocational Education], *13*, 14–15.

Nguyen, Q. C. (2005). *Evaluation of students' research work.* Danang: Danang Publisher.

Nimmannit, S. (1998). Maximizing students' oral skills: The Asian context. *Language Teacher* online journal. Retrieved April 9, 2005, from http://www.jalt-publications.org/tlt/files/98/nov/nimmannit.html

Novak, J. D. (1990). Concept maps and Vee diagrams: Two metacognitive tools to facilitate meaningful learning. *Instructional Science, 19*, 1–25.

Nunan, D. (1989a). *Designing tasks for the communicative classroom.* Cambridge: Cambridge University Press.

Nunan, D. (1989b). Hidden agendas: The role of the learner in programme implementation. In R. K. Johnson (Ed.), *The second language curriculum* (pp. 176–186). Cambridge: Cambridge University Press.

Nunan, D. (2000). *Language teaching methodology: A textbook for teachers.* Edinburgh: Pearson Education.

Nunan, D. (2005). Important tasks of English education: Asia-wide and beyond. *Asian EFL Journal, 7*(3). Retrieved December 8, 2005, from http://www.asian-efl-journal.com/September_05_dn.php.

Oppenheim, A. N. (1992). *Questionnaire design, interviewing, and attitude measurement.* London: Pinter.

Oxford, R., & Shearin, J. (1994). Language learning motivation: Expanding the theoretical framework. *Modern Language Journal, 78*, 12–28.

Pennycook, A. (1994). *The cultural politics of English as an international language.* London: Longman.

Pennycook, A. (1998). *English and the discourses of colonialism.* London: Routledge.

Perry, L. (2001). Beautiful [Recorded by C. Aguilera]. On *Stripped* [CD]. New York: RCA. (2002)

Pierson, H. (1996). Learner culture and learner autonomy in the Hong Kong Chinese context. In R. Pemberton, E. S. L. Li, W. W. F. Or, & H. D. Pierson (Eds.), *Taking control: Autonomy in language learning* (pp. 49–58). Hong Kong: Hong Kong University Press.

Postiglione, G. (2005). Editor's introduction. *Chinese Education and Society, 38*(4), 3–10.

Pratt, D. D. (1992). Chinese conceptions of learning and teaching: A westerner's attempt at understanding. *International Journal of Lifelong Education, 11*(4), 301–319.

Randall, M., & Thornton, B. (2001). *Advising and supporting teachers.* New York: Cambridge University Press.

Richards, J. (1996). *Teacher education for language teachers: Content and process.* Auckland: Institute of Language and Learning, University of Auckland.

Richards, J. C. (1998). *Beyond training.* New York: Cambridge University Press.

Richards, J. C. (2001). *Curriculum development in language teaching.* Cambridge: Cambridge University Press.

Richards, J. C., & Farrell, T. S. C. (2005). *Professional development for language teachers: Strategies for teacher learning.* New York: Cambridge University Press.

Richards, J. C., & Lockhart, C. (1994). *Reflective teaching in second language classrooms.* New York: Cambridge University Press.

Richards, J. C., & Nunan, D. (Eds.). (1990). *Second language teacher education.* Cambridge: Cambridge University Press.

Rohlen, T. (1983). *Japan's high schools.* Berkeley: University of California Press.

Ross, H. (1993). *China learns English: Language teaching and social changes in People's Republic*. New Haven, CT: Yale University Press.

Rothery, J. (1996). Making changes: Developing an educational linguistics. In R. Hasan & G. Williams (Eds.), *Literacy in society* (pp. 86–123). London: Longman.

Ruddock, J. (1991). *Innovation and change*. Buckingham: Open University Press.

San Mateo County Office of Education. (n.d.). *Why do project-based learning?* Retrieved February 12, 2006, from http://pblmm.k12.ca.us/PBLGuide/WhyPBL.html

Schleppegrell, M. J. (2004). *The language of schooling: A functional linguistics perspective*. Mahwah, NJ: Lawrence Erlbaum.

Schmich, M. (1997). Everybody's free (to wear sunscreen) [Recorded by B. Luhrmann & Q. Tarver]. On *Something for everybody: Baz Luhrmann* [CD]. Hollywood, CA: Capitol Records (1998).

Schmidt, R. (1995). Consciousness and foreign language learning: A tutorial on the role of attention and awareness in learning. In R. Schmidt (Ed.), *Attention and awareness in foreign language learning* (pp. 9–64). Honolulu: University of Hawaii Press.

Schoenhals, M. (1993). *The paradox of power in a People's Republic of China middle school*. New York: M. E. Sharpe.

Scovel, T. (2001). *Learning new languages: A guide to second language acquisition*. Scarborough, Ontario: Heinle & Heinle.

Shen, H., & Li, W. (2004). *A review of the student loans scheme in China*. Bangkok, Thailand: UNESCO Bangkok/International Institute for Educational Planning, Paris.

Shulman, L. (1987). Knowledge and teaching: Foundations of the new reform. *Harvard Educational Review, 57*(1), 1–22.

Shumin, K. (1997). Factors to consider: Developing adult EFL students' speaking abilities. *Forum, 35*(3). Retrieved July 8, 2005, from http://exchanges.state.gov/forum/vols/vol35/no3/p8.htm

Sinclair, B. (1997). Learner autonomy: The cross cultural question. *IATEFL, 139*. Retrieved January 30, 2006, from http://www.eayrs.com/ELT/publications/IATEFL_Issues/Archives/Texts/139Sinclair.html

Slimani, A. (1989). The role of topicalisation in classroom language learning. *System, 17*(2), 223–234.

Spargo, E. (1989). *Timed readings*, books 1-10. Lincolnwood, IL: Jamestown.

Spargo, E. (2001). *Timed readings plus*, books 1-10. Lincolnwood, IL: Jamestown.

Stanley, C. (1998). A framework for teacher reflectivity. *TESOL Quarterly, 32*(3), 584–591.

Stephens, K. (1997). Cultural stereotyping and intercultural communication: Working with students from the People's Republic of China in the UK. *Language and Education, 11*(2), 113–124.

Stewart, T., Sagliano, M., & Sagliano, J. (2002). Merging expertise: Developing partnerships between language and content specialists. In J. Crandall &

D. Kaufman (Eds.), *Content-based instruction in higher education settings* (pp. 29–44). Alexandria, VA: TESOL.

Stracke, E. (2004). Voices from the classroom: Teaching in a computer-assisted foreign language learning environment. *New Zealand Studies in Applied Linguistics, 10*(1), 51–70.

Strauss, A., & Corbin, J. (1998). *Basics of qualitative research: Techniques and procedures for developing grounded theory* (2nd ed.). Thousand Oaks, CA: Sage.

Sturtridge, G. (1997). Teaching and language learning in self-access centers: Changing roles? In P. Benson & P. Voller (Eds.), *Autonomy and independence in language learning* (pp. 66–78). London: Longman.

Taylor, N., & Coll, R. K. (1999). Concept mapping as a tool for monitoring student learning in science. *Teaching & Learning, 20*(2), 84–90.

Temple University, Japan Campus. (n.d.). Academic Preparation Program [Web page]. Retrieved May 4, 2006, from http://www.tuj.ac.jp/newsite/main/app/index.html

Thanasoulas, D. (2000). Learner autonomy. *ELT Newsletter*, 32. Retrieved January 30, 2006, from http://www.eltnewsletter.com/back/September2000/art322000.htm

Toledo, P. F. (2005). Genre analysis and reading of English as a foreign language: Genre schemata beyond text typologies. *Journal of Pragmatics*, 37, 1059–1079.

Tsui, A. B. M. (1996). Reticence and anxiety in second language learning. In K. M. Bailey & D. Nunan (Eds.), *Voices from the language classroom: Qualitative research in second language education* (pp. 145–167). New York: Cambridge University Press.

Tsui, A. B. M. (2003). *Understanding expertise in teaching: Case studies of second language teachers.* Cambridge: Cambridge University Press.

Turner, J., & Hiraga, M. (1996). Elaborating elaboration in academic tutorials: Changing cultural assumptions. In H. Coleman & L. Cameron (Eds.), *Change and language* (pp. 131–140). Clevedon: BAAL and Multilingual Matters.

Turner, Y., & Acker, A. (2002). *Education in the new China.* Aldershot, Hampshire, England: Ashgate.

Ur, P. (1991). *A course in language teaching: Practice and theory.* Cambridge: Cambridge University Press.

Van Bruggen, J. M., Kirschner, P. A., & Jochems, W. (2002). External representation of argumentation in CSCL and the management of cognitive load. *Learning and Instruction, 12*(1), 121–138.

Vandergrift, L. (2003). From prediction through reflection: Guiding students through the process of L2 listening. *Canadian Modern Language Review, 59*(3), 425–440.

Vygotsky, L. S. (1978a). *Mind in society: The development of higher psychological processes* (M. Cole, V. John-Steiner, S. Scribner, & E. Souberman, Eds.). Cambridge, MA: Harvard University Press.

Vygotsky, L. S. (1978b). *Thought and language.* Cambridge: M.I.T. Press.

Wadden, P. (Ed.). (1993). *A handbook for teaching English at Japanese colleges and universities*. Oxford: Oxford University Press.

Wallace, M. J. (1991). *Training foreign language teachers: A reflective approach*. Cambridge: Cambridge University Press.

Wang, M. C., & Peverly, S. T. (1986). The self-instructional process in classroom learning contexts. *Contemporary Educational Psychology, 11*, 370–404.

Wang, M. M., Brislin, R. W., Wang, W., Williams, D., & Chao, J. H. (2000). *Turning bricks into jade: Critical incidents for mutual understanding among Chinese and Americans*. Yarmouth, ME: Intercultural Press.

Wen, W. P., & Clement, R. (2003). A Chinese conceptualization of willingness to communicate in ESL. *Language, Culture and Curriculum, 16*(1), 18–38. Retrieved July 8, 2005, from http://www.multilingual-matters.net/lcc/016/0018/lcc0160018.pdf

Wenden, A. L. (1987). How to be a successful language learner: Insights and prescriptions from L2 learners. In A. Wenden & J. Rubin (Eds.), *Learner strategies in language learning* (pp. 103–117). Englewood Cliffs, NJ: Prentice Hall.

Wenden, A. L. (1991). *Learner strategies for learner autonomy*. Hertfordshire: Prentice Hall.

Wenden, A. L. (1998). Metacognitive knowledge and language learning. *Applied Linguistics, 19*(4), 515–537.

White, C. (1999). Expectations and emergent beliefs of self-instructed language learners. *System, 27*, 443–457.

White, M. (1987). *The Japanese educational challenge*. New York: The Free Press.

Widdows, S., & Voller, P. (1991). PANSI: A survey of ELT needs of Japanese university students. *Cross Currents, 18*(2), 127–141.

Williams, G. (2000). Children's literature, children, and uses of language description. In L. Unsworth (Ed.), *Researching language in schools and communities* (pp. 111–129). London: Cassell.

Williams, J. (1995). Focus on form in communicative language teaching: Research findings and the classroom teacher. *TESOL Journal, 4*, 12–17.

Wilson, V. (1997). Focus groups: A useful qualitative method for educational research? *British Educational Research Journal, 23*(2), 209–224.

Wolff, D. (1994). *New approaches to language teaching: An overview*. CLCS occasional papers No. 39, Trinity College, Dublin.

Zeichner, K. M., & Liston, D. D. (1996). *Reflective teaching: An introduction*. Mahwah, NJ: Lawrence Erlbaum.

Zhao, Y., & Campbell, K. P. (1995). English in China. *World Englishes, 14*(3), 377–390.

Zhu, X., & Liu, C. (2004). Teacher training for moral education in China. *Moral Education, 33*(4), 481–494.

Zuengler, J. (1993). Encouraging learners' conversational participation: The effect of content knowledge. *Language Learning, 43*, 403–432.

Index

Page numbers followed by an *f* or *t* indicate figures and tables.

Applied Linguistics unit, 113–114
Applied science model of professional
    education, 109
Apprenticeship of observation, 47
Asian Institute Technology Center, 107
Asian learning styles, 157–158
Authentic learning, 158
Authentic materials, 79, 84, 177
Autonomy. *See also* Learner autonomy
    in East Asian cultures, 76–77
    kinds of, 36
    self-regulation in, 37
    teacher-dependence as form of, 72
    universality of desire for, 77

B

BaFa BaFa simulation, 154
Ballard, B., 141, 158
Bamford, J., 129
Barkhuizen, G. P., 142, 143, 153
Basturkmen, H., 125
Bazerman, C., 10
BBC World Service's Learning English, 96
"Beautiful" (Perry), 177
Beckett, G. H., 159
Beijaard, D., 48
Beliefs. *See* Prior beliefs
Benson, P., 64, 76, 77, 80
Bilingual approach, 110
Biographical/narrative approach, 64
Block, D., 142
Bloor, M., 10
Bloor, T., 10
Bowls, Steve, 12
Braddock, R., 76
Breen, M., 153
Brinton, D. M., 126
Brislin, R. W., 173
Brown, A., 58
Brown, G., 92
Brown, J. D., 123, 124, 125
Bruhn, J., 49
Bruner, J., 158

C

Campbell, K. P., 65, 66, 72
Carrell, P. L., 174
Carson, J., 126
Casanave, C. P., 127
Cause and effect relationships, 118
Chao, J. H., 173
Character depiction, in genre-based
    approach, 8
Charos, C., 171
Cheng, K. M., 72
Cheng, X., 61, 62, 63, 73, 77
Chik, A., 76, 77
China
    exam-oriented learning in, 66–67
    language learning in, 167–168
    learning strategies in, 173
    learning styles in, 157–158
    reticence and motivation in, 173–174
    SARS in, 160
    teacher-dependence in, 62–63
Chinokul, S., 24
Chopin, Kate, 177
Christie, F., 10, 11
Chulalongkorn University, 21
Clanchy, J., 158
Class observations, on learner autonomy,
    38
Class participation
    data collection on, 175–176
    extrinsic motivation in, 182
    reticence in, 173–174
    self-image and, 183
Clayton, P., 38
Clement, R., 62, 171, 173
Cleverley, J., 62, 65, 67, 73
Cognitive strategies
    in listening tasks, 98, 103, 104
    in narrative writing, 10–11
Coll, R. K., 50
Collectivists, 173
Communicative competence, 171
Communicative language teaching (CLT)
    challenges to, 173
    film discussion in, 178
    in L2 use, 171

Expert teacher *(continued)*
  learning approaches of, 27, 28*f*
  learning experiences of, 25*t*
  lesson plans of, 28–30, 29*t*
  teaching behaviors of, 30*t*–31*t*
Explicit instruction
  benefits of, 11
  in genre approach, 8–9
  on grammar, 11, 125
  in language learning, 152–153
Extrinsic motivation, 182

F

Face protection, 173
Facilitator, 40
Farrell, T. S. C., 1, 33, 34, 153
Ferris, D., 76
Finch, A., 168
Firth, A., 159
Fischer, F., 49
Flavell, J. H., 92
Flower, L., 9, 14, 15
Flowerdew, J., 76, 92
Form- and meaning-focused instruction,
  125–126, 132
Forsyth, D., 109
Fotos, S., 125
Freeman, D., 1, 2
Freedman, A., 11
Fried-Booth, D. L., 159, 168
Fry, H., 109

G

Gabriele, A. J., 48
Gallo, M., 49
Gardner, D., 80
Garrott, J. R., 63
Genesee, E., 143
Genre approach
  in content choice, 16*t*, 17
  emotive response in, 10
  explicit instruction in, 8–9
  journal writing in, 14
  as sociocultural practice, 10
  to writing instruction, 7
Ghaye, A., 23

Ghaye, K., 23
Goal setting
  in independent learning, 45
  in learner autonomy, 36
  negotiation in, 44
  by teacher, 40–41
Goh, C. C. M., 92, 93, 94, 95, 96, 97,
  100
Golombek, P. R., 64
Gorman, G. E., 38
Gorsuch, G., 75, 77, 78
Grading, English proficiency as factor in,
  120
Grammar
  explicit teaching of, 11, 132
  in reading process conceptualization,
    52
  as TOEFL preparation focus, 124
Grammar-translation method (GTM)
  materials supporting, 78–79
  preferences regarding
    overview of, 82*t*
    students disliking, 84–85
    students preferring, 83
  priorities of, 77
  self-access center use by students
    preferring, 86
  in teacher-centered system, 75–76
Grammar/vocabulary course, 129
Grasel, C., 49
Graves, K., 125
Grounded-theory approach, 64
Guanxi, 172
Guided-listening lessons
  feedback on, 98, 99*t*
  task procedures for, 95, 96*t*
Gupta, A. F., 11
Guzman, T., 76

H

Hamelin, O., 49
Handouts, and student expectations, 114
Haste, H., 22
Hativah, N., 109
Hato, Y., 75, 77
Hayes, J. R., 9, 14, 15
"Headache, The" (Hunter), 12

Hinkel, E., 11
Hiraga, M., 76
Ho, J., 76
Holec, H., 36, 37, 93
Holliday, A., 109
Hollingsworth, S., 59
Horton, P. B., 49
Horwitz, E. K., 93
Hot issue-based language projects
    framework for, 162*f*
    learner autonomy in, 168
    SARS as, 160–164
    as task-based strategy, 159
    uses of in EFL context, 160
    vs. top-down approach, 159–160
How Languages Are Learned
    (Lightbown & Spada), 114
Hu, G., 62, 171, 173
Hu, J., 67, 72
Hunter, Ann, 12
Hurd, S., 37
Hwang, C. C., 166
Hyun, T. D., 168

I

Ideational tokens
    affect and, 10
    definition of, 12
    discordant, identification of, 15*t*
    genre practices in use of, 9
    increased use of, 16*t*, 17*t*
Independent learning. *See also* Learner
    autonomy
    class observations in, 38
    data collection in, 41–42
    definition of, 37
    goal setting in, 40–41, 45
    in learning process, 37
    need for, 70–71
    self-regulation in, 37
    skills needed for, 45
    teacher role in, 36–37
    terms for, 39
    vs. independent work, 39–40
Independent work
    definition of, 37
    difficulties in implementing, 42–43

student perception of, 43–44
    vs. independent learning, 39–40
Individual autonomy, 36
Informational-oriented approach, 109
Instructivist approach, 37
Interviews
    on concept mapping process, 50
    on learner autonomy, 38–39
    on students' expectations of teacher,
        64
Intrinsic motivation, 182
Introduction to Language, An (Fromkin,
    Blair, & Collins), 111
Issues in Applied Linguistics (McCarthy),
    114
Issues in cross-cultural communication
    course, 142

J

Jamestown Publishing, 129
Japan
    perception gap in, 141–142
    self-access language learning center in,
        75
    test focus in, 123–125
Jargon, 119
Jin, L., 61, 62, 63, 73, 76
Jochems, W., 48
Johnson, K., 26
Johnson, K. E., 22, 64, 142, 143
Johnson, P., 174
Jones, J., 76
Joram, E., 48
Journal writing
    for genre-based approach, 14
    learning logs
        in perception assessment, 144–146
        sample prompts for, 155
        student, 146–147
        summaries of, 147–149
        teacher, 147
    listening diaries, 100–101
    in self-monitoring process, 45
Juku, 123

K

Kagan, D. M., 49, 59
Kang, L., 63
Kennett, P., 110
Kern, R., 9, 11
Ketteridge, S., 109
Khanh, D. T. K., 1
Kiasu, 58
Kirschner, P. A., 48
Knowledge
    content, 174
    metacognitive, 92–93
    person, 93
    strategic, 93
    task, 93
Knowles, M., 37
Kohonen, V., 36
Kramsch, C., 109
Kumaravadivelu, B., 143, 153, 154

L

Language
    emotive, in genre approach, 10
    explicit instruction in, 152–153
    metalanguage, 119
Language Change unit, 113, 115, 116
Language learning centers. *See* Self-access
    language learning centers
Language Teaching: A Scheme for
    Teacher Education, 109–110
Language use. *See* Communicative
    language teaching (CLT)
Larsen-Freeman, D., 108
Learner autonomy, 35–36. *See also*
    Independent learning
    class observations in, 38
    in East Asian cultures, 76–77
    in exam-oriented system, 77–78
    in hot issue-based language project,
        168
    kinds of, 36
    need for, 70–71
    in self-access center growth, 75
    self-regulation in, 37
    teacher-dependence as form of, 72
    teacher role in, 36–37
    universality of desire for, 77

Learner-centered problem-based learning
    model, 110
Learning approach
    Asian, 157–158
    constructivist, 37
    deep *vs.* surface, 27, 28*f*
    grammar-translation method, 75–76
    vs. conversational emphasis, 84
    instructivist, 37
    metacognitive knowledge influence on,
        93
    preferred, in self-access learning
        centers, 82
Learning centers. *See* Self-access language
    learning centers
Learning logs
    in perception assessment, 144–146
    sample prompts for, 155
    student, 146–147
    summaries of, 147–149
    teacher, 147
Learning process
    exam-oriented, 66–67
    independent learning in, 37
    role of teachers in, 72
    student monitoring of, 45
    teacher-dependence in, 62–63
    teacher/learner perception gap in,
        142–143
Lecturing techniques, 118–119
Lee, I., 157, 159, 167
Lee, J. F., 124, 125
Leki, I., 126
Lesson plan analysis, 28–30, 29*t*
Li, M. S., 157
Li, W., 72
Liddicoat, A. J., 159
Likert scale, 130
Lim, H., 76, 77
Linguistics. *See also* Applied linguistics
    in TESOL, 118
Listening comprehension, 92
Listening diaries, 100–101
Listening strategies
    choice of, 97–98
    cognitive, 98, 103, 104
    difficulties with, 92

guided-listening lessons
 feedback on, 98, 99*t*
 task procedures for, 95, 96*t*
metacognitive
 description of, 102–103
 in different tasks, 105–106
 instruction in, 98, 100
perceived problems in, 103
prediction as, 93
process-oriented, 93
self-directed
 comparison of, 104–106
 feedback on, 99–100
 guide for, 101–102
 task procedure for, 95–96, 97*t*
social-affective, 102, 104
Listening tasks
 guided, 96*t*
 metacognitive strategies in, 98
 self-directing, 97*t*
Liston, D. D., 22, 23
Little, D., 36, 37
Littlejohn, A., 90
Littlewood, W., 37, 62, 72, 76, 77, 168
Liu, C., 72
Liu, N., 77
Lo, R., 72
Lo Bianco, J., 159
LoCastro, V., 141
Lockhart, C., 23
Loewen, S., 125
Lortie, D., 47

M

MacIntyre, P. D., 171
Mandl, H., 49
Mariani, L., 36
Marincovich, M., 109
Marshall, S., 109
Martin, J. R., 10
McConny, A. A., 49
McDonough, J., 143
McGraw-Hill, 129
McKay, S., 77
Meaning-focused context, 124
Medgyes, P., 78
Meijer, P. C., 48

Mendelsohn, D., 94
Mergendoller, R., 48
Metacognitive knowledge
 categories of, 92–93
 influence on learning approaches, 93
 in listening tasks, 98
Metacognitive listening strategy, 102–
 103, 105–106
Metalanguage, 119
Metastrategic awareness, 94
Methods course. *See* TESOL methods
 course
Miller, L., 75, 76, 80
Ministry of Education, Culture, Sports,
 Science, & Technology, 123
Misson, R., 10, 11
Mnemonics, 168
Mohan, B., 109, 126
Morine-Dershimer, G., 49
Moss, D., 157, 158
Motivation
 in Chinese classroom, 173–174
 extrinsic, 182
 in L2 learning, 172, 181
 in reading process conceptualization,
  51
 self-image and, 183
 student-teacher rapport and, 66
 topic choice and, 176
Multidimensional methodology data
 collection, 80

N

Narrative writing
 cognitive strategies in, 10–11
 emotive language in, 10
 genre-based approach to, 7–8
Nassaji, H., 125
Nation, I. S. P., 129
Nelson, G. L., 174
Nguyen, D. C., 36
Nguyen, Q. C., 36
Nimmannit, S., 171, 173, 176
Nonexpert teacher
 definition of, 24
 learning approaches of, 27, 28*f*
 learning experiences of, 25*t*

Nonexpert teacher *(continued)*
  lesson plans of, 28–30, 29*t*
  teaching behaviors of, 30*t*–31*t*
Nonstructured approach, 49
Novak, J. D., 48
Nunan, D., 22, 108, 109, 110, 141, 143,
  153, 159

O

Oppenheim, A. N., 38
Oral presentations
  lecturing techniques, 118–119
  rehearsals for, 42
  student control in, 41–42
Oxford, R., 172, 181

P

Participation. *See* Class participation
Pennycook, A., 65, 72, 158
Perception gap
  in Asian context, 141–142
  in class participation study, 179–180
  course changes in response to,
    151–154
  literature on, 142–143
  task-based assessment of, 144–146
  between Western and Asian teaching
    styles, 157–158
Perception task, 154
Perry, L., 177
Person knowledge, 92
Pierson, H., 76
Postiglione, G., 72
Pratt, D. D., 173
Prior beliefs
  acknowledgment of, 59
  in concept generation, 49
  in preservice teachers, 47–48
Proactive autonomy, 37
Problem-based teaching, 158
Process-oriented listening, 93
Professional development and education
  acceptance of change as integral to,
    22–23
  three models of, 109
Proficiency-focused activities, 109

Project-based learning. *See also* Task-
  based learning
  framework for, 162*f*
  implementation issues in, 166–167
  literature on, 158–160
  material accessibility in, 166
  SARS project as, 160–164
  teacher skills in, 167
  vs. top-down teaching, 158–159

R

Randall, M., 22
Reactive autonomy, 37
Reading aloud
  ineffectiveness of, 54
  as lecture technique, 119
  in reading process conceptualization,
    52
Reading-based writing course, 126–127,
  131
Reading process
  concept mapping of, 49–50
    comprehension in, 51
    grammar in, 52
    motivation in, 51
    reading aloud in, 52
    vocabulary in, 51–52
  methods course in, 47–48
  teaching strategies in, 53–54, 53*f*
Reflective model of professional
  education, 109
Reflective teaching, 22–23
Reinders, H., 75
Research approach
  biographical/narrative, 64
  grounded-theory, 64
Rhetorical goals
  categories of, 14*t*
  definition of, 12
  student awareness of, 16*t*
Rhetorical problem, 9
Richards, J. C., 1, 22, 23, 33, 34, 59,
  109, 110, 125
Roberts, P., 76
Rohlen, T., 75, 77
Ross, H., 65, 67, 72

T

Text awareness, 54
Text-responsible writing, 126
Thanasoulas, D., 36
Theory-based approach, 26
Thinking process
    explicit instruction in, 8–9
    in narrative writing, 8
    rhetorical goal in, 13
Thornton, B., 22
TOEFL. *See* Test of English as a Foreign
    Language (TOEFL)
Toledo, P. F., 10
Top-down teaching. *See*
    Teacher-dependence
Topic choice, and motivation, 176
Tree technique, 48
Tsui, A. B. M., 21, 22, 157, 171, 173
Turner, J., 76
Turner, Y., 65
2R2C principle, 23, 33

U

University of Canberra, 107
Upshur, J. A., 143
Ur, P., 108

V

Values task, 154
Van Bruggen, J. M., 48
Van Duzer, C., 157, 158
Vandergrift, L., 93, 94, 95, 96, 98
Verloop, N., 48
Vietnam
    applied linguistics in, 107–108
    learner autonomy in, 35–36, 43
Vocabulary
    as common student concern, 121
    in reading process conceptualization,
        51–52, 54
Voller, P., 77
Vygotsky, L. S., 21, 33, 158

W

Wadden, P., 141
Wagner, J., 159
Wallace, M. J., 22, 109
Wang, M. M., 173
Wang, W., 173
Watch-and-report news presentation, 155
Webb, G., 109
Wen, W. P., 62, 171, 173
Wenden, A. L., 92, 93
Wesche, M. B., 126
Western teaching styles, 157–158
White, C., 39
White, M., 123
Widdows, S., 77
Williams, D., 173
Williams, G., 11
Williams, J., 124, 125, 126
Wilson, V., 50
Wolff, D., 37
Woods, A.L., 49
Writing process
    genre-based *vs.* product-based
        methods of, 7
    goal-directed nature of, 9
    rhetorical problem in, 9, 13
    as sociocultural practice, 9–10
    text-responsible, 126

Y

Yakudoku system, 76. *See also* Grammar-
    translation method (GTM)
Yamashita, S. O., 123
Yobiko, 123

Z

Zeichner, K. M., 22, 23
Zhao, Y., 65, 66, 72
Zheng, C., 76
Zhu, X., 72
Zone of proximal development, 21
Zuengler, J., 174

Also Available From TESOL

Interaction and Language Learning
Jill Burton and Charles Clennell, Editors

Internet for English Teaching
Mark Warschauer, Heidi Shetzer, and Christine Meloni

Journal Writing
Jill Burton and Michael Carroll, Editors

Literature in Language Teaching and Learning
Amos Paran, Editor

Mainstreaming
Effie Cochran, Editor

PreK–12 English Language Proficiency Standards
Teachers of English to Speakers of Other Languages, Inc.

*Planning and Teaching Creatively within a
Required Curriculum for School-Age Learners*
Penny McKay, Editor

Professional Development of International Teaching Assistants
Dorit Kaufman and Barbara Brownworth, Editors

Teacher Education
Karen E. Johnson, Editor

Teaching English From a Global Perspective
Anne Burns, Editor

Technology-Enhanced Learning Environments
Elizabeth Hanson-Smith, Editor

For more information, contact
Teachers of English to Speakers of Other Languages, Inc.
700 South Washington Street, Suite 200
Alexandria, Virginia 22314 USA

Toll Free: 888-547-3369   **Fax on Demand:** 800-329-4469

Publications Order Line: 888-891-0041 or 301-638-4427 or 4428
9 am to 5 pm, EST

Order online at www.tesol.org/

T E S O L